Common Scents

COMMON SCENTS

COMPARATIVE ENCOUNTERS

IN HIGH-VICTORIAN FICTION

Janice Carlisle

OXFORD

UNIVERSITY PRESS

2004

OXFORD
UNIVERSITY PRESS

Oxford   New York
Auckland   Bangkok   Buenos Aires   Cape Town   Chennai
Dar es Salaam   Delhi   Hong Kong   Istanbul   Karachi   Kolkata
Kuala Lumpur   Madrid   Melbourne   Mexico City   Mumbai   Nairobi
São Paulo   Shanghai   Taipei   Tokyo   Toronto

Copyright © 2004 by Oxford University Press, Inc.

Published by Oxford University Press, Inc.
198 Madison Avenue, New York, New York 10016

www.oup.com

Oxford is a registered trademark of Oxford University Press

Library of Congress Cataloging-in-Publication Data
Carlisle, Janice
Common scents : comparative encounters in high-Victorian fiction /
Janice Carlisle.
p. cm.
Includes bibliographical references and index.
ISBN 0-19-516509-8
1. English fiction—19th century—History and criticism.   2. Odors in
literature.   3. Melancholy in literature.   4. Smell in literature.   I. Title.
PR878.O46 C37 2004
823'.809353—dc21   2003004248

1 3 5 7 9 8 6 4 2

Printed in the United States of America
on acid-free paper

In memory of Carol Kay

ACKNOWLEDGMENTS

In writing this book, I have incurred a number of debts, and I am pleased to have this opportunity to acknowledge them. As I have discovered, the vocabulary of gratitude is almost as limited as that which pertains to olfaction, but I hope that I can begin to indicate how much I appreciate the support that I have received.

Sustained research on this project was made possible by the National Endowment for the Humanities, and the year's leave during which I held its fellowship was also funded by Tulane University. During that time I profited from the collections at Yale University and the aid of the staff at Sterling Memorial Library, Mudd Library, and the Beinecke Rare Book and Manuscript Library. An early version of the argument of this study appeared in *Victorian Literature and Culture*, and revised portions of it are reprinted with the permission of Cambridge University Press. To the Dickens Project, particularly to all those present at the 2000 "Universe" when we studied *Our Mutual Friend* and to all those individuals who ensure the continuance of the opportunities for encounter and exchange that the consortium offers, I extend my thanks. It has been my good fortune to have worked with Elissa Morris of Oxford University Press. Her thoughtful support of this project and her ability to expedite its evaluation are greatly appreciated. My thanks as well to Stacey Hamilton and Jeremy Lewis at OUP.

A number of readers, including those whose reports were solicited by Elissa Morris, have enriched the experience of working out the ideas that I present here. Annabel Patterson, Jonathan Arac, and Linda Peterson all read and commented on versions of this project. Rosemarie Bodenheimer offered particularly insightful advice on a draft of its introduction. I am grateful to Paul Morrison and Alison Booth for sharing my interest in olfaction and joining me on the "Smell" panel at the Narrative Conference in 1998. Paul Morrison also kindly sent me a draft of a chapter of *The Explanation for Everything*, the importance of which to my analysis in the second chapter of this book I hope I have made clear. At the earliest stages, Richard Rambuss provided advice on the shape of this study and on its publication. Mary Poovey, Catherine Gallagher, Linda Peterson, Jay Clayton, and

James R. Kincaid aided my efforts at the beginning of this project, and at its end Elsie Michie provided timely suggestions. I am grateful to all these individuals.

Members of my family have once again given me more support than they can know. My mother, Hazel Lagerstedt Carlisle, has consistently offered her encouragement. For drawing the visual mantra that has brightened my desk throughout the process of writing this book and for sharing both my taste for Victorian novels and last-minute chores of proofreading, I am particularly grateful to my daughter, Catherine Roach. My son, Joseph, provided computer expertise, and he has made Tulane a better place to be with his presence there. To his father, Joseph Roach, I owe debts both professional and personal. He willingly read multiple drafts of this study, offering his characteristically astute advice on matters large and small. More important still, Joe has made the future something worth working for, and for that gift I am every day more and more deeply grateful.

The completion of this book has been to a large extent dependent on the support of my friends. At Tulane, Rebecca Mark, Supriya Nair, and Lois Conrad have consistently found ways of making work a pleasure. Maaja Stewart's contribution has been material in more ways than one: over many a supper of her making, we discussed one draft after another as I defined the scope of this project, and it has gained much from her insight. Only Elizabeth Reed knows how often and how generously she has offered a sense of perspective.

Finally, I would like to try to acknowledge what I owe to Carol Kay, the friend whose loss remains impossible to accept. As I have been writing this book, I have repeatedly thought of how often I have benefited from the strength of her confidence in my work. When we were living across the street from each other in St. Louis, for instance, she took care of my young children for an afternoon every week so that I could have time for research. Although I cannot know that Carol would have agreed with the "political constructions" that I have put on the materials that I treat in this project, I am certain that she would have cheered me on to complete it. Carol's generosity to members of my family and to me cannot be repaid. As at least a gesture in that direction, however, I offer this book to her memory.

CONTENTS

Common Scents

INTRODUCTION

When does a cigar give off an odor? Why is a particular woman's presence fragrant? Whose food is appetizingly aromatic; whose, wholly inodorate? What work smells more, storing refuse or selling cheese?

High-Victorian fiction posits precise answers to these questions when it represents the odors that its characters notice as they go about the business of their everyday lives. Unlike sight, a sense whose functions are almost inevitably intellectualized, smell seems stubbornly material in both origin and effect. As such, it constitutes a basic—some might say, a negligible—form of physical experience; but it is the sense that Victorian novelists frequently invoke to depict what happens when one character encounters another. Such meetings constitute only one category of the many kinds of events that Victorian plots typically include: characters are born, marry, and die; they study and work, visit and gossip; they lose or gain reputations, honor trusts or betray them; their endeavors succeed or fail. Yet all such activities and outcomes depend on the interactions that occur when characters come face to face. Focusing on fiction written during the high-Victorian decade of the 1860s, this study examines those meetings between two individuals of unequal status whose differences are registered when one of them perceives an odor. Presented as the lived experience of inequalities, such *comparative encounters*, as I term them, quickly and even automatically identify one character as better, more highly valued than the other. In high-Victorian novels, I argue, olfaction is the sensory modality in which such discriminations are most reliably cast.

In the fiction of the 1860s, meetings marked by smells take place anywhere and everywhere—in enclosed rooms, in the open air, in cities, in the provinces. Eugene Wrayburn in Dickens's *Our Mutual Friend* uses his nose to register the invasion of his London chambers by the destitute tailor Mr. Dolls, and a potential victim of the enchantress of Trollope's *Phineas Finn* notices that her curls fill the air of her sitting room with "the same soft feeling of [the] perfume" that scents her stationery (2: 174). Meetings depicted as odorous also take place outdoors, as happens after a would-be gentleman in Meredith's *Emilia in England* is covered in beer when he collides with a

3

pot-boy on a city street and when Maggie Tulliver in Eliot's *The Mill on the Floss* is taken aback by the unappealing aromas of gypsy food being cooked at the side of a country lane. Significantly, such events often transpire in the liminal spaces located between the privacy of the home and the public realm of the street—outside on the grounds of an estate when Squire Wentworth of Oliphant's *The Perpetual Curate* walks among fragrant lime trees or, more revealingly, in railway carriages like the one into which the wealthy farmers of Braddon's *Aurora Floyd* track the smelly soil of their barnyards. Olfactory responses to meetings can occur even in the realm of imagined possibilities. The narrator of Hughes's *Tom Brown at Oxford* goes so far as to conjure up for his readers the smell of fustian that they would perceive if they ever rode a train in third-class. Similarly, the finicky second wife of the doctor in Gaskell's *Wives and Daughters* dreads the prospect of "county" ladies noticing in her home the smells of cooking food or, even worse, the aroma of cheese that would put in question her husband's and, by extension, her own gentility (177–78).

In all these instances, characters are known by the odors associated with them: their scents provide olfactory evidence of the food that they eat, the work that they do, the clothes that they wear, and the homes in which they live. As etiquette manuals point out, however, it would be more polite to ignore such sensory evidence than to heed its existence. Since most cultural and literary critics have tended not to pay attention to smells,[1] the decision to chart their meanings raises questions that require consideration. Why and how do texts recognize odors? Why and how might it be profitable to study their implications in Victorian fiction? Although there have been times in the history of Western culture when smell has risen to the middle of the hierarchy of senses, the great majority of commentators on bodily experience have placed it at the bottom, well below the other chemical sense, taste, which in at least some forms can be the proof of refinement and the source of aesthetic interest. Smell, by contrast, seems inveterately low: corporeal, animalistic, primitive, and therefore degraded. Even in their most acceptable contexts, odors are associated with the relatively involuntary and unconscious processes of memory and desire. More often smells seem to be evidence of not fully evolved forms of human life, if not simply the material traces of disease and death.[2] Finding odorous those whom one despises is a common practice of both Western and non-Western cultures: accounts of bigoted relations of difference in Anglo-American experience offer numerous examples of groups marked as less than human by their supposedly distinctive scents; similarly, the Serer Ndut of Senegal turn their noses away from Europeans, whose urinous odor is attributed to their hopelessly uncivilized lack of hygiene.[3]

The fictional practices of high-Victorian novels, however, argue for a different understanding of the sensory processing involved in smelling out those whom one meets. Defining the 1860s as the epitome of the era typically called mid-Victorian, this study examines representations of olfaction so that it can gauge as precisely as possible the anxieties that predominated after the crises of poverty and popular politics in the early Victorian period and before the depression and decadence of the fin-de-siècle. Recognizing an odor, registering its effects, comparing what smells to what does not—all such perceptual activities when recorded in a novel of the 1860s provide access to the common sense of that decade, the rarely articulated, taken-for-granted result of experiences supposedly shared by all one's fellows, if not by all humankind. Like the sense of smell, common sense was understood during the Victorian period as the source of responses that are immediate, instinctive, and automatic.[4] Some of the self-evident truths conveyed in high-Victorian fiction by the supposedly natural processes of olfaction are conventionally and predictably negative. By identifying certain objects as odorants, a novel of the 1860s often relegates the men and women associated with them to the domains of a contemptible sensory modality, and that point is central to many of the analyses that I offer here. Yet at other moments in this fiction, the base materiality of olfaction occasions more positive responses: when characters catch whiffs of substances that they might prefer to ignore, they may be sensing value in what smells. The effects of such perceptions may be ambiguous or ambivalent, and their implications are frequently disguised or indirect. Yet once they are recognized, they reconfigure standard accounts of what high-Victorian culture prizes or denigrates, particularly as that culture sorts out the opposing claims of matter and spirit, men and women.

Attending to Odors

Gathering the evidence for this study involved reading for their smells eighty novels that were written or published at least in part during the 1860s—titles, authors, and dates of which are listed in the appendix. Although seven of these novels are singled out for more-or-less sustained attention, all the fiction that I read came to serve as a collective repository of olfactory data. Combining interests in the textual representation of things and the history of sensory experience,[5] I noted in each novel references to any object or body explicitly described as giving off a smell: even obvious odorants like pigs and sewers do not count if no one, character or narrator or reader, is depicted as noticing their exhalations. The pleasures of this research agenda can easily be imagined, even if it routinely elicited from my colleagues predictable puns and expressions of amusement. Odors are traditionally the source of comedy, often evoking a laughter of unease, because they witness in unpredictable and uncontrollable ways to the materiality of human experience, but I have chosen to take smells seriously because Victorian novelists did. I can think of no instance in the fiction of the 1860s in which an odor occasions even a knowing smile, much less a chortle. Although *Punch* in the same decade is not above finding funny the girl who mistakes her brother's mustache wax for perfume or the housewife who has her stable boy dose himself in eau de cologne before he waits on her table,[6] fiction in the 1860s typically treats odors as simple matters of fact. Looking at Victorian assumptions about bodily responses to the physical world, however, begins to suggest why the meanings conveyed by odors justify extended analysis.

At the Victorian midcentury there was enough interest in sensory experience to establish a school of common sense on its import.[7] Some of the scientists writing on this subject were trying to merge philosophic conceptions of the mind, which were based largely on methods of introspection, with research on the anatomy and physiology of nerves and brain. Their treatises are therefore often confusing amalgams of tradition, speculation, and anatomical fact, and they can seem messy and impressionistic by the standards of the experimental science that psychology became by the end of the century, but they are especially pertinent here because they often took as their purview what George Henry Lewes called "common life." Lewes's conception of himself as both a research scientist and a writer aiming to interest a relatively wide, though generally educated audience is characteristic of a number of these commentators, whose works were often widely distributed. *The Five Gateways of Knowledge*, for instance, written by George Wilson, the Regius Professor of Technology at the University of Edinburgh, reached an eighth edition by 1860 after being published only four years earlier. This slight and charming essay frankly blends science and religion, taking its title from Bunyan's metaphor for the senses as five gates to "the famous town of MANSOUL" (epigraph). It is not surprising that Dickens found this book particularly to his taste; as he told its author, "Wise, elegant, eloquent, and perfectly unaffected, it has delighted me" (*Letters* 8: 218). Along with Wilson's *Five Gateways*, a variety of mid-Victorian commentaries attempted both to analyze and to popularize scientific understandings of the senses. Prominent among them are works to which I refer throughout this study: Alexander Bain's materialist and associationist exercise in psychophysiology, *The Senses and the Intellect* (1855); Lewes's *The Physiology of Common Life* (1859–1860); *The Senses* (1853), published by the Religious Tract Society; A. B. Johnson's *The Physiology of the Senses; or, How and What We See, Hear, Taste, Feel and Smell* (1856); Henry Maudsley's 1867 *The Physiology and Pathology of the Mind*; William B. Carpenter's *Principles of Mental Physiology* (1874); Julius Bernstein's *The Five Senses of Man* (1876); and Grant Allen's *Physiological Aesthetics* (1877).

Whether the writer of one of these texts is a self-declared scientist intent on establishing the authority of psychology as a discipline, a doctor dedicated to the treatment of the insane, or an essayist glorifying his maker by celebrating the opportunities for sensory perception offered by the created world, these works express a surprising consensus on the basic reliability of the senses. For George Wilson, sensory impressions are "ambassadors from the material world," and they are to be greeted with "child-like faith and adoring wonder" (18), not with hesitancy or skepticism. That a materialist like Karl Marx would accept Baconian doctrine on the reliability of the senses is hardly surprising. That such certainty also provided the premises for these quite different treatments of sensory experience is, however, more revealing.[8] The most important of these texts, Bain's *The Senses and the Intellect*, which was republished in a condensed form in 1868, defines the uses to which the reliability of olfaction may be put: "Smell . . . is an important instrument in the discrimination of material bodies" (170). As Bain's identification of odors and matter suggests, these commentaries offer a conventional hierarchy of the senses that puts sight at the top and smell at the bottom. For Wilson, sight is the "Queen of the Senses" (25). Bain labels taste and smell as "Sensations of Organic Life" and defines touch and hearing and sight as "Intellectual Senses" (121–22). Despite such devaluations or, perhaps, because of them, Victorian scientists and moral commentators are particularly anxious to establish that even a sense as humble as that of smell can be educated to perform its proper duties.

A number of the most scientifically inclined of these writers also theorize a remarkably direct and simple connection between sensory experience and mental life, one that explains why Victorians might have found occasions for sensory response in the olfactory images of the novels that they read and, therefore, a form of sensory training. According to Bain, "mental agencies alone" have the power to revive "past or extinct sensations," and that power is one of the chief distinctions of "Intellect" (315). More emphatically than most, Carpenter insists, "*real Sensations are producible by Mental states*" (164). At the Victorian midcentury it was an article of scientific faith that, as Bain also insists, "the imagination of visible objects is a process of seeing" (339); and theorists typically argued, even as they conceded that the effect might be less intense, that imagining a smell is a process of smelling. For that reason, *The Senses*, richly illustrated with wood engravings and colored plates, includes in one of its chapters on smell an elaborate picture of a bouquet of flowers, a visual cue presumably able to elicit an olfactory response from those who see it. Moreover, verbal references to sensory responses—words like *shiny* and *putrid*—were themselves deemed to be "suggested feelings" (Allen 225) or "sensory representations" (Maudsley 115); as such, they were taken to excite sensations in anyone who reads or hears them.[9] The odors depicted in a novel therefore invite its readers to experience physically the distinction between what smells and what does not, to recognize some kinds of people and not others as capable of either giving off or responding to odors.

As such, reading is a form of olfactory exercise—a way of practicing when and how and why to notice an odor.

A scene in the fifth chapter of George Eliot's *Felix Holt* reveals what sorts of values such olfactory exercise entails. This episode, to which I return several times in this study, offers an unusually lengthy meditation on olfaction.[10] When Felix Holt enters the sitting room of the dissenting minister Rufus Lyon to introduce himself, the two men begin their acquaintance by discussing the tastes of Mr. Lyon's daughter, Esther. The minister is afraid that Felix will misjudge him because he is reading by the light of an expensive wax candle. Hastily, the older man explains, "You are doubtless amazed to see me with a wax-light . . . but this undue luxury is paid for with the earnings of my daughter, who is so delicately framed that the smell of tallow is loathsome to her" (54). Yet Esther is not the only character in *Felix Holt* who is presented as responding to such olfactory stimuli. Both the reader and Felix are quickly described as alert to similar sensory impressions. The narrator offers a lesson on the kind of audience that the novel demands by explaining, "any one whose attention was quite awake must have been aware" of the "things" that identify Lyon's room as one inhabited by a refined lady, and the first among those "things" is the "delicate scent of dried rose-leaves." Felix, declaring that he is "not a mouse to have a nose that takes note of wax or tallow" (53–54), thinks himself above caring whether a candle smells because it is made of fat. Yet he goes on to demonstrate how frequently he too uses his mouse-like nose to evaluate the things that meet it: he epitomizes a period of debauchery in his past by remembering the "smell of raw haggis" that pervaded his lodgings, and he despises those members of "the middle class" who present themselves as "ringed and scented men of the people" (56, 58). Although Felix prides himself on having transcended the realm of physical comforts, his supposed superiority to bodily experiences simply makes more significant his representation—not to mention the reader's imaginative apprehension of him—through responses to the material traces of substances like fat and food. At such moments in a Victorian novel, senses respond to things in ways that reveal what William A. Cohen has recently called "the materiality of human subjects"[11] or, as Mr. Lyon would say, the inescapable effects of "our sojourn in the flesh" (54). This scene therefore demonstrates at length what other high-Victorian novels take for granted: noses sometimes know more about what matters than their owners would be able to articulate.

In the opening chapters of *Felix Holt*, Eliot also depicts Esther Lyon in ways that explicitly comment on the most significant characteristic of odors represented in high-Victorian fiction—their constitution of what cultural anthropologists call an *osmology*, a system of categories that uses smells to classify people and objects in ways that define their relations to each other and their relative values within a particular culture. Even before Esther enters the narrative of *Felix Holt*, its readers learn that she cannot stand the odor of her servant's warmed ale. The narrator later explains that Esther's "exceptional organization"—"quick and sensitive without being in the least morbid"—makes her "alive to the finest shades of manner, to the nicest distinctions of tone and accent; she had a little code of her own about scents and colours, textures and behaviour, by which she secretly condemned or sanctioned all things and persons" (68). According to the tenets of this "little code," which tellingly gives priority to "scents," Esther judges all the "things and persons" she meets. On the level of individual experience, therefore, it does what the larger osmology of high-Victorian fiction accomplishes: it sorts "things and persons" into categories of less or more appealing, less or more valuable.

During the Victorian period, the word *osmology* indicated simply "a treatise on smells," according to the entry under *Osmologia* in R. G. Mayne's *Expository Lexicon of the Terms, Ancient and Modern, in Medical and General Science* (1860). Yet anthropologists now use the term to identify how peoples "from Africa to the Amazon and from China to New Guinea" use olfactory perceptions "to order the world,"[12] and in this sense it is applicable as well to the no-less-exotic realm of Victorian fiction. Responses to smells have been characterized as so deeply personal as to "bypass all forms of coded communication" (Sperber 118), but as Esther's experience reveals, the odors represented in high-Victorian fiction argue otherwise. Even more accurately than the single glance that frequently proves whether a man is or is not a gentleman, one whiff is often enough to place a character in relation to those granted the capacity to perceive it: the aroma of warm ale is one bit of data in an osmology that distinguishes between Esther and her servant. In this sense, Victorian fiction, whose primary orientations seem so much more obviously moral and social than physical, has much to say about what Bain calls "the discrimination of material bodies."

The novelistic representations of smells and smelling ultimately constitute a structure of sensations, to use a version of Raymond Williams's phrase "structures of feeling,"[13] and the first task of this study is to describe that osmology and explore its diverse meanings. The sampling of fiction surveyed here is large enough and diverse enough to reveal such patterns as well as variations and frequencies. Whether a novel like Payn's *The Lost Sir Massingberd* contains one odor or another like *Our Mutual Friend* contains dozens, an olfactory reference in one text tends to echo and therefore to reinforce the effect of those found in another. Despite the obvious dissimilarities of their subjects, aesthetic ambitions, original popularity, or staying power, these novels are remarkably consistent in their evocation of smells, in the occasions that they offer their readers to perceive their stories through imaginative olfactory responses. So dependable are such references that they came to have predictive power: I began to expect and to find a certain kind of smell at a certain point in a narrative. So rarely disappointed were such expectations that after reading dozens of novels, I realized that I had read widely enough since each addition to my list was offering only new instances of the osmology already well established. Not every novel contains every kind of smell that is important in constituting this structure of olfactory sensations, but each of them does convey the cultural values toward which those odors point once they are understood in relation to each other: even relatively inodorate texts enact the common sense displayed by the implications of the smells of their more odoriferous counterparts.

Encounter and *Exchange*

Rufus Lyon remarks that the "niceties" of Esther's discriminations seem simply marvelous to him, "reports of a sixth sense which I possess not" (62). Yet her exceptional sensitivity to the evidence of her five senses does its work in the context of her otherwise unremarkable daily experiences. Defining even the most refined sensory impressions as grounded in the mundane, the fifth chapter of *Felix Holt* therefore provides a fitting introduction to the terms, along with *osmology*, that are central to this study. Because Eliot's chapter begins by depicting two men coming face to face—one a preacher, the other a worker—it exemplifies what I identify as a *comparative encounter*. More or less explicitly setting two characters in evaluative relation to each other, such a meeting declares one the superior of the other: because Mr. Lyon does not work with his hands, he is presumably Felix's better. Whether that is the case is a question answered by gauging the import of a second, related process, which I call an *exchange*.

Although the term *encounter* often appears in ethnographies dealing with distant peoples,[14] I use it here to stress the far-reaching implications of occurrences so casual and ordinary that they easily escape notice. The term also carries with it a sense of danger and risk, a recognition that a meeting may have high stakes—and the stakes are, I think, often highest when the meeting is most routine. Novels of the 1860s can be remarkably self-conscious about the import of such events. Oliphant's fiction seems most so: the narrator of *Miss Marjoribanks* uses the word *encounter* repeatedly to identify a confrontation, usually in a street, that effects unsettling recognitions; and the plot of *The Perpetual Curate* depends on a complex architecture of encounter that multiplies the opportunities that characters have to observe others coming together. More often, however, such meetings simply move a story unobtrusively from one complication to the next. By treating comparative encounters as the basic narrative components of their plots, Victorian novels tacitly acknowledge that such incidents constitute a significant portion of nearly everyone's everyday life.[15]

Meetings between individuals—whether they are strangers or acquaintances, relatives or friends—take place repeatedly throughout any given day. Encounters may consist only of glances, never extending to words or introductions. They may be momentary and evanescent, never to be repeated; alternatively, they may serve as prologues to or episodes in lengthy associations. Despite such variations, however, face-to-face meetings invite their participants or those observing them to engage in processes of judgment and evaluation—to compare gestures and manners, clothing and scents, the shapes and sizes of bodies, the textures and hues of skin and hair, the tones of speech or the qualities of silence. These often unremarked negotiations of daily life engage, in short, not only all the impressions offered by the objects, including the bodies, that a particular culture creates and with which particular individuals present themselves, but also all the varying significances that attach to physical impressions. As such, encounters constitute a kind of perceptual politics: they involve cultural values enacted through and by the senses—seeing, smelling, hearing, and touching. Because meetings necessarily encourage their participants to judge themselves in relation to others—Am I better than he? Is she my inferior?—such events almost invariably involve social valuations at their most personal. The intimacy, the closeness of an encounter, even if it occurs only for a moment between individuals who have never met and will never meet again, is precisely the quality that gives it the power to be felt, not only along the pulses but also in the bone. That such practices are, for most people, second nature, that they are often unconscious, largely taken for granted, can simply magnify the significance of their unacknowledged effects.

When high-Victorian fiction renders such meetings in olfactory terms, it capitalizes on their narrative potential not only to define the relative status of two characters but also to transform it through an *exchange*. This specific, though not necessary effect of a comparative encounter reverses conventional valuations when either the superior party to such a meeting or its observer recognizes that they no longer obtain, that the inferior embodies the values that the superior lacks.[16] The two participants to an encounter exchange the positions that they would usually hold in relation to each other. Although Victorian society is often characterized in the terms that Thomas Carlyle offered when he deplored the cash-payment nexus or that Marx proposed in his theory of the commodity fetish, exchanges depicted in the 1860s often do not involve transfers either of money or of the characteristics that usually differentiate persons from things; rather, they transform the valuations that usually attach to different persons or things. Exchanges are, therefore, structurally similar to more easily recognized instances of hierarchies undone, such as the servant's revelation of the shortcomings of the master or the worker's denunciations of a gentleman's behavior as effete foppery, but they require that the reversal taking place be viewed from the perspective of the relative superior. Still attached to the hierarchical notions that supported a society based on deferential relations, whose importance Walter Bagehot stressed in *The English Constitution* (1867), Victorian culture was capable of recording as significant those encounters that had the potential to alter the status of the parties to them.[17] Demonstrating what it means when a fictional encounter is cast in olfactory terms and what effect it has when it issues in an exchange is my project throughout this study.

Although the differences of status indicated by scents in high-Victorian fiction may involve factors as varied as age and respectability, olfactory encounters often depend for their significance on what Bagehot called his society's "system of *removable inequalities*" (2: 308). Such events both assume and confirm a particular understanding of the phenomenon that Victorians pointed toward when they used the terms *class* and *status* and *rank*.[18] The inescapable presence of inequalities explains, I think, why representations of comparative encounters abound in the records that Victorian society made of and for itself: journalism, economic treatises, and parliamentary debates often base their analyses of contemporary life on social models that resemble in structure and effect the face-to-face meetings of daily life. Yet Victorian novels invoke the model of encounter with a result that is more vividly and palpably comparative than it is in such nonfictional prose because their representational conventions frequently record the physical bases of the differences that encounters reveal. Meetings rendered in olfactory terms are more significant still. Odors evoke sensations that necessarily convey the force of the economic determinants of social distinctions, no matter how they are labeled or where they are taken to have originated.[19] For those who believed that culturally recognized and approved differentiations reflect a divinely ordained, moral order of material relations, as natural and unavoidable as instinct, smell seems to have been the obvious register of those relations. Felix Holt explicitly recognizes that fact when he uses the formulation "the middle class."[20] As shifting but inextricable entanglements of social and economic valuations, class distinctions in Victorian culture were frequently experienced in the terms that Mary Poovey uses in defining "the binary logic that governed the Victorian symbolic economy" (*Uneven* 12), the logic that is replicated in the structure of an encounter: upper versus lower, genteel versus vulgar, middle versus working. Olfactory encounters suggest why class might have seemed to hold priority over other measures of inequality: such meetings bring into play all sorts of distinctions—gender, nationality, religion, and region—but they also array the individuals so identified against each other in the evaluative terms that class naturalizes, high versus low.[21]

Within the context of an olfactory encounter, then, class is a practice of everyday life, a way of comprehending quotidian, individual experience, rather than a sociological formulation or a political agenda. Less a structure that sorts out large groups of people into two or three categories, it is a process of setting one person in comparative relation to another. As often as class was formulated during the high-Victorian period in terms of clearly and absolutely differentiated groups, the experience of such categories was insistently represented as involving two individuals, at least one of whom was perceiving and responding to specific sensory stimuli.[22] High-Victorian fiction depicts encounters in ways that suggest what class might have meant in the daily lives of those who experienced it because such meetings constitute both the subject and the form of a novel: just as characters meet and come to know each other, creating connections and extending acquaintances, imaginative encounters of readers and characters, about which novelists like Dickens and Eliot and Trollope could be quite explicit, encourage the former to engage in processes of comparison and judgment, to apply codes "little" or large, in the ways similar to those typical of the face-to-face meetings of daily life. Both for readers and for characters of high-Victorian fiction, class is a measure set to do its work when two individuals come together.

The analysis that I offer in this study therefore confirms understandings of class proposed by early cultural theorists whose basic claims have often been obscured in subsequent commentaries on or qualifications of them. George Orwell's assertion in *The Road to Wigan Pier* (1937) that class is a matter of "*physical* feeling" is relevant here, even though the "*lower classes*" represented in the fiction of the 1860s do not "*smell*" as rankly as he claimed of the workers among whom he lived (128). More important, defining class as a practice of everyday life ratifies the distinction with which E. P. Thompson began *The Making of the English Working Class* (1963): class is not a thing, but a relation, even more an event, "something which in fact happens (and can be shown to have happened) in human relationships" (9). Finally, finding in olfactory encounters the sensory evidence of material differences reaffirms the importance of the questions about class that Raymond Williams posed. In the few pages of *The Long Revolution* (1961) that he devoted directly to the subject when he identified "the reality of differential treatment [as that which] makes a class system," he insisted on "looking rigorously at what [class] is there to do." According to Williams, "The question we need to ask . . . is what all this classification is for, what actual purposes in the society it serves" (317). Like the literary conventions that Williams analyzed in *The Country and the City*, class distinctions work "to promote superficial comparisons and to prevent real ones" (54). Representations of encounters rendered in the osmology of the 1860s often have the effects that Williams more generally attributed to class as a system of "differential treatment," whose consequences, as Orwell painfully established in *The Road to Wigan Pier*, are often most impressive when they are acted out in the encounters of one person with another.

Smells of the 1860s

High-Victorian fiction depicts a wide variety of distinctive sensory impressions—from the salt scent of a sea breeze in Yonge's *The Trial* and the disagreeable fumes of paint in Collins's *The Moonstone* to the smell of brandy in Robinson's *Beyond the Church* and the odor of rum on a midwife's breath in Wright's *Johnny Robinson*. Not surprisingly, historical novels like Le Fanu's *The House by the Churchyard* and Blackmore's *Lorna Doone* tend to describe more frequently than novels of contemporary life the fresh breezes and fragrances of rural existence. The scholastic, mediated flavor of the historical experience narrated in Eliot's *Romola* results, however, in its characters consistently speaking of smells rather than actually perceiving them—a distinctive quality that it shares with none of the other texts that I have read for this study. Novels conventionally labeled "realistic" tend to be more responsive to the documentary potential of smells than do those called "sensational." Such a generalization holds true for fiction by George Eliot and Mary Elizabeth Braddon—*Silas Marner* versus *Lady Audley's Secret*—and even for those novels by a single author like Braddon that are usually distinguished from each other as either more or less sensational—*Lady Audley's Secret* versus *The Doctor's Wife*. Some novelists record few olfactory stimuli. Trollope's *Orley Farm* contains no smells at all if one excludes, as I do, the narrator's reference in its first sentence to the cliché about a rose "by any other name," the rose in this case a metaphor rather than an odorant. Other novelists write fiction redolent of scents, good and bad. Dickensian smells are typically distinctive and sometimes highly unusual: the acrid odor emitted by the singed feathers in Mrs. Boffin's cap as she leans too close to a candle in *Our Mutual Friend* and the sickening stench of burning flesh that Pip cannot forget after Miss Havisham goes up in flames at the end of *Great Expectations*. The odors depicted in a novel can be numerous and varied, as they always are in the case of Dickens, or they can be numerous and numbingly unvaried, as they are in the only twenty-number serial novel that Thackeray wrote in the 1860s, *The Adventures of Philip*, which repeats again and again the same two odors, those of flowers and tobacco. Yet even this repetition, which might be dismissed as the effect of the exhaustion otherwise apparent near the end of Thackeray's career, helps establish a characteristic of the fictional osmology of the 1860s: flowers and cigars are its most frequently mentioned odorants.

As the prominence granted early in *Felix Holt* to the odors of rose leaves and candles suggests, the smells that provide the olfactory data for this osmology, including those that elicit negative responses, are relatively mild and sometimes even potentially pleasing. Although in many different historical and cultural contexts, smells are typically treated as automatically evocative of disgust or even nausea,[23] the fictional smells of the 1860s tend to be more subtle than otherwise—the lingering odor of Miss Havisham's burning flesh being the quite rare and most extraordinary exception to that rule. Of all the noxious smells that life in the 1860s no doubt exuded—effluvia from industrial waste, barnyard products, and cesspool collections—high-Victorian fiction registers almost exclusively the emanations that come from relatively innocuous sources, and they usually cause only faint distaste. Absent in the novels of the 1860s is the stench of the poor typical of fiction of the 1840s, the decade during which the sanitary reformer Edwin Chadwick felt justified in generalizing that "all smell is disease."[24] In novels of the 1840s, the working classes give off the fetid odors of decay and death, the most memorable instance of which is the suffocating stink in the Davenports' cellar in Elizabeth Gaskell's *Mary Barton* (1848). Lesser known but more emphatic still is the "scent-fiend" that haunts and kills the heroine of Charles Kingsley's *Yeast* (1848) after she nurses a fever patient (172). The depiction of bad smells in *Yeast* is so self-conscious that its hero actually proposes writing a *Chadwickiad* in honor of the 1842 *Sanitary Report*, an epic that would begin: "Smells and the Man I sing" (54). Even relatively genteel poverty can stink in the 1840s: during the outbreak of typhus at Lowood in Charlotte Brontë's *Jane Eyre* (1847), the school is described as "steam[ing] with hospital smells: the drug and the pastille striving vainly to overcome the effluvia of mortality" (85).

By contrast, rank odors of death and destitution rarely figure in novels from the 1860s, and they make their presences known, if at all, in only attenuated forms. Yonge's *The Trial* contains several discreet references to the kind of water pollution so important to the plot of *Yeast*; and when Eugene Wrayburn fends off the odor of Mr. Dolls by burning pastilles, the former never explicitly explains why the latter prompts their usage. Lower-class smells reckoned offensive in these novels may seem oddly unimpressive if judged by the standards of the 1840s. The odors of the poor that annoy the fastidious maiden aunt of Linton's *Lizzie Lorton* when she enters a cottage are those of "stale pie-crust and peat smoke" (84). Bertie Cecil, the aristocratic second son of Ouida's *Under Two Flags*, judges as intolerable, not the stench of sewage or diseased flesh, but the relatively mild, though "disagreeable odour of apples and corduroys." He finds this aroma so unpleasant that he indulges in a fantasy about a parliamentary "Bill for the Purifying of the Unwashed," which would call into action "a couple of fire-engines . . . playing on [the masses] continuously with rose-water and bouquet d'Ess" (10, 9). When Aurora Floyd encounters the "powerful odour of the stable-yard" on the wealthy farmers with whom she shares a railway carriage in Braddon's novel (289), she is less repelled by that odor than she is concerned that the men will notice her. Similarly, when *The Mill on the Floss* describes the deprivations felt by the multitudes participating in Britain's "wide and arduous national life," it refers to "unfragrant deafening factories" (255) as if a more direct and positive indication of their noisome odors would be impolite.

In the fiction of the 1860s, London, accordingly, seldom evokes any olfactory response at all, except when a particularly genteel young woman falls upon luck hard enough to impoverish her there, as happens to the heroine of Norton's *Lost and Saved*, or when a more prosperous young lady takes on the charitable duties of district visiting in the slums, as do the heroines of Broughton's *Not Wisely but Too Well* and Reade's *Hard Cash*. Even in *Our Mutual Friend*, the novel of the '60s most concerned with what we would call environmental pollution, London's filth is rendered visually in terms of the dust and debris that float through the city;[25] the dirty Thames may yield up bodies, but only one reference to its "ill-savoured tide" suggests that it produces odors (33). Two of the very few references to smells in Trollope's *Phineas Finn* evoke the "stinking" Thames (2: 80), but that stench is experienced, not when a character visits the poor, but when the members of Parliament gather in the House of Commons, as had been the case during the Great Stink of 1858 (Wohl 81). Urban smells, however, are more often represented indirectly. The narrator of Gilbert's *De Profundis* remarks on the discomfort caused by London's airless habitations and close streets. Similarly, Collins's *No Name* describes a particularly unappealing set of "cheap lodging-houses" in York by ironically locating them in a narrow street called Rosemary Lane (148). Such a designation emphasizes that this part of York lacks the healthy smells of the natural world that do occasionally enter the novels of contemporary life written during this decade or, more frequently, the stories depicting an earlier, simpler period like that portrayed in Howitt's *Woodburn Grange*.

The relatively inoffensive smells characteristic of the novels of the 1860s may attest, in part, to the success of midcentury hygienic campaigns, the widely touted "olfactory revolution" credited with sanitizing and deodorizing urban life, but they more directly reveal, I think, a change in perception effected by those campaigns.[26] Chadwick's identification in 1842 of smell with disease came at the opening of the first of the sustained attempts to improve public health, but such efforts did not quickly eradicate the sources of olfactory offense. Despite significant legislation that in 1848 established, for instance, a central board of health, it was not until 1866 that local authorities were required to hire sanitary inspectors and not until 1871 that a new central department was created to oversee public health. Many early parliamentary measures passed to deal with sanitary problems "proved useless until heavily amended and defined" (Hoppen 108). The "professionalized, bureaucratized apparatuses of inspection, regulation, and enforcement" characteristic of "the modern state" (Poovey, *Making* 116) were envisioned as early as the 1840s, but even decades later such instruments of government had not completely or even largely eliminated the overcrowded and unsanitary conditions in which the poor lived.

As Chadwick had definitively established, the poor smell, but they smell more in some kinds of texts published in the 1860s than in others. The various reports of 1864 and 1865 from public-health officers and child-labor commissions that Marx quotes in the first volume of *Capital* refer typically to the "unbearable" smells of the cottages where "children of 2 and 2½ years" make lace or to "places where 'the stench is enough to knock you down'" (598, 609). John Hollingshead's report on *Ragged London in 1861* notes specifically that the "dreary swamp of black manure-drainage" in Kensington "is in nearly the same condition now as it was some ten years ago, when attention was called to it in *Household Words*" (156). Describing the "sickening" odor in a house near Regent Street, he explains, "when a room-door was opened this stench came out in gusts" (119). If the poor and the locales in which they live continue to reek in such accounts, they do not do so in the novels of the 1860s: the deodorization project proposed by Bertie Cecil in *Under Two Flags* seems to have been applied, not to the Great Unwashed of the London streets, but to the representations of them in high-Victorian fiction. What is at work here, as Alain Corbin suggests in his commentary on French instances of the same effect, is a change, not so much in the material circumstances in which such fiction was being written, but in responses to those circumstances: a "new form of perception, [a] new intolerance of traditional actuality," now determines what sensations are to be ignored (156). It is almost as if Chadwick's campaigns, having taken hold of middle-class imaginations, made it more difficult for novelists to attend to the evidence of the unsolved sanitary problems around them—much as feminist principles, currently demonized as supremely powerful in the popular imagination, are mistakenly assumed to have magically eliminated the inequalities in response to which feminism initially developed.

Novels of the 1860s, therefore, reflect a highly refined sensibility to often subtle aromas, turning their imaginative noses away from the disgusting, contaminating stench of the poor to apprehend fainter, though sometimes distinctly distasteful odors. Such sensory capacities are as unlike those appropriate to the odors of the 1840s as they are to the intoxicating aromas that dominate the late-nineteenth- and early-twentieth-century fiction written by Wilde and Huysmans, Proust and Woolf, novels that treat an acute sensibility to positive olfactory stimuli as typical of the heightened aesthetic sensitivities of the so-called creative artist.[27] So obtrusively symbolic are the scents of such fiction that the *Quarterly Review* in 1899 labeled Huysmans's latest novel "a treatise on . . . mystical osmology, for the author sees hidden meanings in smells" ("Modern" 91). The only harbinger of such excesses in the fiction of the 1860s appears in the novel that Swinburne neither completed nor published in his lifetime: when brother and sister kiss in *Lesbia Brandon*, her "sweet-scented flesh," to which he presses his "violent lips," seems to "smell of flowers in a hot sun" (264). In no other novel of the decade—including Swinburne's *Love's Cross-Currents*, whose odors are chastely conventional—is sensory experience rendered through such aromatic intoxications, though Norton late in *Lost and Saved* does associate the fragrance of orange blossoms with the overwhelming feelings of awakening, though not incestuous, love.

The emphasis placed in the 1860s on ensuring the purity of fictional reading matter may have contributed to the widespread banishment of strong odors from the novels of that decade, but if the smells represented in texts like *The Mill on the Floss* and *Lizzie Lorton* are generally less potent than those found in the fiction of earlier and later decades, they are, arguably, even more effective in indicating the values that underwrite the osmology of high-Victorian fiction. As the intensity of the smells recorded in such works decreases, their significance in evaluating the subtle distinctions charted in the encounters of everyday life seems actually to increase.[28] Interestingly, two late-twentieth-century attempts to rewrite *Great Expectations*—*Jack Maggs* by Peter Carey and the novelization of the 1998 movie featuring Ethan Hawke and Gwyneth Paltrow—cannot imagine a Victorian world or even a modern version of one that is not rank with openly deplored, disgusting odors: the characters in the former frequently respond to the elaborately described "foul smells" of London (68); and in the latter, Estella tells the incarnation of the young Pip when she first meets him, "You smell like horseshit" (Chiel 41). Victorian noses were more refined than such recreations insist, and the evaluative potency of the odors of the 1860s depends at least in part on their relative subtlety. Moreover, audiences now seem to be able to experience olfaction only in the presence of objects that physically excite it—witness the odd phenomenon of odorama, the more recent fad of publishing children's books that purport to exude historically accurate smells, and the 2001 London exhibit of dinosaurs that offered, along with conventional models, the stench supposedly typical of their prehistoric environments.[29] Unlike such uses of specific odorants, representations of smells in the fiction of the 1860s are capable of constituting an osmology because they are so varied, distinct, finely nuanced, and perceptible.

The sense of society portrayed through the odors that high-Victorian fiction records is anything but calm and complacent.[30] Rather, such sensory responses illuminate the often uneasy and contradictory reactions of middle-class culture to its own productive and commercial successes. The 1860s constituted an historical watershed between the small-scale, kinship enterprises of the 1830s and 1840s and the corporate capitalism of the 1880s and 1890s, with its purpose-built office buildings and armies of female and German clerks: during the 1860s, almost all the legal, economic, and technological developments required for this transformation were being effected.[31] The fact that the odors of particular kinds of work appear in the fiction of those years reflects, I believe, contemporary responses to the economic tran-

sitions then taking place, particularly as they affected conceptions of genteel manhood. Prominent among such responses was an often unrecognized
but nonetheless profound nostalgia for an idealized materiality located in the
past. More generally, odors in the fiction of the 1860s tend to convey a deeply
conservative sense of both the small scale and the large import of traditional
forms of daily life. High-Victorian novels, wherever their stories are set,
portray spaces dense with social interactions, and they are typically the close,
sometimes uncomfortable relations more characteristic of the village and the
town than of the city.[32] Within such nostalgically conceived locales, the olfactory encounters of particular kinds of persons with particular forms of
matter revive earlier values even as they also often acknowledge the impos-
sibility of sustaining those values in the present.

Analytic Encounters

"Comparisons are odorous," as Dogberry would have it, but they constitute
both the subject and the method of this study. Throughout the following
chapters, I stage comparative encounters between the specific odors, characters, and plots of novels of the 1860s as well as between fictional representations of smells and Victorian commentaries on the senses. Setting out the
osmology of high-Victorian fiction and the principles that explain its structure and begin to account for their significance, the first chapter treats the
odors depicted in the novels that I have read without regard to the identity
of their authors, their generic features, or the kinds of social issues that they
variously engage. Although female characters often respond to odorants and
such impressions are frequently included here, descriptions of three comparative encounters in which working-class men sniff out their supposed superiors provide the central texts of this chapter: an instance from *Great Expectations*,
an example again featuring the hero of *Felix Holt*, and a meeting between a
worker and his employer depicted in the first volume of *Capital*. Putting Marx
in the company of English novelists, whose social insights he on occasion
praised, reveals the wide reach of the fictional osmology that I identify, and it
also demonstrates the centrality to olfactory exchanges of the characteristics
conventionally attributed to members of the working classes. As Bruce Robbins
has argued in *The Servant's Hand*, workers other than servants are typically
absent in British fiction, yet in the 1860s some artisans do participate in encounters registered through smells and smelling. What that fact says about both
the qualities of their manhood and their class status is a more complicated
question, one that I treat at length in subsequent discussions.

Implicit in such depictions of working men is the conviction consistently
conveyed by high-Victorian fiction that a particular kind of man matters more

than others—the kind of man whose gentility can be counted on to register the smells that others give off. Hughes's *Tom Brown at Oxford* is typical in describing "the marks of that thorough, quiet, high breeding, that refinement which is no mere surface polish, and that fearless unconsciousness which looks out from pure hearts, which are still, thank God, to be found in so many homes of the English gentry" (2: 44). Conversely, this standard applies as a way of quickly recognizing the qualities that some men lack. When Mr. Prong, a minor character in Trollope's *Rachel Ray*, is introduced to readers of the novel, the narrator insists three times that the Evangelical cleric is "not a gentleman." The narrator, however, declines to define what he means by the term *gentleman*, arguing that such a judgment is instantaneous and invariably reliable.[33] Gentlemen are known as easily as one recognizes a good coat: "As it is with coats, so it is with that which we call gentility. It is caught at a word, it is seen at a glance, it is appreciated unconsciously at a touch by those who have none of it themselves" (77). The validity of such social judgments is recognized immediately by all who see or touch or even hear about their material markers. Yet olfaction as a test of gentility sorts out the men who have it from "those who have none of it" in ways that even the narrator of *Rachel Ray* might find surprisingly accurate.

From its second chapter through its conclusion, this study explores the effects of olfactory encounters and of the exchanges that may issue from them by dealing with the characters and plots of specific novels. Chapter 2 treats the principal male characters of Oliphant's *Salem Chapel*, Dickens's *Great Expectations*, and Meredith's *Evan Harrington*, each of whom suffers from a particular condition of Victorian manhood that I define as melancholia, in some cases a nearly pathological insubstantiality that reflects an unacknowledged loss of direct physical contact with the products of artisanal labor. Bringing together the thinking of Freud and Marx for the purposes of this analysis, I identify the causes of an apparently idiopathic psychological state in the circumstances of material production characteristic of the 1860s. The third chapter, which returns to *Evan Harrington* and *Salem Chapel* to deal with their principal female characters, also considers the heroines of Yonge's *The Clever Woman of the Family*, Eliot's *Felix Holt*, and Trollope's *Miss Mackenzie*. These novels attribute to such female characters the capacity to offer their men the substance not only of their reproductive bodies but also of their money and their land. A woman's attempt to treat the ills of her melancholic man in the context of the domesticity that they share, however, often merely reveals that his cure must be sought elsewhere. To illustrate the implications of this point, a final chapter deals with *Our Mutual Friend*. In John Harmon, I argue, Dickens creates the supreme melancholic of the 1860s. A woman's ability to assuage Harmon's suffering is ultimately less efficacious than the opportunities that the plot gives him to display the physical strength conventionally associated with working-class men. Through the exchanges effected during the olfactory encounters depicted in *Our Mutual Friend*, the negative projection by which such workers are usually understood to contribute to middle-class subjectivity[34] is transformed into a process of positive embodiment.

In the afterword, I comment briefly on Eliot's *Middlemarch*, a novel begun in the last year of the 1860s, to indicate the historically specific political analysis to which my argument leads. The preceding chapters examine the plots of the fiction of the 1860s by assuming, as Rosemarie Bodenheimer explains, that a novel's politics inheres in "the shape and movement of narrative." That principle applies whether the term *politics* is defined generously as the realm of day-to-day negotiations that determine who holds power over whom or as the arena in which the workings of a particular government sort out which group's interests will prevail.[35] The narrative of *Middlemarch* addresses both understandings of the political, thereby providing the most telling, if still indirect demonstration of the connection between the osmology of high-Victorian fiction and parliamentary activity in the 1860s. The debates surrounding the 1866 and 1867 reform bills, I argue, involved on a national scale the kind of exchange that Victorian novels enact on the level of relations between individuals, and seeing the former in the context of the latter is a way of understanding the distinctive qualities of the culture that created both—the explanatory power of fiction, if not its agency, extending to historical events far removed from the erotic and domestic concerns with which Victorian novels are so preoccupied, even obsessed.

The argument with which this study concludes, like those in the previous chapters, is therefore based on the olfactory data provided by the many novels surveyed earlier: it could not have been developed without the perspectives on materiality that they offer. Yet it also extends beyond issues directly related to the sensory modality of smell so that franchise reform in particular may be understood as a distinctively high-Victorian exchange. Ultimately, olfactory encounters reveal that the material and the immaterial in Victorian culture, despite the many and eloquent insistences at the time to the contrary, do not necessarily compete with or oppose each other: rather, matter and spirit are often conjoined so that the sensory data of the former support the shared assumptions and beliefs specific to the latter. The evocative smells of *Middlemarch* exemplify that relationship, connecting olfactory experience to the larger, normally inodorate arena of parliamentary politics, to which such sense impressions apparently have little relevance but to which they actually point.

Victorian understandings of olfaction differ markedly from our own: verbal images of specific smells were deemed more immediate and thus more potent; the ability to note such odors more refined and thus more meaningful, than current formulations would allow. If everyday experience taught Victorian writers and readers that people do not have olfactory receptors as powerful as those of dogs, which Bain found to be "almost miraculous" (170), the human nose was understood to be more than adequate to meet human needs. The basic physical mechanism of this sensory modality was a mystery to Victorian science, as it remains today,[36] but the cultural purposes served by the discrimination of odors were and are more readily open to analysis and explanation. Olfactory encounters in high-Victorian novels, therefore, reveal the common sense of middle-class culture as it was both enacted in and obscured by the unremarkably ordinary practices of daily life.

I

Smelling Others

Of all the fictional figures of the 1860s who use their noses to recognize those whom they meet, three men serve here as their representatives. Early in Dickens's *Great Expectations*, Pip encounters the as-yet-unnamed lawyer Jaggers on the stairway in Miss Havisham's house. Pip, whose chin is held firmly in the hand of the "gentleman" who is examining him, listens to a predictable, if blessedly short homily on the bad behavior of boys: "With those words, he released me—which I was glad of, for his hand smelt of scented soap—and went his way down stairs" (83). In a similar first meeting, the hero of Eliot's *Felix Holt* is introduced to his future wife in an olfactory encounter. The odors of wax and tallow have been the subject of the conversation between Felix Holt and Esther Lyon's father, but when she enters the room where they are seated, smell is the first sensory modality, before even vision or hearing, that records Felix's surprise at her gentility: "A very delicate scent, the faint suggestion of a garden, was wafted as she went" (60). Finally, in a passage from the first volume of *Capital* that adapts the techniques characteristic of high-Victorian fiction, Marx's archetypal worker responds to the "odour of sanctity" that he notices when he comes face to face with his employer (343). In each of these instances, a man responds to another person by recognizing matter, an object giving off fragrance, and he thereby registers the physical trace of a physical presence.

Although at least the first two of these incidents seem unremarkably ordinary, they all serve as occasions for a number of exemplary questions. Why are particular smells represented rather than others? Why, for instance, does Pip perceive the scent of soap on Jaggers's hand rather than, say, that of wine on his breath? Why does Felix note the floral fragrance given off by Esther rather than the aroma of the tea that they are about to share? Why does it make sense to see Marx's worker as the colleague of such characters? In what way does the odor of sanctity emanate from matter as well as spirit? Even more pertinently: Why does one character rather than another perceive a smell? What does it mean that three workers are the ones doing the smelling here when workers, at least in most Victorian imaginations, were considered more often the source of olfactory stimuli than the sensitive agents of its perception? That final question is more fully addressed in the following chapters when I deal at length with the ways in which the characteristic odors of high-Victorian fiction identify Pip and Felix as melancholics, but these three instances of olfactory processing exemplify, as I argue in this chapter, the conventions that govern the osmology of high-Victorian fiction. The depiction of smells in novels of the 1860s is so highly formulaic that it amounts to a kind of aesthetic second nature, one that seems to have been supplied to Victorian writers along with the paper and pens with which they created their novels. Its code, more extensive and capacious than Esther Lyon's, is as refined in its discriminations as hers but ultimately much more revealing.

To understand why that is so, one needs to ask a simple question of the olfactory responses recorded in the encounters of high-Victorian fiction: Who smells? In the clumsy terminology characteristic of discourses of olfaction, that question actually contains two queries: Who does the smelling? And who—or what—gives off the odors that are smelled? Setting the experiences of Pip, Felix, and Marx's worker in the context of a range of other different but equally typical olfactory encounters begins to answer these questions by identifying the osmology that gives meaning to the responses that such characters have when they smell others.

The structure of sensations that I outline here is based on the novels that I have surveyed for their smells, for the traces of matter that they recognize as occasions for olfactory sensations. Because the scents that these texts have in common when they represent smelling outweigh the distinctions that their status as works by different authors would imply, in this chapter I cite the novels from which I draw my examples only by title, and they appear alphabetized in that form in the appendix. Discussing three specific and representative comparative encounters, however, also allows me to explain the relevance to them of the nonfictional commentaries on the senses provided by such writers as Alexander Bain, George Henry Lewes, and George Wilson. In the kind of exchange that I have come to expect of this material, Victorian fiction, presumably the inferior of such works in matters of observational accuracy and scientific insight, offers more subtle, if less direct, analyses of olfaction than Victorian psychophysiology can provide.

Olfactory Encounters

Smelling soap on Jaggers's hand, Pip is responding to the kind of odorant typical of the 1860s. The most prominent characteristic of the fictional osmology of the 1860s, as I point out in the introduction, is the relatively inoffensive nature of the smells that high-Victorian novels register: subtle odors matter more than rank ones. Like the fragrance that Felix notes as Esther Lyon walks toward him and the balsamic aroma that Marx's worker perceives, such odors are mild; in other contexts they could easily be pleasing. Yet equally characteristic is the kind of reaction, the unease, that the aroma of soap elicits from Pip. During his encounter with Jaggers, the boy has every reason to be uncomfortable. He is being held in the grasp of an unknown "burly man of an exceedingly dark complexion" with "disagreeably sharp and suspicious" eyes, a man who subjects him to a cross-examination that takes as its premise the younger party's guilt simply because he is male and young: "I have a pretty large experience of boys, and you're a bad set of fellows." Pip here becomes merely one of a lot, made to stand for all those who cannot be trusted to behave. Yet Pip says that he is "glad" to be released, not because he is tired of being verbally abused, as he no doubt soon becomes, not because the man's grasp is rough, as it no doubt is, but specifically because Jaggers smells: "With those words, he released me—which I was glad of, for his hand smelt of scented soap" (83). The *for* in this sentence carries the weight of causality, portraying Pip's discomfort with Jaggers's grasp wholly and remarkably as the sensation caused by smelling perfumed soap.

Such a response is typical of the 1860s—a function of the time of Pip's telling of his story rather than of the earlier decade in which this incident presumably has taken place—and why that is so is a question that can be addressed by posing another, perhaps prior question: Why is the sense of smell privileged here? Being able to answer such a question depends on recognizing a principle that is virtually inviolable in the representations of odors in the fiction of the 1860s: smell is the sensory register that unerringly responds to the differences between one individual and another. Pip's meeting of Jaggers immediately emphasizes a number of factors that distinguish the two characters from each other—one young and provincial, the other mature and worldly; one weak and vulnerable, the other powerful and dominant—precisely because that meeting involves olfactory stimulus and olfactory response. Similarly, the many differences that separate Felix Holt and Esther Lyon, but particularly the major factor that distinguishes them, his masculinity as opposed to her femininity, like the opposing stations in the "production process" held by Marx's worker and capitalist (342), are registered by smells because they are differentiations of such magnitude and wide-ranging import.

These three encounters are exemplary of dozens and dozens of such meetings in the novels that I have read, and the olfactory sensations that they typically elicit involve responses to a wide range of culturally constructed differences. The "Oriental strangers" of *The Moonstone* imbue their lodgings with a "faint" but clearly recognizable "odour of musk and camphor" (239). A particular French woman, like all of her kind, is "strongly scented," according to *Grasp Your Nettle* (2: 3); and Tourbillon, the aristocratic French villain of *The White Rose*, is associated with the sickeningly sweet aura of the perfume that remains in a room even after he has left it—so much so that when he stays in London, he lodges over a perfumer's shop in Bond Street. Odors distinguish the sane from the insane: in *Hard Cash*, a novel explicitly crusading against the cruelty of imprisoning those of sound mind along with the mad, the latter are recognized by the former because the insane give off "the peculiar wild-beast smell that marks the true maniac" (482). Subjecting not only Jaggers to such sensory processing, Pip later differentiates the criminal from his law-abiding counterpart by smell, "that curious flavour of bread-poultice, baize, rope-yarn, and hearth-stone, which attends the convict presence" (228). Scenting another sort of differentiation, the mature villainess of *Armadale* dismisses the charms of her rival by quoting Byron to the effect that young girls "always smell of bread and butter" (428). Most frequently, however, smells allow those perceiving them to sniff out social distinctions. Like the flashing of a diamond ring on a male hand, perfume on a male body warns of an aristocrat or a ne'er-do-well pretending to be one—Francis Levison in *East Lynne* or Stephen Guest in *The Mill on the Floss*. Tourbillon's scent in *The White Rose* is therefore overdetermined: his perfume marks both his questionable status and his nationality. A stable boy, like the one in *John Marchmont's Legacy*, may make "the air odorous with the scent of hay and oats" (313); or he may, as in *Eleanor's Victory*, give off the less appealing fragrance of other odorants characteristic of his work. Whatever the difference at issue—British versus French, sane versus insane, lawful versus criminal, young versus old, genteel versus common—it can be sensed, experienced through the senses, because the nose knows infallibly the matter that meets it. Why this might be so, why it makes such representational sense, becomes clear if one considers the scientific and popular theories about sensory experience that were current when these novels were being written.

Victorian conceptions of the workings of the sense of smell demonstrate Thomas Laqueur's thesis that "powerful prior notions of difference or sameness determine what one sees and reports about the body" (21). Although Western thinking about sensory experience tends to view "perception as a physical rather than cultural act" (Classen 1), there is plenty of evidence in mid-Victorian treatises and their popularizations that olfaction in particular was conceived to be more the latter than the former. In part, the understanding of olfaction as culturally determined reflects Victorian conceptions of the relative lowliness of this sensory modality. According to writers whose works on the moral and physical dimensions of smell I cite in the introduction here, the sense of sight transcends the limitations of time and place. The eye was for Victorians the "preeminent organ of truth" (Christ and Jordan xx), and mid-Victorian commentators make clear that the truth that the eye recognizes is universal and unchanging. Like visual images, the sounds heard in music are also assumed to mean the same things to all those who experience them. George Wilson discovers in music a "universal language": its meanings are the same for "the white man and the black man, the red man and the yellow man," for "both sexes and all ages" (50). Smell, however, is conceived in entirely different terms.

According to Victorian psychophysiology, smell is the sense of difference. Because olfaction is the "least intellectual and most purely emotional" of the senses (Allen 83), it is also the most primitive. *Primitive* in this context means animalistic, and Victorian commentaries on sensory experience typically associate olfaction with the physical requirements of human existence—most notably, with eating and sex. Wilson identifies smell as the sense "closely related to the necessities of animal life," and he finds that it is therefore "more largely developed in the lower creatures" than it is in human beings (52–53) or, as Grant Allen puts the point, more evident in children and savages, "whose nerves are fresh and strong" (43). The olfactory organ, the "Nose-Brain" or rhinencephalon, according to Bain's citation of the "best works on human Anatomy," is "in man . . . a very insignificant mass," predominant only in the "lowest vertebrate animals" (24–25n). The links between emotion, instinct, and even animality identify this particular sensory modality as, in the phrase that Allen uses twice, "a mere relic" (81, 83).[1] Wilson, alone of all these writers, regrets the relative and inevitable anosmia of modern life, but in doing so he makes the point that Bain presents as a simple matter of physiological organization: "in these later days," writes Wilson, it is only "natural that the sense of smell with which we are not highly endowed, and which we cannot very easily gratify, should become to us an object of less concern than any of the other senses" (71–72).

As Allen's reference to children and savages and Wilson's lament for the blunted olfactory capacities of highly civilized peoples both demonstrate, such commentators find in olfaction a sensory response that differs from one culture to the next. In *The Physiology of Common Life*, Lewes offers with his characteristic self-assurance one of the fullest and most remarkable treatments of this Victorian commonplace, in the course of which he provides anecdotal evidence from a German source that Carpenter cites with less fanfare in his *Principles of Mental Physiology* (141). Noting that "in few things do human beings differ more widely than in their sense of Smell," Lewes attempts to prove his point not by citing the variations of individual experience that, for instance, allow a person to associate specific memories with a particular smell. Rather, Lewes instances cultural differences: "Peruvian Indians can, in the dark, distinguish by the smell the different races, European, American-Indian, or Negro" (2: 315–17). This assertion has two meanings: different races give off different olfactory stimuli—Europeans do not smell like American Indians—and different races have different capacities for olfaction—Peruvian Indians are more fully capable of smelling others than Europeans are. Offering an example that confirms the point made in Lewes's reference to Peruvian Indians, Wilson can locate no universalized responses when he discusses perfumes, which, he argues, are more important to ancient than to modern peoples, more prevalent in their uses among "Oriental and Southern peoples, than . . . those of the North and the West" (62). Such differences not only depend on physical organization—southerners, who have "quicker blood and keener physical perceptions" than northerners, are more attuned to the effects of perfume—but they also reflect training— those living in warm climates are often exposed to the kinds of fragrant plants capable of "educat[ing] the sense of smell" (69–70). Smell, as all these works agree, is the major register of such cultural differences, which in turn always reflect material differences, both in the smeller and the smelled. Because odor is so inextricably defined as a characteristic of matter, even in the more refined emanations characteristic of the culture of the high-Victorian 1860s, it can communicate what distinguishes one person from another by representing one individual as having a smell to be perceived and the other as perceiving it. For Victorian science, those who perceive smells are, by definition, closer to animals and savages than those who do not. The two roles, smelled and smelling, are, however, apportioned differently in fictional encounters.

Lewes's insistence on the olfactory genius of Peruvian Indians puts a global perspective on the various examples of olfactory perceptions that I have cited: foreigner and countryman, sane and insane, young and old, gentle and common are differentiated from each other through the perception of odors. Lewes's distinctions are also based on similarities: all Europeans smell the same to the Peruvian Indians who can sniff them out even in the dark, and all members of a given "race" smell the same, be they "European, American-Indian, or Negro." Unlike Lewes's formulations, however, instances from high-Victorian fiction prove that not all Britons smell alike. By comparison, then, commentaries offered by writers like Lewes provide a way of understanding the full subtlety of the messages that a Victorian novel conveys when it presents an encounter by invoking a smell. Yet the osmology of high-Victorian fiction goes well beyond simply differentiating one person from another; it also evaluates the relative worth of the parties to an encounter, and it does so in quite specific ways. Once again Pip's encounter with Jaggers provides a test case. If scents mark the participants in an encounter as high or low in relation to each other, which position does Pip hold? The answer would seem simple: according to all the conventional physical markers of a comparative encounter, to which Estella's previously registered contempt for Pip's "coarse hands" and "thick boots" have pointed (61), Pip is low, Jaggers high. That is literally the case as the older man towers above the slight, young boy, the rough clothing of the latter justifying and explaining his subjection to the power of the former's grasp. One is "a gentleman," the other a "common labouring-boy" (83, 61). No mystery here. According to writers like Bain and Wilson, Pip's role as the character who uses his nose simply identifies him as lower on a scale of development than Jaggers: Pip is a working-class version of a Peruvian Indian able to smell out his European better. Yet Pip's olfactory encounter with Jaggers is also, according to the characteristic practices of high-Victorian fiction, an exchange: the event presumably ratifying the kind of inferiority that Pip's elders inevitably attribute to him actually allows the boy to register his superiority to yet another brow-beating adult. Understanding that exchange depends on putting Pip's olfactory experience in two larger contexts, one constituted by the data drawn from the fiction of the decade and the other by the physiological principles that illuminate their import.

Olfactory Evaluations

Repeatedly in the fiction of the 1860s, comparative encounters are depicted in terms of an inodorate perceiver of smells and his or her smelly other. In the novel named for her, Rachel Ray attends a ball and notices the lack of gentility in one of her dancing partners when she encounters the scent of perfume with which, along with too much jewelry, he has adorned himself, just as the eponymous Miss Mackenzie recognizes her superiority to her would-be suitor Mr. Rubb by responding to the "perfumed grease" (139) that he wears. Similarly, Maggie and Tom in *The Mill on the Floss* know in their olfactory nerves the full extent of the disgrace of their father's bankruptcy when they are "startled" to find in their own house the "strong smell of tobacco" given off by a bailiff, "a coarse, dingy man . . . smoking, with a jug and glass beside him" (176). The heroine of *Cometh up as a Flower* carries soup in an act of unwilling charity to an impoverished widow, at whose gate the young lady smells "a mixed flavour of pigs and of that objectionable herb called southernwood . . . in [her] small nose" (51), the delicacy of which clearly distinguishes her from the object of her charity. Most explicit in this regard is a scene recollected by the socially ambitious countess of *Evan Harrington*, when she refers to a British newspaperman whom she has known in Lisbon: "The man was so horridly vulgar; his gloves were never clean; I had to hold a bouquet to my nose when I talked to him. That, you say, was my fault! Truly so. But what woman can be civil to a low-bred, pretentious, offensive man?" (33). Making much of her sense of her social superiority, the countess casts it in terms of a sensory delicacy that forces her, like the witnesses to Magwitch's trial in *Great Expectations*, to use her nosegay as a defense against a journalist, a gesture that identifies him as a kind of social criminal.

Because such encounters underscore the primarily affective nature of smelling as a sensory process, they cast those who experience them as relatively refined, even if the characters in question are the children of a penniless miller. Rachel feels more or less mild distaste, Maggie and Tom experience shame, the young lady of *Cometh up as a Flower* and the would-be lady of *Evan Harrington* register disdain; and these characters respond in such ways immediately and automatically, as if they were reacting instinctively to the inferiority of the persons whom they have just encountered. None of these responses, moreover, seems to need any explanation. Each stimulus prompts an instantaneous and unmistakable physical reaction on the part of the character who experiences it. The unfortunate Mr. Griggs, earlier described as "odious with the worst abominations of perfumery" (73), is rejected as a dancing partner not only by Rachel Ray but also by every self-respecting young woman at the Tappitts's ball. Likewise, Maggie and Tom flee the room where the bailiff is sitting; Tom, aware of what that "hateful" presence means, does so without answering the man's embarrassed greeting (177). The heroine of *Cometh up* escapes the object of her charity as quickly as possible, and the countess of *Evan Harrington* raises her bouquet to her nose. Such responses to the registration of smells as sensory stimuli, moving quickly and directly as they do from feeling to action, are based on the physiology of olfaction, characteristics of which were well known to Victorian commentators on the senses.

Smells and the affective reactions they trigger can provide rich and even subtle perspectives on cultural valuations because, by an only apparent paradox, the basic classification that differentiates odors is so crude and limiting. Odors provide sensory data that Victorian science was particularly hard pressed either to categorize or to describe.[2] In *The Senses and the Intellect*, Alexander Bain thinks himself equal to both challenges, but as soon as he starts classifying olfactory sensations by adducing simple binaries (*fresh* vs. *close*), the future grammarian comes up with failures of parallelism (*sweet* vs. *stinks*), and he finally gives up by proposing the anomalous category of *appetising*. Throughout this discussion Bain indulges in neologisms like the awkward term "nose-pain" or the more graceful "'mal-odour,'" but he continues to emphasize the insufficiencies of the language of olfaction: "something beside sweet is wanting to express" the effects of ethereal aromas (165–69). The difficulties that Bain faces seem to reveal shortcomings not only of science but also of language itself. The "olfactory-verbal gap" is experienced every day in Western culture as the linguistic poverty that attends the sense of smell,[3] which has no vocabulary of its own, no words that function, as do, for instance, *red* and *blue* in the realm of vision. Smells are either labeled in relation to their source—it smells like a rose—or by analogy—it smells like a rose. Using repetitive diction seems the fate of any discussion of this particular sense.

The categories that sort one kind of smell from another are equally crude. As Bain puts the point, a smell produces either "the sentiment of liking or [the sentiment of] aversion" (343). Using the hedonic distinction that goes back at least as far as Plato's *Timaeus* (Rindisbacher 10), Victorian commentators distinguish between odors that are either pleasing or unpleasing, good or bad, odors that, accordingly, evoke reactions of attraction or repulsion. In a widely reprinted treatise of the 1870s, Julius Bernstein admits that science cannot explain "the existence of different kinds of sensations of smell," yet he takes for granted the force of the difference "between the irritations produced by good and bad smells" (294). George Wilson recognizes this basic distinction when he explains that "sympathies, common to all mankind, . . . lead us to connect fragrance with health, happiness, and joyous existence, and revolting odours with disease, suffering, and death" (84). Anthropological research has confirmed Wilson's speculation that the hedonic distinction between smells is virtually a cultural universal: all societies differentiate between good and bad smells, though which smells fall into which category varies greatly, with odorants like onions and urine serving as perfumes in some cultures but not in others.[4] The unsubtle affective responses typically evoked by smells—pleased, displeased—quickly become translated into action—yes, no; do, don't. A smell excites "the carnivorous appetite, and rouses the animal to pursuit" (Bain 169–70), with eating and sex again as the most obvious outcomes of such incitements. Physical stimulus creates affect; affect leads to action.

As the instance of Esther Lyon's "little code" suggests, the action most often prompted by olfaction in a high-Victorian novel is that of judging, of placing in categories of relatively good or bad the object or person perceived as giving off a smell. Encounters as they are represented in such fiction, therefore, typically exhibit the bluntly categorical power of the evaluations prompted by olfaction. Even metaphoric invocations of the term *odor* demonstrate the relation between olfactory cause and the immediate, active effect of passing judgments. Used in a figure of speech, *odour* indicates an individual's reputation, as the *OED* records, drawing its examples exclusively from the nineteenth century. In recounting the incident from *Capital* that I have cited, Marx adopts the phrase "odour of sanctity" from a workers' manifesto published during the London builders' strike of 1859–1860 so that he can convey its authors' skepticism about their employer's reputation for piety (343). Fictional uses of this metaphor tend to embody in action its evaluative implications. Thus, one character in *Armadale* recognizes that another is shunned by the townspeople because he is "in bad odour in the neighbourhood" (288), and the unpopular candidate for Parliament and his supporters in *East Lynne* are "entirely alive to the odour in which they [are] held," even before the would-be M.P. receives a dunking by the "mob" in a literally "stinking" pond (389, 391). Judging is an action that can lead to other, more physically impressive actions.

The process of arriving at such judgments, therefore, necessarily distinguishes the character whose body or accessories smell from the one who does the smelling. Casting the relatively superior character as inodorate and the relative inferior as odorous is a practice that high-Victorian fiction invokes with particular consistency when the differences between two individuals being acted out in a comparative encounter involve inequalities of social status. The only very rare exceptions to this rule occur when a character of lower standing perceives the attractive aroma of his or her superiors—when, for instance, the publican of *Evan Harrington* says of another tradesman that he "smel[ls] of good company" after having dined with the gentry (6). Disapprobation almost inevitably attaches to what is odorous as a way of registering the social inferiority of a character associated with a smell. By contrast, none of the characters whose perceptions of smells are recorded in the examples I have cited—the sane, the legitimate, British, mature, or male—is represented as giving off an odor at which others, including the reader, might sniff. As important, then, as what these characters smell is what they do not smell: themselves. And here again, in the impoverished but usefully ambiguous language of olfactory experience, this assertion has two meanings: these characters do not smell their own bodies, and they do not emit odors that others might smell.

According to the convention that is perhaps the most powerful of those governing the representations of olfactory experience in high-Victorian fiction, then, encounters between equals are depicted as wholly inodorous; those between unequals apportion olfactory responses only to the inodorate superior. Novels of the 1860s use this convention to make series of sometimes gross and sometimes quite subtle social differentiations. When Gerard, the cleanly Dutch hero of the historical novel *The Cloister and the Hearth*, is forced by a storm to take shelter in a German inn, he is assaulted by the smells of its inhabitants. Once he is able to overcome the sensory shock of entering the room and encountering there "compound odours inexpressible," he distinguishes a fantastic range of distinct "fetors": "habiliments, impregnated with . . . the dirt of a life, . . . the peculiar sickly smell of neglected brats. Garlic . . . Odour of family . . . stewed rustic. . . . a flavour [of] ancient goats or the fathers of all foxes" (154). Clothes, dirt, children, food—all are so rancid that they smell like animals, making Gerard feel as if he were dying. This passage, the most sustained and graphic description of olfaction in any of the novels that I have read, records a variety of potentially annihilating smells presumably because they indicate the rustic brutalities of Continental life in the late fifteenth century, and the novel may defy for that reason the convention that calls for relatively inoffensive odors in the fiction of the 1860s. Yet even this excessive recording of stench is quite typical in its granting to its social superior the ability to recognize and evaluate the smells that others give off. Presumably, Gerard is the only guest at this particular inn who finds in its inhabitants the stimuli for olfactory offense. Their responses to his relatively sanitary person are never registered. Each of the groups represented—families, rustics, garlic-eaters—Gerard finds rank, while he remains inodorous.

A similar series of discriminations is also typical of the olfactory responses to the more subtle stimuli encountered closer to home in Victorian England. Over the course of a number of chapters in *Tom Brown at Oxford*, the hero differentiates the fellow students he meets at Oxford through the odors that he perceives when he encounters them, odors that typify the various styles of life that they represent and sort them out according to criteria that are moral and religious as well as economic and social. In the rooms of Drysdale, the foremost of the "fast" set of wealthy gentlemen-commoners, Tom encounters the mingled scents of flowers, denoting Drysdale's effete refinement, and tobacco, denoting his dissipation. Hardy, the servitor or working student, is marked by the smell of the whiskey that he drinks in place of the wines that he cannot afford. In the rooms of one of the High Church party, Tom is offended to find what he calls "three sorts of scent on the mantelpiece, besides eau de Cologne," clear proof to Squire Brown's sturdy son that the men inhabiting such a room are engaged in a religious version of what he calls a "man-millinery business" (1: 130, 132). In each of these cases, Tom, the standard by which the novel measures the various qualities associated with gentility, even when he strays slightly from the path of manly purity, is as wholly without odor as those he judges are found by him to be odorous. If the fine port with which his father supplies Tom gives off any scent, the reader is never told so. Like Lorna Doone, a seventeenth-century aristocratic character whose "olfactory powers" are a mark of her breeding (427), Gerard in the fifteenth century and Tom two hundred years later perform their superiority by responding to the olfactory stimuli presented by their inferiors.

Like the hedonic distinction between pleasing and unpleasing smells to which it is related, the practice of identifying the superior participant in an encounter as inodorate seems to be a cultural universal, the most powerful group among the Suya Indians of Brazil, for instance, being the ones who are most odoriferously "bland" (Classen, Howes, and Synnott 101). Smells, therefore, provide particularly potent ways to draw distinctions between the marked and the unmarked. According to Peggy Phelan's account of this distinction, any culture based on inequalities renders invisible—representationally unmarked—the qualities or phenomena that it invests with value.[5] What lacks visibility—white, male, hetero—is the unmarked, the dominant and powerful norm. What has representational visibility—black, female, homo—is the marked, the supposed inferior. Translated into olfactory terms, the principle that representations typically feature and therefore mark those whom a culture devalues informs the osmology of high-Victorian fiction: when it comes to smells, top dogs do not mark their territory; they know it because their inferiors are presumably powerless not to mark theirs. As one of Gaskell's characters from the late 1850s explains in more genteel terms, "nothing show[s] birth like a keen susceptibility of smell" (qtd. Classen 82). Moreover, the specific physiological reactions typical of olfaction explain why those individuals granted the capacities to perceive the odors of others are, as if by definition, dominant over those who give off odors.

Smell is a particularly apt register in which to chart the distinctions between marked and unmarked because, as Victorian commentators recognized, olfaction, much more than sight or hearing, is a modality in which nerves inevitably become adapted and therefore desensitized to the stimuli that they most frequently encounter: the more one smells a particular odor, the less one can smell it; the stronger a particular odor, the more rapid and apparently complete the adaptation to it.[6] The effects of this process are widely recognized in daily life—walking into a room, one can be overwhelmed by an odor that seems to disappear shortly thereafter. As the narrator of *John Marchmont's Legacy* explains, invoking the language of science, if a man tests the contents of too many bottles of perfume, his "olfactory nerves" become "afflicted with temporary paralysis" (391). More important, what is the norm in one's olfactory experience is not perceived as experience at all. Victorian commentators often associated the process of adaptation with the primitive, even animalistic nature of olfaction. As a sailor comes not to feel the rocking of his ship, "the muskrat possesses an unintermitted odour, which, therefore, is undiscoverable to the animal. . . . It smells nothing" (Johnson 45, 57). The muskrat's presumed inability to perceive its own stench was often attributed to the similarly animalistic poor. Speaking specifically of olfaction, George Wilson defines the lower classes, perhaps wishfully underestimating their numbers, as the "one half of the community [so] steeped in such physical degradation and wretchedness that they cannot use their senses aright" (71–72). Chadwick notes the same phenomenon in his *Sanitary Report* (165),[7] and Hollingshead concludes his *Ragged London in 1861* by deploring the way in which the "senses" of the poor are "blunted by long familiarity" with the squalor in which they live: "they cannot see . . . the mass of rotten filth that surrounds them; they cannot smell the stench" (222).

In the context of the relatively genteel and inodorous regions charted by the fiction of the 1860s, adaptation is not noted in relation to the poor, whose stench, as I have pointed out, is all but absent there. It pertains consistently, however, to their betters, the ladies and gentlemen who smell others but do not smell themselves. *The Adventures of Philip* offers an effective demonstration of this phenomenon. Philip's relation to virtually all those whose homes he visits is charted by their responses to the smell of the cigar or pipe smoke that he carries with him as a sign of his life as a journalist: his old nurse is delighted by it, his fiancée finds it attractive, his social-climbing relations are revolted by it, and his old friends Pendennis and his wife, Laura, barely notice it; but Philip's fellow journalists are never recorded as having any responses to the aura of tobacco that invariably attends him. Since tobacco creates an "endless fog" in the Bohemian dens in which Philip joins other newsmen and writers, smoking is presumably a habit that they share with him (60). Their lack of response to the traces of matter that he carries on his body is therefore a function of adaptation, but it is also the result of his superiority to them. To depict Philip's colleagues perceiving him as smelling of smoke would mark him as their inferior, a judgment that the novel's investment in his status as a true gentleman cannot countenance. Conversely, the olfactory offense that Philip's mean-spirited relations find in his tobacco-trailing presence is their way of trying to deny his standing. Identifying individuals who meet each other as either high or low, as either more or less culturally valuable, is what, to adopt a phrase used in another context by Raymond Williams, such smells are "there to do" (*Long* 317), and Philip's case demonstrates how complicated but assured such distinctions often are.

According to the most significant convention of the high-Victorian osmology, then, Pip's olfactory encounter with Jaggers can be read in only one way: the working-class boy is being depicted as the gentleman's better. Pip associates Jaggers with scented soap at five different points in his story—it is the one smell repeatedly mentioned in the novel—and every reference to it as a sensory stimulus to which Pip responds identifies Pip as the inodorate standard and Jaggers as his materially defined other. Such a conclusion depends on recognizing that Victorian fiction understands better than Victorian science the power inherent in using one's nose: by the standards of the latter, Pip is the primitive, his olfactory capacities a "mere relic." According to the fictional osmology that explains this encounter, however, Pip's sensitive nose makes representationally sensible Jaggers's marked and therefore lowly status. Pip thus takes his place among the inodorate genteel, even while he is "coarse" and "common" and "low" (79). Like the changeling he wants himself to be, the younger Pip is from his earliest years endowed with the refined physical organization that both renders him without odor (unless he has been dosed with tar) and acutely aware of the odors that announce the inferiority of those whom he meets, their otherwise profound domination of him notwithstanding.

What is true of Pip pertains as well to Felix. The rough worker's olfactory delicacy, his noticing of the fragrance that Esther gives off as she walks, declares his ascendancy over her, one granted not only by a culture that values men over women but also by a novel straining to portray the renunciation of material comfort as a form of heroism. When Felix recognizes Esther through her scent, he is conveying in that almost involuntary response to her physical presence his judgment on her "fine lady" ways (60). He is unmarked, she marked; he already senses that her physicality is relatively more impressive, at least to him, than his own. In this exchange in *Felix Holt*, gender seems to trump class: the refinements associated with rose leaves, standing as they do for manners and education and Esther's as-yet-unrevealed gentle birth, are tested and found wanting by Felix's typically masculine olfactory sensitivities. According to the osmology of high-Victorian fiction, one smell declares Felix's ascendancy over Esther, just as another odor announces the superiority of Marx's worker over his employer.

Olfactory Exchanges

In his early writings, Marx had concluded, "The *forming* of the five senses is a labor of the entire history of the world down to the present,"[8] and in *Capital*, his most direct testament to the topical issues of the 1860s, he depicts what that history has come to when he describes an olfactory encounter. Rendered with a physicality that makes it comparable to Pip's meeting with Jaggers, this event specifies more clearly than the latter does the role in such meetings of conventionally understood working-class characteristics. Pip's awareness of the soap on Jaggers's hand may reflect either what the "common" boy has experienced or what the older narrator, now claiming to be a gentleman, wants to remember himself as having noticed. No such uncertainties attend Marx's depiction of his worker. In the preface to the first edition of the first volume of *Capital*, Marx explains, as he reiterates later on, that he deals with "individuals . . . only in so far as they are the personifications of economic categories, the bearers of particular class-relations and interests" (92), and his creation of an individual worker is nothing if not a "personification" of such a classification. In *Capital*, according to the rhetoric made appropriate by Marx's conception of the commodity fetish, commodities "speak" (176), and their voices are heard even more prominently than those of the human witnesses who testify to their own typicality in the sources that he cites—reports of factory inspectors, royal commissions, and parliamentary select committees. At times, however, the human personifications of particular economic positions do become more specifically individualized. In one particularly flamboyant rhetorical flourish, for example, Marx casts Dickens's Bill Sikes as a capitalist so that the fictional character can offer a speech defending the knife that he uses on his victims, thereby exposing the villainy of the industrialism's use of machinery (569). The comparative encounter in which Marx depicts a worker smelling his employer extends in novelistic fashion the effect of such rhetoric.[9]

At the opening of the chapter called "The Working Day," Marx brings alive his analysis of the economic origins of working-class sufferings by asking his readers to witness a meeting between a representative worker and the equally representative capitalist who employs him. Marx introduces the words of the worker as if he, Marx, were playing the role of the narrator of a novel written in the historical present:

> Suddenly . . . there arises the voice of the worker, which had previously been stifled in the sound and fury of the production process:
> "The commodity [labour-power] I have sold you differs from the ordinary crowd of commodities in that its use creates value, a greater value than it costs. That is why you bought it. . . . You and I know on the market only one law, that of the exchange of commodities. . . . You are constantly preaching to me the gospel of 'saving' and 'abstinence.' Very well! Like a sensible, thrifty owner of property I will husband my sole wealth, my labour-power, and abstain from wasting it foolishly. . . . [But by] an unlimited extension of the working day, you may in one day use up a quantity of labour-power greater than I can restore in three. . . . You pay me for one day's labour-power, while you use three days of it. That is against our contract and the law of commodity exchange. I therefore demand a working day of normal length, and I demand it without any appeal to your heart, for in money matters sentiment is out of place. You may be a model citizen, perhaps a member of the R.S.P.C.A., and you may be in the odour of sanctity as well; but the thing you represent when you come face to face with me has no heart in its breast. What seems to throb there is my own heartbeat." (342–43)

Here the worker addresses his employer to demand the full value of his labor, turning the employer's previous economic homilies into a dialogue by repeating the substance of such "gospel." The worker then lectures his silent interlocutor on the laws of the marketplace and, in another section of the speech, proves his point with the kinds of mathematical formulas that are so distinctively characteristic of the argumentative methods of Marx himself.

Yet for all its rationality, this encounter could not be more physically concrete: when the capitalist comes "face to face" with his worker, the former feels beating in his chest the heart of the latter. Nor is that heartbeat the only sensory impression registered in this encounter. In this instance, as in uses of the phrase *odour of sanctity* throughout the nineteenth century, the aroma that the worker sarcastically attributes to the capitalist is not simply metaphorical. Rather, it recalls in either straightforward or ironic fashion, as Scott or Southey respectively employed the phrase, the balsamic fragrance that is said to issue from saints' bodies at their deaths in aromatic testimony to their holiness (*OED*). Alternately, as the footnote in *Capital* explains, since the phrase identifies the employer depicted here as a specific building master, who during the London builders' strike of 1859–1860 was reputed to be "in the 'odour of sanctity'" (343–44n6); it could therefore communicate, along with the hypocrisy that it obviously identifies, a typically English prejudice against Catholic beliefs: as *Punch* noted in an article published in the same year as the first volume of *Capital*, "Popish saints" smell because they do not bathe (11/16/1867: 203). The sensations involved in this encounter are, therefore, both tactile and olfactory: by the end of the passage, the capitalist can feel the worker's heart beating beneath his own flesh, and the capitalist's scent has entered the worker's nostrils.

Central to this encounter is a simple and apparently inviolable contrast: workers are bodies, and they exist, for good or ill, primarily by virtue of their collective numbers; each of their betters, however, is a unique individual defined as superior to the often animalistic physicality of the masses who constitute the working-classes. Yet this encounter also disrupts such conventional distinctions. Although worker and capitalist begin in Marx's text as "personifications of economic categories," as he has promised they will be, they quickly take on individual characteristics. The detail about membership in the R.S.P.C.A., like the topical reference to a "certain Sir M. Peto," tends to identify a specific employer. More strikingly, however, and more clearly in violation of conventional judgments, the worker's formulations, which portray the capitalist as "the thing you represent when you come face to face with me," emphasize the worker's relative humanity: the thing has no heart of its own; the "me" here does. The exchange wrought in this description of an encounter ultimately involves not only valuations but also body parts: so dependent is the employer on this worker that without the latter's heart beating in his breast, he could not live.

The full extent to which Marx makes his worker the articulate superior of the silent and silenced capitalist can be gauged in relation to the conventions of economic discourse and the valuations of workers that Marx uses this encounter to attack. In the complicated debates that attended the passage of legislation to control the conditions of industrial labor throughout the nineteenth century, debates to which "The Working Day" was a late but still pertinent contribution, workers are most typically portrayed as unfeeling matter, as cogs in a machine. Yet here the employer is the inhuman "thing." Even more telling in its unconventionality is the passage's distribution of the roles played by employer and worker. Typical of Victorian social commentary on industrial relations is Carlyle's practice in *Past and Present* (1843). There he addresses what he calls the primary social problem of his time, what to do with the working-class population, by casting workers as the inarticulate masses, unable to understand their own conditions or even to describe their own sufferings.[10] Yet in *Capital*, the worker, in his reiterated "I demand . . . I demand," is more articulate and more intelligent than his better: he is able to state his claims and to do so with both mathematical specificity and rhetorical eloquence.

Marx's rendition of an encounter, not surprisingly, casts the worker as the participant who is aware of the power granted him—perhaps only wishfully—by his relation to his supposed better. The beating of Marx's worker's heart in the chest of his employer makes more explicitly the point conveyed by Pip's implicit judgment of Jaggers when the former finds in the latter the occasion for olfaction. Both instances exemplify the reversals made possible when olfaction is the register through which two characters recognize or unconsciously mark their relation to each other as they trade sensory responses with each other. As indisputably as Pip or Felix declares his superiority, Marx's worker demonstrates his ascendancy over the person he meets, the employer whose hypocrisy the worker can smell. Marx's invocation in this passage of the fictional conventions governing the representation of olfaction reverses conventional expectations: workers are supposed to smell; they are not supposed to do the smelling. The case of an inodorate worker like Pip or Felix might be explained either by the gentility that a worker may attain or by his atypicality. Marx's encounter is less compromised and compromising: its distinctive exchange therefore points to the final convention that I examine here, the characteristically high-Victorian association of smells with work.

Men as Matter

Marx's worker and capitalist are distinguished by their opposing positions within "the production process," and that measure of difference also emerges as the most significant in the osmology of the 1860s for the simple reason that work, more than any other activity, is the source of its smells. More than half of the over thirty odors in *Great Expectations*, for instance, emanate from the various kinds of labor that Pip has occasion to observe. This convention, along with the principle that the inodorate perceiver of smells is superior to the one who gives off a smell, explains, for instance, the ways in which the odors of tobacco enter high-Victorian novels. Whether a cigar mentioned in this fiction gives off an odor has less to do with the quality of its tobacco than with the quality of its smoker. When he is securely positioned as a member of the middle classes or the gentry, when a gentleman enjoys a cigar, it may create a haze hard to see through, as the example of *Philip* testifies, but rarely an odor difficult to bear. In accordance with this convention, pleasant or neutral scents do not often issue from the cigars mentioned in these novels, the response of Philip's nurse being an exception that proves this rule. The aroma of fine tobacco is registered, rather, through the narrators' and characters' silence on the subject. When cigars do smell, their odors are usually unappealing, thereby demonstrating the relative social inferiority of their smokers. Underlying this alignment of class and smell is the explanatory factor of work.

Numerous instances attest to the consistent application of this representational distinction. In *Our Mutual Friend*, Eugene Wrayburn smokes multiple cigars in one of his more painful and ostentatious displays of contempt for the teacher Bradley Headstone, but no one—neither of the two men, neither reader nor narrator—perceives an odor. Phineas Finn and Lord Chiltern enjoy similarly inodorate tobacco. In *Lady Audley's Secret*, the plot actually turns on the smoking of bad cigars, those provided to Robert Audley by the landlord of the inn where he and his friend George Talboys are staying, but neither of these men explicitly notices the smell of the cigars whose foulness keeps Robert in bed the next day and delays their departure to London, a departure that would have saved George from the trip down the well that occasions his unsettling disappearance. The cigars that do smell in these novels are not the ones enjoyed—or even deplored—by the likes of Eugene Wrayburn or Robert Audley, but rather those consumed by their social inferiors. The only time that Robert Audley acknowledges the possibility that his cigar could exude an odor to which others might object is when his comment on the subject allows him to mark his distance from his social inferiors, the surgeon Dawson and the dissolute and pathetic Captain Maldon. Although tobacco in nineteenth-century French culture may have served to indicate the "increasing male domination of social life" (Corbin 150), the smell of tobacco smoke or the lack thereof in English novels of the 1860s indicates the dominance of some men over others as the differences between men are determined by the kinds of labor that they do.

Significantly, Eugene Wrayburn and Robert Audley, both barristers without briefs, both gentlemen who do not work, smoke odorless cigars; their underlings, who scrape together livings in dishonorable ways, are marked by the perceptibly distasteful fumes that their cigars emit. Although the narrator of *Our Mutual Friend* is not certain whether the men who populate Alfred Lammle's study are men of business or men of pleasure, the fact that they pollute his house with noxious smoke as they trade or talk of trading in spurious and unstable investments proves unequivocally that they are less than gentlemen. In novels as otherwise dissimilar as *Lizzie Lorton*, *Great Expectations*, *The Mill on the Floss*, *Cometh up as a Flower*, *At Odds*, and *Castle Richmond*, the combined odors of tobacco and alcohol conventionally indicate the work done in inns and public houses. The clerk who teaches Tom Tulliver his lessons in business "smell[s] strongly of bad tobacco" (214). Smoke in *No Name* marks Wragg's less-than-genteel labor as an impresario; combined with the fumes of liquor, it identifies the lowly actor Bruff of *The White Rose* and a cab driver in *John Marchmont's Legacy*. Men of the lower-middle or lower classes smoke perceptibly odorous cigars or pipes because they are the accoutrements of the often disreputable work that such men do—hanging around racetracks, betting, trading in horseflesh. Thus, the narrator of *Aurora Floyd* describes a dog seller by specifying that the "fumes" of his cigar are "rank" even before mentioning the bull-terrier poking its head out of his coat (24). So conventional is this association that a character in *The Last Chronicle of Barset* complains that "no good" can be expected "when men sit and smoke over their work" (328), and the narrator of *The Rector* explicitly speaks of "light whiffs of smoke, such as accompany a man's labours" (41).

What can be said of the tobacco smoke of men at work can be said of work in general. Even more numerous than images that conjure up delicate floral scents, olfactory references to labor have a consistent source: they emanate from the work done by members of the lower-middle classes and of what it is tempting to call, at least for consistency's sake, the upper-lower classes, those shopkeepers and artisans who were both identified by the Victorian term *tradesmen*, the small businessmen who directly handled commodities as they bought and sold them, and the so-called skilled workers or "labor aristocrats" who still made their products with their own manual labor. Such characters smell of their work. Brisket, the butcher of *The Struggles of Brown, Jones, and Robinson*, is "always greasy and smel[ls] of meat" (26). Pip, his nose ever vigilant, equates artisans with the odors of their products. Hubble, the wheelwright, is "a tough high-shouldered stooping old man, of sawdusty fragrance" (25). Pumblechook's corduroys have a "general air and flavour" of seeds and vice versa (55). Vintry Mill in *The Trial* is the source of both musty smells and the telltale odor of a villain's cigar, and the whaling trade of *Sylvia's Lovers* gives off a reek that is "intolerable" but only to those not accustomed to it (3). Jaggers's case is again pertinent. His work in *Great Expectations* is defined by an odor, that of the soap he uses at the end of each day to wash the criminal taint from his hands. This practice, which makes part of his office "smel[l] of . . . scented soap like a perfumer's shop" (210), indicates both Jaggers's lowly status in the legal hierarchy—no barrister he—and the disreputable nature of his legal dealings. Like another lawyer who gives off odors, the perfumed Jermyn of *Felix Holt*, Miss Havisham's "man of business" makes the law a trade, not a profession (175). Unlike the butcher of *Brown, Jones, and Robinson*, Jaggers does not actually handle the products he sells by touching the disreputable witnesses he creates for use in his cases; like Brisket, who "smell[s] strongly of yellow soap" (245), however, the lawyer tries but fails to wash the olfactory evidence of his labor from his hands.

The association of work with perceptible odors is confirmed, though not fully explained, in nonfictional Victorian discussions of olfactory experience. In their treatises and essays on the senses, Victorian eyes are open to sublime vistas or the wonders of painting, ears respond to the celestial harmonies of music, tongues register the refinements of culinary art, but noses, more often than not, smell work. George Wilson, the purpose of whose *The Five*

Gateways of Knowledge is to demonstrate the relation between the senses and "our Moral Instincts" (4), provides a lengthy commentary on smells, explaining the providential design whereby good odors soon fade and bad odors quickly become less obvious because the former are associated with pleasure, which is to be eschewed, and the latter indicate duty, which is to be embraced. The particular kind of duty that Wilson has in mind is work; and adaptation, the process that he does not directly name, is a blessing because all sorts of occupations are inherently smelly: "the metal worker labours heartily among the vapours from his crucibles and refining vessels; and the bleacher inhales without a murmur the fumes of his chlorine; while, most tried of all, the busy anatomist asks no one for pity, but forgets the noisome odours about him, in delight at the exquisite structures which he is tracing; and the heroic physician thinks only of the lives he can save." Conversely, the most perceptive of modern noses are those belonging to men who sell wine and tobacco, distill perfumes, produce drugs, or grow plants (59–61; cf. Johnson 58, 102).

Alexander Bain's discussion of the smells of work in *The Senses and the Intellect* is even more revealing. Coming as it does after long passages of blandly scientific nomenclature for the chemical compounds responsible for various odors, this passage is unexpectedly and uncharacteristically lively. Even Bain's earlier comments on "animal effluvia" (161) do not trouble the impassive, plodding exposition typical of his prose. But he does respond to his own evocations of the odors associated with labor: following a brief description of the "damping and discouraging" effects of the "effluvia of crowds," Bain continues, "The effluvia of warehouses, stores, and mills, where cotton, wool, cloths, &c., are piled up, and ventilation is defective, are of a like unwholesome description. The smell of a pastrycook's kitchen is peculiarly sickening. The action of highly-heated iron stoves seems of the same nature" (165). This list of odorants includes some apparently unaccountable items. Why should the smells encountered in a pastrycook's shop be "peculiarly sickening"? Why does Bain find offensive the emanations from a hot iron stove?

Novels of the 1860s provide one answer to such questions by identifying a specific condition of work as odorous, as distasteful, though not typically nauseating. Smells in this fiction almost invariably indicate the close proximity to their dwellings of the work done by shopkeepers and artisans, labor that therefore does not conform to the distinction between work and home that is central to Victorian definitions of middle-class culture. *Rachel Ray* offers an explicit formulation of this phenomenon when the narrator describes the longing for a seaside retreat felt by the wife of the brewer Tappitt: "To what lady living in a dingy brick house, close adjoining to the smoke and smells of beer-brewing, would not the idea of a marine villa at Torquay be delicious?" (288). The title character of *The Doctor's Wife* similarly and more seriously laments the smell of drugs that emanates from the household surgery, particularly when her husband trails into her own room "the odious flavour of senna and camomile-flowers" (263). Mrs. Glegg of *The Mill on the Floss*, who makes a trade of her housekeeping, has cupboards distinguished by a "peculiar combination of grocery and drug-like odours" (107). Although Mr. Glegg actually finds olfactory pleasures in this mingling of domesticity and business, an example from *Salem Chapel* suggests how high-Victorian readers might have evaluated it. In that novel the realm of Tozer, the butterman and cheesemonger, is frequently represented as a distasteful mixture of the smells of food for sale in the shop with those of the food to be consumed in the rooms above the shop: the "drawback" to the "most substantial and savoury" supper that Mrs. Tozer offers her visitor is "that whenever the door was opened, the odours of bacon and cheese from the shop came in like a musty shadow of the boiled ham and hot sausages within" (40). This mingling of work and domesticity is clearly assumed to be as unappealing to the readers of the novel as it is to Mrs. Tozer's would-be-genteel guest.

Once again the physiology of sensory response helps to explain why olfaction would be the appropriate register of such unseemly mingling. Smells are preeminently the sensory stimuli that involve involuntary mixture and association, the stimuli that most often demonstrate the presence of borders, the movement across them, and therefore their inevitable permeability. As Hans Rindisbacher notes, "Smells help to mark off territories, indicate transitions and warn of transgressions" (56).[11] The light reflected off an object may enter one's eye, but the physical stimulant of the sensation of smell, the odorant in a gaseous state, has actually to invade one's nostrils before it can be recognized. Unlike sound waves, which have to penetrate only to the ear drum, odors must reach "deeply lodged parts" of the "*organ* of smell" before there can be sensation (Bain 162, 161).[12] Moreover, unlike taste, the other sense dependent on incorporation, smell involves invasions of one's bodily cavities that are largely involuntary. Smells also mark the transitions from one state to another in ways that anthropologists have profitably studied: because odors are formless, mobile, difficult to categorize, they, like the great transitions of birth and death, are virtually impossible to control. Finally, smells are threatening because, as David Howes explains by adapting the formulations of Mary Douglas's *Purity and Danger*, they constitute a "category muddle." Like matter out of place, Douglas's definition of dirt, smells illustrate another central anthropological concept, Victor Turner's principle that "the unclear is the unclean."[13] Tradesmen's homes in high-Victorian fiction are a preeminent example of "category muddle," but for that reason they clearly distinguish tradesmen from their male and female betters. As the countess of *Evan Harrington* says definitively of the house where her father worked as a tailor and where she was raised, "The shop smells!" (395).

Women as Matter

In this context Felix Holt's olfactory encounter with Esther Lyon takes on added significance. Before she enters the room where her father and Felix have been talking, the latter establishes his inodorate superiority by disdaining those who smell. Along with his dismissal of "scented men" of the middle classes, he disowns the dissolute time he has spent in Glasgow by referring to his fellow lodgers as "old women breathing gin as they passed me on the stairs" (58, 56). In the same conversation Lyon invokes olfactory sensations as metaphors, talking of Christians whose "names have left a sweet savour," and he tries to humble Felix by warning him, "The scornful nostril and the high head gather not the odours that lie in the track of truth" (55, 59). Yet neither this chapter of *Felix Holt*, obsessed as it is with smells, nor Felix is likely to lift a nostril too high to ascertain the truths told by odors. As soon as Felix recognizes the "very delicate scent" reminiscent of a garden that attends Esther as she walks, he is "repelled" by this mark of her pretensions to gentility (60). Here, as in Victorian fiction more generally, the primary role of olfaction is to classify, to identify, and to label in ways that those "quite awake" will instantaneously understand. Any reader whose imaginative olfactory sensibilities have been trained by reading the fiction of the 1860s knows immediately that Esther's association with the scent of a garden, like the earlier mention of rose leaves, also marks her as a marriageable young woman. The moment that Esther's body gives off this aroma, she is defined not only as matter but also as the form of matter most useful to unmarried men. Moreover, like the odor of cigars that cling to certain kinds of men, the scents of the natural world that high-Victorian fiction so often attributes to certain kinds of women have everything to do with the work for which they are most suited.

The association of women and flowers is a long-standing convention in a wide range of cultures—East and West, ancient and modern[14]—although it does not seem as universally applicable as the distinction between good and bad smells. Men and women of the ancient world, for instance, both wore attar of roses; and the ascendancy, beginning in the late eighteenth century, of floral scents over such animal odorants as civet and musk became the mark of a clear gender divide only in the nineteenth century when men, by and large, ceased wearing perfume.[15] Yet English novels of the 1860s use the scents exuded by flowers to make finer distinctions than those that set apart the sexes. With extraordinary consistency, such natural floral fragrances—but not, significantly, floral perfumes—identify marriageable women likely to wed their social equals. Unmarried young ladies in these novels often declare their suitability as mates, not by giving off any odor themselves, but by being associated with the explicitly perceived fragrances of flowers.

Characterized in this way are a wide variety of figures: Lilian Ashleigh in *A Strange Story*, Lorna in *Lorna Doone*, Agnes and Charlotte in *Philip*, Lucy Wodehouse in *The Rector*, Josephine in *Barrington*, Nora in *The White Rose*, Mary in *Tom Brown at Oxford*, Sylvia in *Sylvia's Lovers*, both wives of Edward Arundel in *John Marchmont's Legacy*, Clara in *The Belton Estate*, and the late-blooming wife and foster mother, Ermine Keith, of *The Clever Woman of the Family*. Like the olfactory encounters involving Pip and Marx's worker, therefore, Felix's response to Esther epitomizes the effect of many other encounters in the fiction of the 1860s, and the range of fine distinctions that its osmology draws when it categorizes women is a subject that I examine more fully in the third chapter of this study. All such categories evaluate women according to their reproductive potential. The "airless smell" that hangs in Miss Havisham's rooms in *Great Expectations* may suggest, for instance, her frustrated fertility (84). Such an olfactory notation, however, would be unusual since her unmarried state would more typically be represented as inodorate, while the life-giving scents of flowers associated with younger ladies are, it seems at times, everywhere in high-Victorian fiction.

Mid-Victorian commentaries on the senses help to explain why floral fragrances mark certain kinds of women for their reproductive potential, for the work that they will do as wives and mothers. In Victorian science, the link between sexuality and odor is more often implied than explained,[16] but the slight hints offered on the subject are revealing. Sexual responses constitute an area of inquiry, as Bain notes, not "open to full discussion," so the processes whereby "an individual of one sex . . . produce[s] the excitement in the opposite sex, by sight, sound, or smell, as well as by touch, have not hitherto been fully investigated" (254). Yet even Bain's account of the sense of smell suggests its connection to erotic impulses. He asserts that "*sweet* or *fragrant*" odors, "represent[ing] the pure or proper pleasures of smell," are "closely allied with tender emotion." Among the odorants that he identifies as responsible for such fragrances are violets and "flowering and fruit-bearing plants" (166). By analogy, then, marriageable women are, like fruit-bearing flora, able to evoke the tenderness of love. Having read Darwin on the subject of sex roles, Grant Allen is less guarded in his interest in sexuality than Bain. Allen positively exults in the attractions offered by the "beautiful mates" of newts, pheasants, and peacocks, "not to mention the cherry lips, rosy cheeks, blue eyes, and golden hair of our Aryan maidens" (156). Allen's understanding of floral scents, therefore, seems particularly apposite: both flowers and fruits use odors as "allurements for insects, birds, and mammals, to promote cross-fertilization and the dissemination of seeds" (81). In Victorian fiction, some women are similarly equipped, and they are so for similar purposes. When Maud Ruthyn is described as a lady wreathed by "the glow of flowers in winter, and the fragrance of a field which the Lord hath blessed" (*Uncle Silas* 226), her olfactory status is attributed explicitly to the providential order that grants women their fertility. Exuding as Esther does the "delicate scents" of a garden, such women are like flowers grown for their sweet fragrances, the evidence of their natural but also carefully cultivated fertility.

In Victorian novels the physical work that women do as childbearers is at times explicitly recognized, though it is more frequently a topic of Victorian treatises and essays. Dickens in *Dombey and Son* (1848) notes the contribution that women like the first Mrs. Dombey make to the "perpetuation of family Firms" (51), and Dombey clearly chooses Edith as his second wife for the fertility that she has proved in having had a child, now deceased, by her also deceased first husband. The narrator of *Can You Forgive Her?* is also quite explicit about the value of Lady Glencora's somewhat delayed ability to give her husband a male heir, "the one thing in the world which he had lacked" (2: 340), though the narrator of *Brown, Jones, and Robinson*, who frankly labels matrimony as women's "business" (210), does not specify that children are its product. As Leonore Davidoff and Catherine Hall explain, the main service to the Victorian economy offered by middle-class women was the creation of business personnel: "women bore and raised the next generation of sons and nephews, the future partners and entrepreneurs." Such a function could be seen as exalted, as one cleric explained in 1850: "Women are not to be men in character, ambition, pursuit or achievement: but they are to be *more*; they are to be the *makers* of men."[17] Women's role as the makers of male products may have been one of the factors that convinced Henry Mayhew to list "wives" in *London Labour and the London Poor* as among those who work for a living, those who receive either pay or "comforts" in return for their exertions (4: 9). As late as 1891, Eliza Lynn Linton was referring to the "absolute truth" that maternity is the "*raison d'être* of a woman": "her first great natural duty and her first great social obligation" is to ensure "the continuance of the race in healthy reproduction" ("Wild Women" 188–89). Even when Frances Power Cobbe in her 1862 essay "'What Shall We Do with Our Old Maids?'" argues that women must be trained for work beyond that of marriage, she spends a long paragraph explaining that "the beneficent laws of our nature" give priority to the "great and paramount duties of a mother and wife," duties that will cause any other interests to "drop naturally to the ground, especially when [a woman] has children" (90). The floral scents that surround the bodies of genteel women in novels of the 1860s make manifest such laws of nature.

The osmology of Victorian fiction, moreover, in registering the olfactory effects of women as matter, identifies them as a particular kind of matter to which only particular men have the ability to respond. As Bain says, olfaction discriminates among "material bodies," but it can do so only if, as he also notes, such bodies exist in a gaseous state, only when solids or liquids are "evaporated or volatilized" (158). To be perceived as an odor at all, a material body must take on ethereal form. The logic by which the most highly prized female characters in Victorian fiction are represented in association with the aroma of flowers is, therefore, obvious: the convention spiritualizes or seems literally to disembody what it also necessarily recognizes as indisputably material.[18] The narrator of *Middlemarch* points to the duplicity inherent in smells when commenting, appropriately enough, on "prejudices about rank and status": such "prejudices, like odorous bodies, have a double existence both solid and subtle—solid as the pyramids, subtle as the twentieth echo of an echo, or as the memory of hyacinths which once scented the darkness" (408–9). This series of analogies neatly links questions of social distinction with erotic memories. While characters like Esther Lyon and Maud Ruthyn may not be as substantial as the pyramids, they are as inescapably material, and their association with floral scents allows them to seem "both solid and subtle," both body and spirit, both matter and its twenty-first echo.

Yet since fragrant women are defined by their physicality, a fact to which their future mates are assumed to respond instinctively, their status in these novels is anomalous: in relation to their male inferiors—the farmers on a train or the clerks whom they might meet at a ball—such women are unmarked superiors; in relation to men of their own class, they are marked inferiors.[19] The extent to which middle-class women in high-Victorian fiction are depicted as the objects of sensory perception makes them very much the subjects, in more ways than one, of those men represented as perceiving them. The association of women and matter therefore leads to a more unexpected identification. Privileging the sensory responses of the unmarked genteel man, novels of the 1860s equate the groups that are his olfactory others, middle-class women and lower-class men, because they are both deemed the appropriate and inevitable objects of his olfactory sensitivities. Moreover, the distinctions that are indicated by such smells are presented in both cases as the sensuous effects of the material conditions of work. Just as floral scents render attractive the bodies of the women who will produce children, tradesmen—those wheelwrights, corn factors, butter-and-cheese men, and butchers who make or sell products—are similarly marked by the odors of their wares. The scent that Pip perceives on Jaggers's hand, the aroma that Felix senses on Esther's body, and Marx's worker's response to the capitalist's odor of sanctity—all these olfactory sensations associate with each other those whose labors issue in scents that their betters are depicted as perceiving.

The passage from *The Senses and the Intellect* in which Alexander Bain records the disgust caused by the odors of work confirms this identification when he adds to his already odd list of odorants one that seems at first glance not to belong there at all. Along with the effluvia found in factories and warehouses where cotton and wool are, respectively, made and stored, Bain finds "peculiarly sickening" the "smell of a woollen screen when held too close to the fire" (165). In an oddly similar passage, *The Lady's Mile* describes the "odour of heated iron and singed blanket which attends the getting-up of feminine muslins and laces" (1: 183), thereby connecting Bain's objection to the smell of wool to his earlier mention of that of hot iron. Yet Bain makes a more important association: his analysis links industrial sites to the hearth, the chief location of domestic pieties, by detecting repellent odors both in the manufacture of wool and in its use when protecting the lady of the house from the heat of a fire. Bain's curious conception of both odors as noisome makes sense according to the logic of the osmology that novels of the 1860s establish because it identifies genteel female characters with working-class men. Both the ladies who hold up woolen screens and the men who process and stock wool give off the odors characteristic of their labors, and for that reason they take their proper places as marked inferiors.

By creating distinct categories for those whose smells it records and for those who recognize them, high-Victorian fiction also identifies its own imaginative perspective on such figures. Here Marx parts way with his colleagues in fiction-making: in the encounter depicted in *Capital*, work smells, but its odors issue from unjustifiable sanctimony of the capitalist, not from the manual labor of his employee. In novels of the 1860s, that relation is reversed. As a complex, almost unvarying, and quite rigid system of differentiations, this structure of sensations defines the class position from which readers of these novels are invited to experience physically the encounters depicted in them. The only category of persons allowed always to smell others and never to be smelled consists of men of the middle classes and gentry— and Pip and Felix, I argue in subsequent chapters, are not exceptions to this rule. The novels, then, in which such olfactory encounters occur are themselves unmarked as both genteel and male. What one smells in this fiction is not the presumably subtle and pleasing aroma given off by such well-groomed gentlemen as Eugene Wrayburn, Robert Audley, and Pip's double Herbert Pocket, but rather what such men smell. Remarkably, novels of the 1860s also seem to accept the processes of adaptation as a narrative principle so that the responses typical of such men often begin to fade as the story goes on: in both *Salem Chapel* and *Felix Holt*, there are more references to smells in the first third of these novels than there are in the last two-thirds combined. The desire to attain anosmia, predicated in high-Victorian fiction on the sensitivity of refined male noses, seems to prevail. Despite the relative prominence of women as writers of Victorian fiction, despite the fact that the majority of its readers were (and still are?) women,[20] despite the often numbingly consistent focus of such fiction on the subjects of romance and marriage, topics that presumably constitute a domain more identified with women than with men, the structure of sensations that I have been outlining involves a surprisingly consistent male chauvinism of a particularly genteel variety.

Yet the osmology charted by the comparative encounters in the fiction of the 1860s has another and perhaps more unsettling effect. Marking as odorous the reproductive work of respectable women and the productive work of tradesmen inevitably defines the inodorate figures of middle-class and genteel men in terms of their distance from the material realms of generative and manual labor. The logic of representation and the physiology of olfaction join to explain this phenomenon. To be unmarked, not to be represented, is to enjoy the power of constituting the norm and all its privileges; but it is also to be absent, to exist in negative space, to be an ideal that, by definition, lacks substance. In attaching the smells involved in work to both marriageable women and tradesmen, high-Victorian novels also grant to the representatives of those groups a material reality that their principal male characters all too often lack. Although it may seem perverse to count the cost of being unmarked, resulting as that status does from having the power to set the standard by which others are deemed inferior, novels of the 1860s devote a great deal of attention to depicting and even lamenting that plight. In physical terms, being unmarked may even seem perilously close to not being at all. Only to perceive and never to exude odors is perhaps, after all, not as healthy as one might have thought. To explore how an olfactory exchange may reconfigure male superiority as insubstantiality, I examine in the following chapter specific novels whose main characters epitomize a form of genteel manhood that I call male melancholia.

2

Melancholic Men

Arthur Vincent, Evan Harrington, Pip Pirrip, and Herbert Pocket are all men of a type: they are male melancholics. Suffering from various forms of a condition whose symptoms and implications are defined by the osmology of high-Victorian fiction, these men embody, carry in their senses, their culture's ambivalence toward matter and its significance. Used interchangeably for centuries to indicate either a disposition or a form of mental derangement, the terms *melancholy* and *melancholia* had been freed by the nineteenth century from their humoral associations with an excess of black bile and the anger and irascibility taken to result from it. The terms could still indicate specific psychopathologies like hypochondria or monomania, but they also stood for an affective disorder that sometimes preceded full-blown insanity. The osmology revealed by the olfactory encounters of high-Victorian fiction points, however, toward a more specific, though often less obviously pathological condition, with its own characteristic symptoms, etiology, and treatment. Primarily a young man's disease, it is not simply a form of anxiety or depression, though it may be akin to such feelings, as it is to what Raymond Williams calls "the mood of the 'sixties," a "kind of intellectual fatigue" (*Culture* 107). More important, however, it involves an unrecognized but almost palpable nostalgia, an uneasy but unidentified sense of incompletion and loss. Such feelings are necessarily aroused by smells, sensations that, in Bain's words, register the presence of "material bodies": as I argue in this chapter, what male melancholics lack is direct contact with a materiality so thoroughly a part of their commercial culture that it can be neither escaped nor completely rejected, even though it is being figured as lost.

In the fiction of the 1860s, the causes and effects of male melancholia are charted by the smells that distinguish relatively lower-class men from their inodorous superior; the change in a melancholic's condition that may either save him from or doom him to the annihilation threatened by his disorder is prophesied by the aromas given off by the body of a marriageable virgin. Ultimately, then, the characterization of the unmarked genteel melancholic and the plot that defines his fate both depend on comparative encounters between him and his more substantial others. Because he recognizes in others the materiality to which their odors testify, because he has no odors perceptible to himself or represented as such to the readers of his story, what he smells indicates what he lacks. Such encounters enact exchanges: meetings cast in olfactory terms identify the melancholic as a man who cannot have what his male inferiors possess, pronouncing the possibility of his cure only through what a woman, conventionally his inferior, can provide. The potential for such exchanges is evident whenever the fiction of the 1860s represents the odorous realms of trade and the fragrant promises of fertility. Yet these osmological markings also point to other identifications: tradesmen, both artisans and shopkeepers alike, become associated not only with the smells of work but also with those of food; and middle-class women become defined not only as bearers of children but also as bearers of property. As such, both marked groups represent, not what the melancholic thinks he wants, the identification of which he knows too well, but what he has lost, the value of which he cannot recognize.

Analyzing the constructions of masculinity that emerged in the early nineteenth century, Ed Cohen has pointed to the importance of C. B. Macpherson's conception of "possessive individualism": as Locke puts it, when a man owns himself, "the *Labour* of his Body, and the *Work* of his Hands," he becomes an individual.[1] By the 1860s for some men, however, such simple bases for individuation were neither available nor attractive; and other forms of possession were substituted for it. From this perspective, melancholia, like competing varieties of Victorian manhood, is defined by a man's relation to his others.[2] The melancholic owns; others produce or reproduce. More precisely: he owns what others produce or reproduce. As the narrator of Charles Lever's *Barrington* explains when his young hero contemplates the joys of owning an Irish cottage: "in [the] sense of possession there is something that resembles the sense of identity" (76). Central to my argument about high-Victorian conceptions of male melancholy is a man's relation to the woman he possesses or hopes to possess, as I demonstrate in the following chapter. Here, however, I focus on the relation between the melancholic and the other sorts of men to whom he is supposedly superior, specifically the tradesmen who either make products or sell them. The melancholic's ambivalence toward what he has lost, tactile contact with what in earlier generations would have been "the *Work* of his Hands," is acted out in his responses to such men, whom he thinks he can afford to despise since he, like so many of the most influential forms of Victorian culture, is, as the first chapter title in Meredith's *Evan Harrington* puts it, "Above Buttons," above the demeaning world of production and distribution.

I identify this condition as melancholia in recognition of a number of specifically nineteenth-century understandings of the disease to which men rather than women were traditionally judged to be susceptible.[3] Since Robert Burton's *Anatomy of Melancholy* (1621), the disorder had been defined pri

marily as a form of sadness or fear without apparent cause. Famously finding the source of melancholy in idleness and its cure in busyness, Burton
outlined many of the only apparently contradictory symptoms that its Victorian victims display, including restlessness and torpor. Even more pertinent
here are the analyses offered by nineteenth-century medical commentators
or "alienists," as mad-doctors were beginning to be called in the 1860s.[4] The
two foremost psychiatric authorities of the 1860s were Wilhelm Griesinger
in Germany and Henry Maudsley in England. In *Mental Pathology and
Therapeutics* (1867), Griesinger insisted that the causes of melancholy are
"unaccountable," unknown to its victims; and he explained that the disorder causes either dulled or exacerbated sensibilities ("mental anaesthesia"
or "mental hyperaesthesia") or both. Characterized by "an absence of energy and will," the disease also manifests itself in an aimless and "extreme
restlessness" (qtd. Radden 229, 225). In the third chapter of *The Physiology
and Pathology of the Mind* (1867), Maudsley defines melancholia as a form
of both ideational and affective "alienation," an "unnatural state" marked
by intense feelings of oppression, misery, and incapacitation, from which,
however, more than half of its sufferers can be expected to recover (323, 328).
Exhibiting a lack of interest in his affairs, the melancholic "sits or stands like
a statue," ignoring the needs of his body, suffering from a want of appetite
and, most revealingly, "assigning some most ridiculously inadequate cause
for his gloom" (337, 329). Despite the long tradition of defining melancholia as sadness without cause, in which Maudsley participates, the osmology
of the fiction of the 1860s does identify its source. What the male melancholic suffers is a cultural malaise presenting itself as a psychological state.
Identifying the etiology of the disease in that larger context reveals its importance as a condition of unacknowledged loss and its relation to the differing
degrees of materiality characteristic of producing, owning, and reproducing.
Just as work is the factor that explains the importance of cigars and flowers
in the osmology of high-Victorian fiction, various kinds of labor identify the
sources of the disease toward the diagnosis of which that osmology points.

   In examining how the central male characters and the plots of Oliphant's
Salem Chapel, Meredith's *Evan Harrington*, and Dickens's *Great Expectations* epitomize both the nature of male melancholia and its causes,[5] I proceed here as if I were writing a Victorian essay in psychopathology. In that
emerging field of inquiry, analysis, whether popular or scientific, often took
the form of narrative: stories recounting individual cases were presented after
a description of the disease, its symptoms and signs, and the work of past
authorities that elucidated it.[6] This chapter adopts a similar structure by
examining specific fictional cases. Suffering from the same syndrome in often
mild though sometimes temporarily debilitating forms, the melancholics in
these three novels provide particularly clear instances of a form of middle-
class manhood represented repeatedly in the fiction of the 1860s. Genteel

melancholia oppresses a range of male characters, including briefless barristers such as Robert Audley of Braddon's *Lady Audley's Secret* and Eugene Wrayburn of Dickens's *Our Mutual Friend*, the Blancove cousins in Meredith's *Rhoda Fleming*, Gerald Ainsley of Whyte-Melville's *The White Rose*, the religious "pervert" Gerald Wentworth of Oliphant's *The Perpetual Curate*, three of Trollope's 1860s creations—Herbert Fitzgerald of *Castle Richmond*, Squire Gilmore of *The Vicar of Bullhampton*, and Sir John Ball of *Miss Mackenzie*—and a fair number of military men: the convalescing army officers of Yonge's *The Clever Woman of the Family*, Fred Conyers of Lever's *Barrington*, and Edward Arundel, Braddon's simple soldier in *John Marchmont's Legacy*. Along with Felix Holt and Harold Transome, on whose cases I focus in the next chapter, and John Harmon of *Our Mutual Friend*, the consummation of the type and the subject of the final chapter of this study, these men suffer from a condition that requires that they exchange their positions of relative superiority with those whom they would conventionally dominate. As Henry Maudsley explained in a moment of characteristically Victorian historicizing, "The insanity of any time will be a more or less broken reflection of the character of the events that happen in it" (330). Although the cases of affective disorder that I discuss here typically fall short of insanity, they do reveal the "character" of the decade in which their stories were written. Different as these melancholics are in temperament, training, behavior, and class origins, they reflect their culture's anxieties about the economic determinants of genteel manhood.

First Case: Symptoms, Food, and Substance

Arthur Vincent, the unlikely hero of Margaret Oliphant's *Salem Chapel*, epitomizes male melancholia as a constellation of somatic and affective disorders that attend his inability to accept a settled occupation: nervous irritability, lack of appetite, paralyzing uncertainty, and an overmastering restlessness issuing in pointless travels. I begin with Vincent's case because *Salem Chapel* so insistently presents as a physical condition the insubstantiality that underwrites all these symptoms and signs. Vincent's story is enacted as a contrast between food and words, the former smelling all too often, the latter utterly inodorous. On occasion in Victorian fiction, writing can give off the distasteful smell of trade, as it does when the eccentric maiden aunt of Trollope's *He Knew He Was Right* finds disreputable her nephew's work for a popular newspaper and therefore notes that his ink literally "stinks" (68). More typically, writing as an occupation is part of the genteel world of governance and commentary, sometimes dangerously bloodless, as in the case of *Middlemarch*'s failed author of "The Key to All Mythologies," but irreproachably respectable. The osmology of high-Victorian fiction, not surprisingly, recognizes as unmarked the relative immateriality of such activities. Writing, therefore, both stands for and contributes to what Paul Morrison calls the "sensuous impoverishment" and "longing for disembodied discursivity" typical of Victorian fiction, a discursivity associated with Hamlet, the figure who, according to Morrison, "casts his melancholic shadow over nineteenth-century novelistic characterization."[7] *Salem Chapel* offers a case in point. Vincent's bodily responses become a sensory record of the values represented by substance, specifically food, and its opposite, "disembodied discursivity." The plot of the novel demonstrates the process whereby Vincent rejects materiality and comes to embrace a melancholic state of insubstantiality before, as I argue in the next chapter, he can find in his women a stay against its potentially annihilating effects.

At the opening of the novel, young Vincent is newly arrived in Carlingford to take up his role as the nonconformist minister of Salem Chapel. The plot turns on a series of comparative encounters, principally between Vincent and members of his congregation or between Vincent and the most socially prominent of the ladies of Carlingford, the young, beautiful, and kindly widow, Lady Western. One "remarkable encounter" follows another— "there are such curious encounters in life," as Vincent remarks (36, 149). Raised by his widowed mother in shabby and "painful gentility" (15), having adopted his father's calling after being educated in the newest forms of dissent, Vincent cannot but see his position in Salem Chapel as beneath him precisely because it is associated with trade. The amount of his salary depends directly on the number of pews rented; his success as a preacher and, therefore, as a seller of such seats fills him with disgust: "Salem itself, and the new pulpit . . . dwindled into a miserable scene of trade before his disenchanted eyes—a preaching shop, where his success was to be measured by the seat-letting, and his soul decanted out into periodical issue under the seal of Tozer & Co.," a Carlingford shop (47–48). As a minister, Vincent is here specifically compared to a novelist prostituting his "soul," as he portions it out in the "periodical issue" of the powerful sermons that make him an exceptionally popular preacher. Vincent, however, puts this livelihood in jeopardy when he becomes infatuated with Lady Western and begins neglecting the members of his connection, represented principally by three tradesmen, Tozer the butterman, Brown the dairyman, and Pigeon the poulterer, the last of whose names, like that of Brisket in Trollope's *The Struggles of Brown, Jones, and Robinson*, highlights their roles as providers of foodstuffs, comestible commodities. Despite the sensation-novel complications of the plot of *Salem Chapel*, with its amazing coincidences and crises, the question that it poses is simple: Will Vincent satisfy his social ambitions and win the hand of Lady Western or will he settle into the material comfort and vulgarity of his position as minister of Salem Chapel?

These two alternatives are represented in the novel by two smells, and they are, in fact, the only ones repeatedly mentioned in *Salem Chapel*, the sweet fragrance of the perfume that surrounds Lady Western and the all-too-obvious smell of the food that the tradesmen provide for the inhabitants of the town or offer to the guests in their homes. Vincent compares his responses to these two smells when "the distant odours of all the bacon and cheese" in Tozer's shop jar against his olfactory memories of Lady Western: "From her soft perfumy presence to Mrs Tozer's parlour, with that pervading consciousness in it of the shop hard by and its store of provisions, what a wonderful difference!" (346). The conflicts between Vincent and the members of his congregation are occasioned by their desires either to eat or to feed, to hold tea-meetings of the chapel membership or to have Vincent join them at their own dinner tables. To both such activities Vincent objects. Tozer, that "substantial person" as the narrator calls him (375), constantly begs the young preacher to eat or to let others do so. Objecting to Vincent's Malvolio-like resistance to gustatory pleasures, Tozer pleads, "there's cakes and buns enough in Carlingford" (435). At the other end of the social scale represented in *Salem Chapel*, Lady Western lives in an ethereal haze of perfume. When she gives a dinner party to which Vincent is invited, no food, as far as the text is concerned, appears on her table, an omission that contrasts markedly to the "steaming viands on the hospitable board" depicted as being provided at the Tozers's (178). Wine and conversation are the only things consumed in Lady Western's dining room. Choosing between trade and gentility is a contest between substance and words, between food and talk.

The melodramatic turns of the plot of *Salem Chapel*, which put at risk the virtue and sanity of Vincent's sister, reduce him, through one crisis after another, to a disembodied state in which material comfort seems simply irrelevant. Making a number of exhausting and ineffectual journeys between Carlingford and his hometown or London, Vincent becomes "utterly pale, white to the lips" (429). As he continues to refuse to eat, he loses flesh; he becomes all sensibility. Vincent's body is repeatedly described as "tingling in every nerve" (291). When he enters what the narrator calls a "state of fasting," Vincent exhibits "a kind of weakness incident to excitement of mind and neglect of body" (334, 332). In this condition he decides that he must reject the ministry and take up the still socially ambiguous but potentially more secure middle-class role of the man of letters, thereby satisfying what Paul Morrison calls a "longing for disembodied discursivity." As the narrator explains, stressing the typicality of Vincent's story, "the Nonconformist went into literature, as was natural, and was, it is believed in Carlingford, the founder of the 'Philosophical Review,' that new organ of public opinion" (457). This outcome is the one toward which the plot of the novel has been tending from its beginning. At the point of its greatest crisis, when

Vincent's sister appears to be dying and the members of Salem Chapel are deciding whether to dismiss him, he takes refuge in writing, producing even then "a sentence which was not one of the least successful of his sentences" (401). Near the end of the novel, Vincent remarks on the "neutral–coloured life" (439) that now must be his. This characterization of his drab future contrasts forcefully to his earlier shock at seeing the brilliantly colored dresses of the tradesmen's wives in his congregation and the pink plumpness of Tozer's daughter, whose hand is his for the asking. Life, substance, color, smell—all these Vincent puts behind him as he rejects his marked position as a dissenting preacher who ministers to those in trade.

That Vincent comes close to suffering what Victorian medicine recognized as a pathological state of nervous exhaustion is made clear when he cries out, "I think *I* shall go mad after a while if I get no rest" (401). Such a condition was considered the privilege of middle-class men,[8] and Vincent's self-diagnosis here therefore indicates his longing for such status. His symptoms point more specifically, however, to what I am calling male melancholia. His exacerbated sensibilities, his restlessness, and his discontent are all explicitly contrasted to the stolid self-satisfaction and settled ways of his parishioners, whose lives are defined by the odors of the foods that give them substance. Moreover, the osmology that identifies food as a marked form of lower-class substantiality also clarifies the potential cost of Vincent's melancholic rejection of the trade constituted by his ministry. The often deeply ambivalent olfactory representations of food in novels of the 1860s portray a form of less-than-genteel sociability that is simple-minded, limited, and therefore ultimately unacceptable, but they can also reveal a nostalgia for a way of life presented as real, honest, and solid. The distaste that Vincent experiences when he encounters such smells charts both the severity of his melancholic condition and its potentially untoward consequences.

The aromas of food in the fiction of the 1860s almost invariably signify abundance when they are evoked in lower-middle- or working-class settings.[9] Nearly all the smells registered in Eliot's *Silas Marner* arise from the country cooking done by the wives of small tradesmen and farmers, and nostalgia in this case is clearly linked to fantasies of abundance: "The odour of Christmas cooking being on the wind, it was the season when superfluous pork and black puddings are suggestive of charity" (107). Even the funerary rituals for Mrs. Joe in *Great Expectations* involve displaying an array of foods, one of which turns "the air of the parlour . . . faint with the smell of sweet cake" (278). Like odors emanating from work, the aromas of food are either marked or unmarked according to the class positioning and sometimes even the location of those eating or offering food to others. The meals that Pip shares with Herbert give off no aroma, but the meals consumed by Clara Barley's gout-ridden father, a retired purser who is named for a food, reek so highly of rum that its odor can penetrate through a floor into the room below his. Wemmick's repasts are so powerfully scented that the aroma of a "jorum of tea" served at one of them excites the pig in the backyard (294). In his office Jaggers lunches on abundance, drinking from a "flask of sherry [that] smelt like a whole caskfull" (168). Yet when Jaggers invites Pip and Herbert to join him at dinner in his home, his meals, like Lady Western's bill of fare and the genteel dinners represented in virtually any novel by Trollope, are odorless. A lengthy scene from Meredith's *Emilia in England* makes much of the disagreeable smells of both the beer that the "populace" drinks and the perfume (aptly called Alderman's Bouquet) that tradesmen wear when such olfactory stimuli are encountered by a would-be gentleman (3: 236–39), but more typically in such fiction trades of all sorts are characterized by the invitingly savory abundance of the food that their profits buy.

Not surprisingly, then, the shopkeepers and artisans in novels of the 1860s are all remarkably well fed, and their hands are often fat with the effects of what they have ingested. Their corporeality is the traditional mark of all reaches of Victorian commercial life from the "gorging and gormandising" Pumblechook of *Great Expectations* (56) to the "prosperously feeding" Podsnap of *Our Mutual Friend* (21). Such bodily abundance was doubly stigmatized in the 1860s, when to be fat was to be both ungenteel and old-fashioned, when dieting, called "banting" after the doctor who popularized the practice, had become a fad (Hoppen 347). Broughton's novels depict as particularly repulsive the fat associated with trade. *Cometh up as a Flower* can express its contempt for "Manchester gents with fat, smug faces" only by comparing them to the "accursed Israelitish dog" of the Middle Ages (6, 242). Both the butcher and the elder partner in the firm depicted in *The Struggles of Brown, Jones, and Robinson* are repeatedly characterized by their heavy eating and their resulting fat. Sometimes such indulgence is bluntly condemned by a narrator, as it is in the case of Pumblechook when it, in effect, keeps the boy Pip hungry; but the consumption of food and drink enjoyed by tradesmen is often presented at least in ambiguous terms, sometimes with the mingled condescension and appreciation characteristic of the comic perspective placed on it. Even though the pig whom Pip will later eat is noted as being housed a little too close to Wemmick's house for olfactory comfort, Pip relishes as a form of slumming the meals that Wemmick offers him, "warm and greasy" in their "vigorous reality."[10] The self-styled philosopher-narrator of *Emilia in England* generalizes on the relation between trade and fat, defining the country itself as "our fat England" and discoursing on the emergence of sentimentality from the "fat soil" of a "wealthy" nation whose people have enjoyed "a certain prolonged term of comfortable feeding" (3: 142; 1: 8–9).

"Comfortable feeding" is, according to the evidence offered by high-Victorian fiction, what tradesmen do; and the words *comfort* and *comfortable* specifically and repeatedly characterize it.[11] Even Broughton labels "honest, fat burghers" as "comfortable Sunday-clothed tradespeople" (*Not* 109). Brown in *The Struggles* is proud to offer his children meals "hot and comfortable" (32), the criterion by which Wemmick also judges the pleasures of dining. The high-born heroine of Blackmore's *Lorna Doone* enjoys being in a farmer's kitchen, exulting in "the richness, and the homeliness, and the pleasant smell of every thing" there, qualities that the genteel outlaw of the novel sums up when he refers to "the comfort of this place" (365, 434). Similarly, a London tavern in *Evan Harrington* "smell[s] of comfortable time and solid English fare" (75). Trollope uses the physical solace signaled by the aromas of food to make national and class distinctions. Henry Clavering, finally agreeing to dine with the son of the head of the engineering firm where he is working, a man whose vulgar habits Clavering deplores, is "forced to own to himself that he had never been more comfortable" (*The Claverings* 68). In Cork, by contrast, the odorants at an inn include whiskey, rancid butter, and the "perfume" of onions; they are all signs of characteristically Irish discomfort, of "culinary messes too horrible to be thought of" (*Castle Richmond* 54, 56). The narrator of *Miss Mackenzie* comments trenchantly on a similar lack of comfort, not to mention edible food, in the description of a middle-class dinner à la Russe, typical of the attempts made by "ordinary Englishmen" with £800 a year to ape the "grand banquets" of their betters: "It was all misery, wretchedness and degradation" (106–7). Good eating can be found only in less pretentious settings. Shopkeepers and artisans both give and take comfort in their food and drink, and when the odors of their repasts do not too promiscuously mingle with those of the shop, they invariably smell good.

Placed, then, in the contexts both of the novel in which he appears and of the representational practices characteristic of the 1860s, Arthur Vincent attains an insubstantiality that is defined as distinctly uncomfortable, even threatening. By refusing to eat the food of the tradesmen who are his parishioners or to earn the living that their taste for his startling sermons offers him, Vincent rejects fat and its comforts. As such, he might be in need of the kind of nourishment that the quack doctor of *Romola* champions when he defends the virtues of a medicine "infallible against melancholia" by noting its "savoury odour" (230). To refuse such bodily fortifications, to stand at an unmarked remove from the material realities of smell, as Vincent presumably will, is perhaps to risk not existing in any of the ways that make material life possible. Vincent, seeming to recognize that possibility as his fate, imagines living a "posthumous and nameless life" after he leaves Carlingford to become a journalist in London (439). Yet if the osmology of *Salem Chapel* points out the relation between Vincent's symptoms and his longing for disembodiment, its identification of specific values with specific odorants begins to point toward a diagnosis of the causes of his condition. The novel insistently associates the work of making or exchanging products with acts of offering or eating food by marking as odorous all such activities. The only items for sale that the novel features, besides Vincent's pews and one reference to books, are foodstuffs. The smells in *Salem Chapel* therefore identify things that are made and sold with things that give substance to bodies. Its hero is portrayed as losing flesh because he distances himself from any such form of odoriferous substantiality. More directly than Vincent's story, however, the cases of Evan Harrington and his near contemporary, Mr. Philip Pip,[12] establish the rejection of trade as the central cause of male melancholia.

Etiology: Handling Cheeses

Giving Tom Tulliver of Eliot's *The Mill on the Floss* a lecture on his need to learn "the smell of things" by working on a wharf or in a warehouse, Mr. Deane tells the story of his own rise as a self-made man by casting it in conventional osmological terms: "When I was sixteen, my jacket smelt of tar, and I wasn't afraid of handling cheeses. That's the reason I can wear good broadcloth now." Like jackets imbued with tar, hands holding cheeses presumably smell of the objects that they touch, and Deane uses these concrete examples to convince his nephew to leave behind the insubstantialities of his inappropriately fine education. After all, as Deane explains, "the world isn't made of pen, ink, and paper" (202). Tom takes his uncle's advice, fiercely and doggedly committing himself to the import/export trading that wins him fantastically high rates of return on his investments. Despite, therefore, Tom's status as one of the most depressed and depressing male characters in the fiction of the 1860s, his story stands as a contrast to those of his melancholy fellows, even as Deane's speech epitomizes the terms in which their stories are told. *Evan Harrington* and *Great Expectations* explain in more or less direct ways the source of the malaise from which their melancholics suffer: they refuse, as Deane puts it, to handle cheeses, to do the smelly work of making and selling things. When their stories are set in the context of not only the osmology in which they are cast but also nineteenth-century conceptions of melancholia, the etiology of the disorder from which they suffer becomes clear.

Known as *la maladie anglaise*, the mental condition typically besetting those who profited from both English liberty and English trade, melancholy was traditionally characterized as an unaccountable sadness so intense that it sometimes issued in the suicide of those wealthy men of commerce who seemed to have every reason to want to live.[13] By the mid-Victorian period, however, the relation between trade and melancholy was styled differently. In *Self-Help*, Samuel Smiles follows out the logic of Burton's linking of idleness and melancholy, identifying the disorder as one that results from too much mental work, too little physical exercise. Smiles labels the condition "green-sickness," a term associated with anemic young girls, to emphasize the effeminacy of the men who suffer from it: "manhood [is] withered, twisted, and stunted" because men who use only their brains necessarily have "unused pithless hands, calfless legs, and limp bodies."[14] From a more scientific perspective, Maudsley associates melancholy with "an extreme aversion . . . to exercise, employment, and activity of a beneficial kind" (337). Yet Freud is the commentator whose understanding of the disorder is most pertinent here. In 1895 the term *melancholia* appeared in his early notes for the paper that would become "Mourning and Melancholia" (1917). As a state of unrecognized grief resulting from an "unknown loss," it is defined in that essay as a condition in which "one cannot see clearly what it is that has been lost" and whose self-punishing effects are more severe when one is ambivalent about what has been lost.[15] Though the symptomatology that Freud offers resembles that of earlier models, he explains the unaccountability of melancholia by defining it as a condition unrecognized by its victim. It is not idiopathic; it is unconscious. This formulation effectively distinguishes the malaise that he is describing from the self-conscious pleasures of despair offered by Wertherism or more general forms of Romantic despondency.[16]

Because Freud speaks of the emotional "economics" involved in an "object-loss" (14: 245), his analysis is metaphorically suggestive of the economic determinants of melancholia in the Victorian period.[17] The lost "object" that Freud speaks of in this essay is typically a loved one about whom the melancholic has been ambivalent, and such an identification authorizes the use to which Carolyn Dever has put Freud's thinking in identifying the "dead or lost" mother whose absence haunts the "melancholic" texts of Victorian fiction (xi–xii). Yet the term *object* might also be taken more literally to define what Victorian sufferers of melancholia could not recognize as lost to them. In this sense, the condition is doubly a form of alienation, economic and affective: an unrecognized estrangement from materiality caused by the commercial developments of the period and an affective disorder resulting from such changes. As the case of Vincent in *Salem Chapel* suggests, the "objects" that the fictional heroes of the 1860s are represented as having lost are things made and sold, but the stories of Evan and Pip further specify that such things are the products of the kinds of artisanal labor associated with the past. The "individual commodity," the "elementary form" of capitalist exchange, as Marx defined it in the first sentence of the first volume of *Capital* (125), has outpaced the products of an earlier economy, but commodities are, by definition, abstractions.[18] In a culture so thoroughly given over to production and distribution, machine-made commodities may come "alive," as Thomas Richards has argued (2), but tactile contact with hand-crafted objects remains for some men the test and proof of substantive life: I touch, therefore I am. Neither able nor desiring to make such statements, Victorian men who aspire to or have achieved gentility by being removed from manufacture and commerce may unconsciously long for the sensuous, material reality characteristic of traditional forms of trade.[19] The melancholic's condition seems to be a sadness without cause only because he does not or cannot acknowledge what he regrets having lost. That this malaise should be depicted in Victorian novels—by their nature, relatively immaterial, textual representations—only emphasizes as it exemplifies the inevitability of this result.

Great Expectations and *Evan Harrington* present characters desperate to leave behind the trades that they find demeaning, and both Pip and Evan are made miserable by the restless insubstantiality and the uncertainty of the circumstances in which they then find themselves. Published serially and successively in different weekly magazines—Meredith's *Evan Harrington* in *Once a Week* from February to October 1860 and Dickens's *Great Expectations* in *All the Year Round* from December 1860 to August 1861—the two novels present remarkably similar characters with remarkably similar problems, though Dickens does everything to thwart the kind of analysis that I offer of his character and Meredith does everything to make its terms seem self evident. In no other high-Victorian novels is class featured more significantly as a practice of setting two characters in comparative relation to each other than it is in *Great Expectations* and *Evan Harrington*. Yet the older Pip tells his story without recourse to the word *class* or its Victorian variant *rank*. The repetition three times of the formula "Miss Havisham up town" (52) is as close as the novel comes to acknowledging what is involved in Pip's initial meetings with the recluse and her ward. Moreover, Pip evasively disguises his longing for gentility as the effect of his unaccountable erotic attachment to Estella, not, as it is, the cause of that passion.[20] Evan's story puts in more logical temporal order his social and amatory ambitions since he longs to be a gentleman before ever seeing the lady whose hand in marriage would ratify his status as genteel. At various points in his career, Pip claims that he cannot identify what he wants, who has caused his misery, or why he is so desperately unhappy. Yet he can describe his suffering, and he does so— eloquently, repeatedly, and unremittingly. That his "wretched hankerings after money and gentility" (236) have transformed the former "blacksmith's boy" (248) into the archetypal melancholic is clear even though, as Freud would note, Pip cannot recognize what he has lost. Like *Great Expectations*, *Evan Harrington; or, He Would Be a Gentleman* is a novel obsessed with what its narrator bluntly calls "class-prejudice" (18): as its hero tries to avoid taking over the debt-ridden tailor's shop that his father has left him, he openly acknowledges at every turn the shame that his connection to trade elicits in him. Setting Evan's case against Pip's foregrounds the motivations that the latter, the consummate "self-swindler" (225), would deny.

Both *Great Expectations* and *Evan Harrington* conform faithfully to the osmology of high-Victorian fiction that marks trade as odorous. Like most genuinely arduous physical labor depicted in novels of the 1860s, Joe Gargery's work in his forge is figured as free of even a whiff of manly sweat, but Pip recognizes tradesmen like Hubble, Pumblechook, Barley, and Jaggers because he can smell them out. Similarly, as I have noted, one of Evan's sisters voices her brother's distaste for trade when she announces aphoristically, "The shop smells!" (395). Yet because both Pip and Evan are unmarked characters bent on establishing the anosmic atmosphere of their pretensions and expectations, they often register in sensory modalities other than smell the effects of the comparative encounters that reveal the distance between what they are and what they want to be. Proving the physical nature of class distinctions based on material inequalities, Evan responds to encounters as a form of tactile engagement. The mere idea of becoming a tailor triggers for him "visions of leprosy," in which the woman he loves will draw back her skirts in order not to touch him (73), visions of encountering "a hideous image" of himself "burning" in her face and therefore burning his (216). The older narrator of *Great Expectations*, committed to demonstrating that his younger self has been genteel long before his expectations grant him that status, experiences meetings that reveal his social inferiority primarily in terms of sight, as visions that register affective states of hope and dread. The meanings that accrue to such tactile and visual comparative encounters, however, become clear when they are articulated with the lessons of the osmology set out in the fiction of the 1860s.

In its depictions of one character meeting another in the kind of mundane event typical of everyday life, *Great Expectations* seems to present its story as unconventional and even bizarre. Yet, like other novelists of the 1860s, Dickens presents encounters as the basic constituents of his plot. A young boy happens upon two escaped convicts unaccountably loitering on the lonely marshes. A year later he enters a ruined house; on his first visit there he encounters a witch and an enchanted princess only to return the following week to meet three times as many new faces when the family scavengers have arrived, along with the witch's lawyer, to celebrate her birthday. Pip then spends much of the rest of the novel trying to avoid meeting others, the criminals and villagers whose recognitions of him would reveal his lowly origins—while other characters go out of their way, often literally, to stage encounters with him. These meetings include the novel's heights of both nightmare and comedy: convicts breathing down Pip's neck, the young boys of the village gleefully treating Mrs. Joe's funeral as a parade, repeated visions of which they gain by running ahead so that they can see it pass them again. Behavior bent on proliferating the possibility for such meetings seems to be a characteristic of the minor figures in *Great Expectations*, chief among whom is the novel's comic impresario and its comic star,

Trabb's boy. Confronting Pip three times as he doubles back to meet the would-be gentleman again and again, Trabb's boy mocks Pip's would-be superiority through self-abasement, then mimicry. Ejected from the town by the version of the working-class rough music to which Trabb's boy treats him, Pip is forced to see in the smirking and strutting gestures and hear in the drawling speech of the tailor's apprentice the impressions that Pip himself makes on those whom he meets. Yet even the outcome of this humiliating confrontation cannot compare to the performative cruelty of the repetitions involved in Pip's earlier visits to Satis House:[21] there every other day for up to ten months, Pip is forced to confront again and again the differences between himself and its inhabitants through the sights and sounds that he presents to them, and they to him—his coarse hands and thick boots and untutored diction set against Miss Havisham's faded "satins, and lace" and "bright jewels" and Estella's disdainful denunciations of the "stupid, clumsy labouring-boy" (58, 62).

Although the distinctions that such encounters typically bring into play variously involve age, work, family origins, gender, training, legality, and status, the last of these categories emerges as the most significant. Elaborate and elaborated, nightmarish and tormenting, the most significant of the meetings recorded in *Great Expectations* tend increasingly to confirm Pip's social inferiority to virtually everyone he meets. The effect of such interactions is to transform his consciousness into a kind of loop tape that he must replay in both his memories of the past and his conceptions of the future. Even after his visits to Satis House have been discontinued once he is apprenticed to Joe, Pip cannot but relive them imaginatively, and he figures his abasement as a visionary prospect of encountering Estella while he works at the forge:

> What I dreaded was, that in some unlucky hour I, being at my
> grimiest and commonest, should lift up my eyes and see Estella
> looking in at one of the wooden windows of the forge. I was haunted
> by the fear that she would, sooner or later, find me out, with a black
> face and hands, doing the coarsest part of my work, and would exult
> over me and despise me. Often after dark, when I was pulling the
> bellows for Joe, and we were singing Old Clem, and when the thought
> how we used to sing it at Miss Havisham's would seem to show me
> Estella's face in the fire, with her pretty hair fluttering in the wind
> and her eyes scorning me,—often at such a time I would look towards
> those panels of black night in the wall which the wooden windows
> then were, and would fancy that I saw her just drawing her face away,
> and would believe that she had come at last. (107–8)

This encounter, which exists wholly in Pip's suppositions about the future, is one that never takes place, but it reflects the humiliations of all the previous interchanges between Pip and Estella. Like Evan imagining his shame burning in the face of the young lady whom he cannot hope to wed, Pip envisions his continuing disgrace as the expression on the face of the woman rejecting him. Estella is ethereal, fire and wind, as he conjures up her arrival in a moment that turns the black night into panels on which his fear and longing can paint her image as she leaves, in a final gesture of scorn, even before she has arrived. Yet if the fantastic elements and poetic intensity of Dickens's account in such a passage disguise its typicality as a tale of the 1860s, its lyrically evoked visions of witches, monsters, and ghosts should not distract attention from the extent to which Pip's story, like Evan's, is driven by the "class-prejudice" that both novels acknowledge not only in the encounters that the two characters see and feel but also in the smells that they notice. When measured against each other in an analytic comparative encounter, Evan's case of melancholia makes evident the sources of Pip's.

Pip and Evan Meet

In the second volume of *Great Expectations*, Pip enters upon not only his preparations for a life of gentility but also his career in melancholia. He has all the symptoms and exhibits all the signs of the disease. Having been magically released from his apprenticeship to his blacksmith brother-in-law, Pip trains to be a gentleman by going to London. Once there, like Vincent of *Salem Chapel*, Pip defines his life in terms of its discursivity: the "construction" of his mind is a message that he comes to see "written" in the cobwebs and the tracks left by the spiders and mice in Miss Havisham's rooms (301), the aspect of which he as a boy has recognized as "so strange, and so fine—and melancholy" (60). "Not designed for any profession" (196), Pip finds that he has nothing to do, and he turns to reading as a way of filling his purposeless hours. As he explains, "Notwithstanding my inability to settle to anything—which I hope arose out of the restless and incomplete tenure on which I held my means—I had a taste for reading, and read regularly so many hours a day" (310). Pip makes discursivity his vocation, the inodorous and unmarked proof of his gentility. Magwitch confirms this point when he lists the things that prove Pip's status, his watch and diamond ring and fine linen, and then describes finally and most elaborately Pip's books: "And your books too . . . mounting up, on their shelves, by hundreds! And you read 'em; don't you? I see you'd been a reading of 'em when I come in" (317). Once Magwitch has been sentenced to death, Pip spends his time writing pointless memorials on the convict's behalf, Pip's existence becoming "wholly absorbed in these appeals" to the Home Secretary and the Crown (454). That the older

Pip finally turns his story into a "manuscript confession" like those collected by Wemmick (209) simply ratifies the penchant of his younger self for the relative disembodiment involved in being reduced to the marks of ink on paper.

Equally revealing of Pip's melancholia is his restless wandering from one place to the next and back again. Miss Havisham has engendered in him the habit of such profitless circular motion when she has ordered him to push her in her wheeled chair between her two rooms for three hours a day, every other day for nearly a year. Once set in motion, Pip is unable to stop. In his "restlessness and disquiet of mind" (271), he traverses locations in London, Hammersmith, Richmond, and Kent. To the last of these destinations, he makes ten recorded trips after he leaves his home for London. During these wanderings, he threatens to become nothing, a "ghost" whose "unquiet spirit" finds itself "wandering, wandering, wandering" around the house in Richmond where Estella is living (298). The terms *wretched* and *miserable* become the key words of his tale, expressing both the moral disapprobation that his ingratitude to Joe deserves and the weight of the affective disorder from which Pip suffers. Returning, appropriately enough, from seeing Wopsle's rendition of the Danish prince, Pip notes, "Miserably I went to bed, . . . miserably thought of Estella, and miserably dreamed . . . [of] play[ing] Hamlet to Miss Havisham's Ghost" (258). Traveling back and forth between London and "our town," Pip encounters those who applaud or mock his rise in status, responses that whether positive or negative simply make him more miserable. Seeing Estella in "the place of encounter" where he as a youth had fought with Herbert makes Pip "cry again, inwardly—and that is the sharpest crying of all" (237). Nothing can satisfy Pip, and he, like Arthur Vincent, exhibits an acute sensibility to external stimuli as he makes his way from place to place. Pip starts at the slightest sounds, feeling so guilty that he is sure he is being pursued; and his heightened visual acuity allows him to describe Turneresque landscapes, in which "the coming sun [is] like a marsh of fire" bursting into "millions of sparkles" (430).

In the peculiarly reversed logic of the plotting of *Great Expectations*, which renders a previous event plausible only after a later event appears impossibly as its cause, the second volume of the novel, comprising the action before Magwitch returns to reveal the source of Pip's expectations, presents him as the melancholic whose misery is without apparent cause, while the action of the third volume serves to justify his unhappiness by attributing it to his loss of Estella. Earlier when he sees a convict, Pip notes, "I could not have said what I was afraid of, for my fear was altogether undefined and vague, but there was great fear upon me" (230). His childhood "sense of helplessness and danger" (5) is later more than adequately motivated by his fear that Magwitch will be discovered, a revelation that will threaten the convict's life and his beneficiary's status as a gentleman. Now Pip has reason for the "one dominant anxiety" of his "unhappy life," as he rows up and down the Thames in preparation for flight. He is tormented by both "mental hyperaesthesia" and "mental anaesthesia," to use Griesinger's terms: "the round of things went on. Condemned to inaction and a state of constant restlessness and suspense, I rowed about in my boat, and waited, waited, waited, as I best could" (379–80). The signs of his illness increase in number and severity. After Pip is hurt in the fire that ultimately claims Miss Havisham's life, the innkeeper tending him notes, "Your appetite's been touched like," and Pip concedes, "I can eat no more" (417). Pumblechook, displaying his "five fat fingers," finds Pip "little more than skin and bones" (470). Like the tradesmen of *Salem Chapel*, both of these men want to feed a reluctant melancholic. Like Arthur Vincent, Pip becomes "worn and white" with sickness and anxiety (474). Finally, after Magwitch's death, Pip succumbs to fever. In this crisis of "disease," during which he "often los[es his] reason," he also loses his identity, "confound[ing]" it with other "impossible existences" (458). The most acutely stricken of the victims of melancholia in the novels that I am analyzing, Pip becomes prey to the delusions that would confirm for Victorian alienists a diagnosis of temporary insanity.

Yet if Dickens cleverly orchestrates the action of *Great Expectations* so that its third volume seems to explain the affective disorder to which Pip increasingly becomes victim, what can explain his earlier suffering when all his hopes are apparently about to be fulfilled? According to Freud's formulation, melancholia is unacknowledged loss, and the older Pip manages his narrative so that it is almost impossible to identify Joe's trade as either the lost object of Pip's ambivalent longings or the prominent and respected enterprise that it became during the mid-Victorian period. Pip so thoroughly idealizes Joe's work as a blacksmith that it has no substance that could be either disgusting or attractive.[22] There are very few references to dirty hands in *Great Expectations*, the most important of which occurs when Pip imagines the visit that Estella never makes to the forge. Joe's manual labor, moreover, is defined not by its physicality, but by its status as poetic fancy. Joe never makes any specific product in the novel: he mends a set of handcuffs and torments Pip with a list of the items that Pip might make as gifts for Miss Havisham. Joe's most significant productive act is to hammer out "in a single blow" a rhyming epitaph for his father, a couplet that, significantly, Joe cannot afford to materialize as an engraving on a headstone (48). Pip recognizes that Biddy is "theoretically . . . as good a blacksmith" as he is (125), but Joe is only "theoretically" one as well. Unlike Pip, Joe serves no apprenticeship to the trade, simply taking over his drunken father's place since someone has to earn a living for the family. Even the blacksmith's traditional song, "Old Clem," whose rhythms are vigorous enough to be heard above the sound of hammer blows, is introduced into the novel in a way that divorces it from its origins in a material practice. Before the reader hears Pip and Joe and Orlick sing it, Pip has crooned the song at Satis House, Miss Havisham and Estella both taking up the tune. There, like everything else associated with Joe's trade, the "ditty" appears in a gentrified and attenuated form: "the whole strain was so subdued, even when there were three of us, that it made less noise in the grim old house than the lightest breath of wind" (96). The novel empties of substance the work that Pip has rejected so that he cannot feel the loss of the kind of tactile immediacy that Deane in *The Mill on the Floss* identifies when he speaks of "handling cheeses."

The distaste for trade that *Great Expectations* disguises as a boy's romantic passion is fully acknowledged in *Evan Harrington*. Whereas Joe's work as a blacksmith is idealized as honest, virtuous, and unmarked, Evan's story bluntly articulates the Victorian contempt for production and commerce, a dominant attitude that is well documented, frequently analyzed, and claimed to be powerful enough to persist to this day.[23] One has only to read the first paragraphs of novels like *The Perpetual Curate* and *Miss Mackenzie* to recognize the depth of the scorn for retail trade in particular, especially as it is practiced by small shopkeepers standing behind their own counters. *The Struggles of Brown, Jones, and Robinson*, in my view the most distasteful novel of the 1860s, asks its readers to encounter characters engaged in retail trade in a nasty mockery of its fake gentilities; and *Tom Brown at Oxford* uses the debasing effects of trade to explain why so many of the previously genteel institutions of the country—schools, fox hunts, and Oxford itself—have been devalued by their having become goods sold to the highest bidders. Such trade smells, as Bain's analysis in *The Senses and the Intellect* makes clear and as Grant Allen also suggests when he compares the "poetical" qualities of wine with the "vulgar" attributes of rum, a "modern commercial product" whose scent is "strong and disagreeable" (268–69n). Even fiction can stink of trade: according to the *Quarterly Review*, sensation novels are to be deplored because of the "commercial atmosphere [that] floats around works of this class, redolent of the manufactory and the shop"; so "unspeakably disgusting" is this odor that the reviewer attributes to such fiction a "vulture-like instinct" to devour "loathsome" bits of "social corruption . . . before the scent has evaporated" ("Sensation" 483, 502). Though the olfactory representations of commerce in the fiction of the 1860s are often only mildly distasteful, thereby simply registering its physicality, a few come close to registering similarly intense disgust. In Collins's *The Woman in White*, drawings are said to "smel[l] of horrid dealers' and brokers' fingers" (69), and one character in Trollope's *Framley Parsonage* calls the heiress Miss Dunstable "a gallipot wench whose money still smells of bad drugs" (452). In resisting the smelly world of trade, Evan, like Pip, suffers a dematerialization that threatens his manhood, but his case more directly portrays what Evan has lost as tactile contact with the handmade products that are associated with the past, despite their continued importance in the getting and spending of the high-Victorian economy.

Although the action of *Evan Harrington*, like that of *Great Expectations*, is set in an earlier generation, "in a time before our joyful era of universal equality" (75) as the narrator puts it in his characteristically sardonic way, Evan is a man of the 1860s: attractive, well-educated, well-mannered, well-dressed. His plight is also typical: he is a young man without profession, without goals or ideals other than his love for Rose Jocelyn, the young lady of Beckley Court. When the reader first meets Evan, he is about to learn of the death of his father, the tailor Melchisedec Harrington, the "great Mel" of Lymport-on-the-Sea. One of Evan's sisters, married to a Portuguese count and ennobled by his dubious foreign title, has previously taken Evan off to Portugal to distance him from his father's trade, association with which she and her two sisters have all managed to escape by marriage. Although Evan goes immediately into mourning for his parent by shedding one tear for him, that acknowledged grief is much less significant than Evan's melancholic fears about what that death means for his own future. The story recounts Evan's attempts to confirm the genteel status that seems to accrue to him through his graceful person and the refined education that the social pretensions of the "great Mel" have provided him. Evan must choose between running a tailor's shop, a business encumbered by his father's substantial posthumous debts of roughly £5,000, or pursuing his attentions to Rose, whom he has met during his time in Portugal. Supposedly in training for his career as a tailor, Evan can do nothing more effectual than ride or walk back and forth among London, Beckley Court, and Lymport as he waits for destiny to offer him a future. Evan's liberation from his father's trade is simply an outcome for which the young man longs, not one to be effected by the exertion of his will. Like Pip, Evan epitomizes self-doubting passivity. In the twists and turns of the novel's sometimes obscure plot, Evan tries to avoid encountering those who could reveal that he is a tailor's son. Tempted by one of his sisters to accept an invitation to Beckley Court, Evan exposes himself, even more than the older Pip does in visiting his village, to the chance meetings that will reveal him as a pitiful fraud.

In the sixth chapter of *Evan Harrington*, "My Gentleman on the Road"—where else would he be?—the narrator notes of his gentleman that "he has little character for the moment. Most youths are like Pope's women; they have no character at all" (52–53). If this comment is meant to foretell Evan's eventual maturation into the fullness of manly character, it is deeply misleading. His past actions seem, rather, to predict a future of melancholic insubstantiality. At the age of seventeen, more than two years before the opening of the story, Evan has spent his time in the brewery of his brother-in-law, the affluent M.P. Andrew Cogglesby. Months before Herbert Pocket of *Great Expectations* asserts that it is genteel to brew beer, Cogglesby is making that point to Evan ("Van") but in such a vulgar fashion as to put in question its validity: "I'm a brewer, Van. Do you think I'm ashamed of it?

Not while I brew good beer, my boy!—not while I brew good beer! They don't think worse of me in the House for it. It isn't ungentlemanly to brew good beer, Van" (47–48). Evan evidently does not agree. Rather, he passes "the hours not devoted to his positive profession—that of gentleman—in the offices of the brewery, toying with big books and balances, which he despise[s]" (20). Evan's only positive quality is his commitment to the profession of gentility that he cannot afford to adopt. Such a negative calculus of characterization is all that there is to Evan: he is defined by what he hates more than by what he wants. His exercises in discursivity both before and after he returns from Portugal are notably insubstantial and incomplete. There he has been a private secretary to a British diplomat; he has written half of a history of Portugal. Now back in England, he waits upon his great expectations, which he thinks will come to him in the form of a government appointment. Like Pip, though he is more writer than reader, Evan is heartily miserable. Even after he tries to accept his fate by entering upon a kind of abbreviated London apprenticeship that will teach him to run his father's shop, if not how to sit cross-legged and sew a pair of trousers, he serves as the secretary to a second brother-in-law's company of the Royal Marines, trying to hold on to his identity as a composer of words rather than a cutter of cloth. At this, the nadir of his fortunes, he passes nights of "misery" and "intolerable anguish," sometimes becoming in his sleeplessness "like one in a trance, entombed" (445).

That Evan's manhood is at stake the novel ironically makes clear by having him reject a line of work that is traditionally associated with emasculation. Trade, in general, bore that reputation: a writer in the *Cornhill* for 1860 found emblematic of the attitudes of his own countrymen the story of a young Frenchman whose occupation had driven him to commit suicide and whose last wish was for an epitaph announcing his fate: "Born to be a man; died a grocer" ("Work" 600). If such clerks were deemed unmanly (Davidoff and Hall 269), tailors were more definitively so. Tradesmen in both senses of the word, makers of the products that they sold, they pursued an occupation whose physical accoutrements of cloth, scissors, needle, and thread were so obviously gendered female that, as the proverb has it, it takes nine tailors to make a man. Over and over again in *Evan Harrington* the material markers of this trade serve as badges of unmanly dishonor: as the countess exclaims, "Shop! Shears! Geese! Cabbage! Snip! Nine to a man!" (492). Associated with the smoothing iron called a goose and known in slang as a cabbage because he deals in such leavings of fabric, a tailor is both as foolish as a female bird and as devious as the cook or housemaid who claims as her perquisites the leftovers of the materials on which she labors. The narrator mockingly finds tailoring so unspeakably offensive that he refers to it by invoking a classical euphemism, "the gloomy realms of Dis, otherwise Trade," just as the countess prefers to call it Demogorgon (17, 23). Evan remembers his father Mel as "a pattern of manhood" (52) precisely because he refused to live like a tailor, choosing instead to keep horses, to dine with the neighboring gentry, and to carry himself with such dignity that he was once mistaken for a marquis in disguise. According to the model that his father offers, then, as Evan becomes less and less a tailor, he should become more and more a man, possessing will, energy, determination, and purpose. Yet the result of Evan's experiences is exactly the opposite: the more he removes himself from the shop in Lymport, the less manly he becomes. When his mother tries to convince him that he must take over his father's business, Evan responds as only a melancholic can: he refuses to eat, accuses her of trying to drive him mad, and feels "oppressed by horrible sensations of self-contempt, that caused whatever he touched to sicken him" (74). As Rose aptly notes, he has become Don Doloroso (39).

Moreover, *Evan Harrington* identifies the tactility of trade as its most repellent characteristic by casting responses to it, like those that Evan experiences when he imagines encountering Rose, in terms of the sense of touch. The narrator of the novel opines that in "our civilised state" the act of "touching a nerve" has replaced the bloodshed characteristic of "savage nations" (236), and the thought of being a tailor makes Evan suffer from violent tactile perceptions that seem to rend his flesh, even if they do not draw blood. A snip himself, as slang would label him, Evan seems vulnerable to the kinds of wounds that scissors make and to the burns caused by a flat iron. Evan's skin is alive to both the "smart" and "little slap" of self-loathing, the "innumerable little pricks and stings" that prove him a tradesman (225, 395). The "sensation" caused by the shame of making clothes is that of being "skinned alive" or having "burnt flesh" (216, 219). So sensitive does Evan become that he projects the power to hurt him onto every object around him: "oppressed by horrible sensations of self-contempt" when he thinks of working as a tailor, "whatever he touched . . . sicken[ed] him" (74). Nor is Evan alone in having such physical responses. Told that the man she has mistaken for a fine English gentleman is the son of a tailor, Rose responds as if to a blow: "There was a sharp twitch in her body, as if she had been stung or struck" (190). "It *is* a word—snip!" she later comments, "that makes you seem to despise yourself" (215). Interestingly, Meredith is not the only Victorian novelist to link sensations of smell and touch to tailoring: when Trollope denounces the vulgar pretensions and unreality of Disraeli's novels, such fiction is reduced to "a smell of hair-oil, an aspect of buhl, a remembrance of tailors, and that pricking of the conscience which must be the general accompaniment of paste diamonds" (*Autobiography* 259–60). Both Rose's response to the word *snip* and Trollope's reference to tailors involve reactions as if to the pricking of needles. The power of a word to create such bodily responses in *Evan Harrington* exemplifies the physical effects that Victorian psychophysiologists attributed to "sensory representations" and "suggested feelings." Even the thought of bodily contact with the materialities of trade causes physical suffering: to imagine the handling of cheeses is to be wounded and tortured by them.

That the suffering caused by the unacknowledged loss of such contact results from ambivalence about its value is made clear, therefore, by setting side by side the depictions of trade in *Great Expectations* and *Evan Harrington*, the former idealized as a paradise lost, a realm of duty and manly effort and moral simplicities; the latter, a social hell in which the damned are burned and cut and struck. Yet, as the high-Victorian osmology shared by both novels suggests, not to have such contact is to risk disappearing altogether. Like Arthur Vincent, both Pip and Evan come close to such annihilation before the fairy-godfather plots of both the novels in which they appear resolve their difficulties in quite different ways. How the women in their lives offer to or withhold from these characters the substance that trade can no longer provide is the portion of their case histories that I recount in the following chapter. The power of the disorder from which they suffer, however, is made clear by the extent to which it can afflict even those men least temperamentally prone to depression, prominent among whom is Pip's closest London companion.

Idleness and Impotence, Economy-Style

Herbert Pocket, with his imperturbable good cheer and amiability, would seem a poor candidate for melancholia. Yet he also exhibits its symptoms, and his case reveals both the economic factors that contribute to and the powerlessness engendered by the malaise from which both Pip and he suffer. Herbert, as his friend first encounters him, is a punching bag: he is repeatedly seen lying on his back, like Pip's siblings in the grave; and when Pip and he meet again in London, Herbert is still taking "blows and buffets" (183), this time occasioned by the poverty of his profitless position in a counting house. Like Evan and Pip, his fellow do-nothings of 1860 and 1861, Herbert is powerless to determine the outcome of his own story. The two conditions are linked: those who cannot act can hardly expect to be self-determining. Throughout most of *Great Expectations*, Herbert experiences an unaccountable and anomalous condition of vocationless activity that makes almost parodic the melancholic's characteristic idleness. Less than manly, Herbert becomes an exaggerated and fantastic embodiment of melancholia, the outcome of whose story sheds light on those of his fellow sufferers because it highlights the issue of male productivity.

Anxieties about loss and negation, which characterize melancholia, also pervade the ongoing debate in nineteenth-century political economy over the proper definition of productive as opposed to nonproductive labor.[24] The problem of how to categorize different kinds of work had plagued theorists since the eighteenth century. Adam Smith had objected to the physiocratic practice of "degrad[ing]" the "class of artificers, manufacturers and merchants" by giving them "the humiliating appellation of the barren or unproductive class" (2: 184). Smith developed a test for productivity that prevailed a century later: productive labor is that "which adds to the value of the subject upon which it is bestowed" (1: 351). Yet Smith's was hardly the last word on this question. As John Stuart Mill notes in his *Principles of Political Economy*, "not a little controversy" has arisen because the term *unproductive* is taken to be a "term of disparagement" and those labeled by it are "'stigmatized'" as "wasteful or worthless" (2: 45). Even though Mill argues against such conventional responses, his categorization of "merchants or dealers" as productive laborers (2: 47) is criticized by Mayhew in *London Labour and the London Poor* as itself falling into the trap of conventional thinking because Mill tries to grant those who deal in objects the status of those who make them.[25] According to Mayhew's categorization, however, such men are not themselves productive. Rather, they are "merely" "Auxiliaries," as opposed to "Enrichers, or those who are employed in producing utilities fixed and embodied in material things, that is to say, in producing exchangeable commodities or riches" (4: 9). Mayhew follows out the implications of his reasoning by concluding, "it must be confessed that, economically speaking, the most important and directly valuable of all classes are those whom I have here denominated Enrichers" (4: 10). Uncomfortable as it makes him to admit it, Mayhew therefore grants workers, even so-called unskilled workers, a value that he denies middle-class managers, owners, and dealers; and this value is directly based on the materiality of working-class labor, its ability to "produc[e] utilities fixed and embodied in material things." The middle-class man found to be "unproductive" by the discourse of political economy, then, the man whose work is "merely" auxiliary, to use Mayhew's repeated evaluation, might find himself branded, in Mill's terms, as "wasteful or worthless."

The rhetoric of the ending of *Great Expectations*, with its emphasis on diligence and profits and a company's good name, works hard to counteract such valuations. It installs Pip and Herbert in a shipping brokerage, where their later work as middlemen at the Victorian midcentury would plausibly make them large and ever-increasing profits.[26] Yet on his way to that outcome, Herbert must put in more than three years of idleness. Judged by either Mill's or Mayhew's criterion, Herbert is radically unproductive. Before joining Clarriker's concern, Herbert spends his days at a counting house, time for which he is paid nothing: "it doesn't pay me anything," as he tells Pip, "I have to———keep myself" (183). That his position makes Herbert nothing seems just: he does nothing at the counting house to earn a salary.

Looking always for an opening, he can only look, as Pip explains: "I often paid [Herbert] a visit in the dark back-room in which he consorted with an ink-jar, a hat-peg, a coal-box, a string-box, an almanack, a desk and stool, and a ruler; and I do not remember that I ever saw him do anything else but look about him." Herbert sits among the objects associated with trade, but he never touches them. Once a day he walks to Lloyd's "in observance of a ceremony of seeing his principal," but this ritual of seeing his employer, another form of "look[ing] about," involves no productive labor. Herbert is not even a lowly message carrier; his daily journey to Lloyd's is simply an opportunity for him to look at the man, the partner in the firm, whose position he covets. Herbert's pointless journeys back and forth to Lloyd's, like Pip's and Evan's and Vincent's restless travels, epitomize his confinement within a cycle of nonproductive activity from which there is no escape. Pip rightly notes that Herbert joins him in a companionship of misery: "We were always more or less miserable," he says of the "usual manners and customs at Barnard's Inn" (273). There Herbert suffers daily cycles of the kind of depression that Freud describes in "Mourning and Melancholia": gloomy in the morning, more hopeful as the day goes on, Herbert late at night becomes "so deeply despondent again as to talk of buying a rifle and going to America, with a general purpose of compelling buffaloes to make his fortune" (272).

Released from this misery, not by buffaloes, but by Pip's machinations, Herbert the idle becomes Herbert the impotent. By making him the unsuspecting object of Pip's apparently benevolent conspiracy to install him as a future partner of Clarriker and Co., the novel casts Herbert as both child and dupe. Pip uses first the funds supplied by Magwitch and then those donated by Miss Havisham to make Herbert an articled clerk or apprentice. Herbert can enter into his great expectations only because Pip plays the role of his father and uses his capital to buy his friend both an annual salary and the prospect of partnership on the promise of future payments. Keeping Herbert in the dark about the source of his good fortune simply emphasizes how little he has done to deserve it. Pip's plotting offers Herbert a future as a shipping broker, but Herbert's conception that his own good qualities have gained him access to that position would have been recognized by Victorian readers, conversant as they were with the customs of apprenticeship and its function in commercial concerns, as wildly improbable. In the 1820s, only young men supported by family capital and connected by family ties to particular firms would have been welcomed into them.[27] The idleness that characterizes Herbert's work at the beginning of his career simply makes more apparent the oddity of his later installation at Clarriker's. On the principle that wholesale trade is more respectable than retail trade—a point established early in Trollope's *Miss Mackenzie* (1–2)—Herbert, like Pip and Evan, manages to escape becoming tainted by the least reputable forms of commercial exchange, but Herbert's route to the business that he does embrace reveals its origins in both unproductivity and impotence.

As Herbert's case testifies, powerlessness is the condition of the 1860s melancholic. The peculiarities of Pip's situation, requiring him to wait, as his friend does, on the pleasure of his unknown benefactor, create in him the kind of self-punishing guilt that Freud and earlier commentators found characteristic of melancholia, but Pip's plight also makes him very self-conscious about his own impotence. As he sinks into the fever that will challenge his sanity, he presents symptoms of potentially annihilating and even fatal disease: he has "no purpose, and no power" (457). Similarly, Arthur Vincent must spend most of *Salem Chapel* waiting to discover if his sister has disgraced his family and whether his parishioners will dismiss him. Evan's passive acceptance of whatever events may offer him is embodied in the role that his sisters play as the three "Parcae, daughters of the shears, [who] arranged and settled the young man's fate" (26). Specifying the effects of such passivity, Pip complains to Herbert that "Fortune alone" has "raised" the blacksmith's boy: "I cannot tell you how dependent and uncertain I feel, and how exposed to hundreds of chances." Not to have done anything in the past to have determined one's fate makes one's expectations, no matter how great, seem "indefinite and unsatisfactory" (248).

An understanding of oneself as passive victim is characteristic not only of nineteenth-century conceptions of melancholy but also of anxieties about the Victorian economy. According to Maudsley, those suffering from simple melancholia blame "some external agency" for their "deep sense of individual restriction, . . . the wretched feeling of the oppression of self" (329). Similarly, Grant Allen in his *Physiological Aesthetics* attributes what he takes to be the century's characteristic desire for the pathos of a "melancholy tone in art" to "man's" sense of solitary helplessness and ignorance in the face of the external forces, the "naked realities of nature" (277). Such a conviction that one is subject to ungovernable forces, like the retreat from the physical proximity of commodities that gentility required, was a common response to the Victorian economic system, which seemed to many to be beyond an individual's understanding and control.[28] "The historical experience of large-scale capitalist economy," as Raymond Williams explains, led "many more people than Marxists [to conclude] that control of the process was beyond them, that it was at least in practice external to their wills and desires, and that it had therefore to be seen as governed by its own 'laws'" (*Marxism* 86). In the first volume of *Capital*, Marx makes this point repeatedly: capitalism performs according to certain "natural laws" that he attempts to explain, "but the immanent laws of capitalist production confront the individual capitalist"—and later he includes the worker—"as a coercive force external to him" (92, 381). As Marx puts the point more specifically in *The German Ideology*, "the relation of supply and demand" becomes "like the Fates of the ancients, and with an invisible hand allot[s] fortune and misfortune to men" (*Selected* 170). Like the factory system, which was taken to epitomize new relations based on large-scale production and exchange, basic economic realities appeared to be mysteries, machines driven by their own power and for purposes that were often hard to fathom. Like Darwin's conception of evolution, which Marx adopted as a scientific basis for his study of capitalism, "economic interests" seemed to be an "'elementary force'" that could not be challenged.[29] A system characterized less by order than by chance, the Victorian economy experienced severe ups and downs, which were not conceived of as constituting recurrent and therefore even roughly predictable cycles until late in the 1860s (Sennett 138–39).

Equally effective in diminishing a sense of the possibility of individual control was the development from the 1860s on of corporate capitalism, which was typified by large firms housed in purpose-built structures, staffed by growing numbers of clerks.[30] *Great Expectations*, according to its typical indirections, presents this development in reverse. Herbert's hopeless situation in the counting house is more typical of the plight of clerks later in the century than it is of an earlier period when the family constituted both the basic domestic unit and the primary business organization (Hobsbawm, *Age* 236; Davidoff and Hall). Herbert's first position, therefore, reflects the later, large-scale employment of apprentices and clerks in poorly paid jobs without meaningful responsibilities, while his second position, as a prospective partner at Clarriker's, is more consonant with the earlier nineteenth-century setting of the action of the novel. Significant midcentury legal developments exacerbated the individual's sense of a loss of control. The passing of limited liability acts in the 1850s and 1860s may have encouraged investment, but those changes also gave rise to a proliferation of risky ventures, thus creating what Mary Poovey has called an "unpredictable world of financial speculation," the outcomes of whose ventures individual men could not determine (*Making* 159–60, 166). Middle-class men in the marketplace would necessarily feel less than fully defined by financial dealings for which they were no longer personally responsible. Herbert Pocket comes to stand for such men, the plot of the novel allowing Pip to make painfully obvious his friend's inability to control his own destiny.

Smelling Home

Men whose labor associates them with smells—Brisket with his beef, Jermyn flourishing his scented handkerchief, Jaggers washing with scented soap—are closer to the world of making and selling than those who perceive smells but do not produce them, and like those living in an earlier period of precapitalist productivity, they stand for a more substantial way of life than that of the present. In *The German Ideology*, Marx defines the alienation of workers, "the majority of individuals from whom [productive] forces have been wrested away," as a condition in which they have been "robbed thus of all real life-content, have become abstract individuals" (*Selected* 177). This formulation also defines the condition of the men who profited from the labors of such workers. That at least is how high-Victorian fiction understands their plight as it is epitomized in the case of the melancholic.[31] Men who do not give off odors—Pip and Vincent and Harrington and Pocket—are presented as middle-class melancholics before the plots of the novels in which they appear allow them to be categorized as such. Their stories have to be told, it seems, so that they can fully accept and therefore represent the disembodied and "abstract" existence characteristic of high-Victorian conceptions of respectable manhood. Yet novels of the 1860s also demonstrate that their successful and presumably fulfilled middle-class characters suffer a form of alienation unknown to those below them, the small tradesmen who still directly produce and sell things. More specifically, the osmology of the novels in which such figures appear charts their distance from sites of production that are also figured as homes that they have left behind them.

Since Joe Gargery is old enough to play the role of Pip's parent, both Evan and Pip are represented as having turned their backs on the trades practiced by members of the previous generation. As such, each of these melancholics acts out in familial terms, in the course of one young life, the effects of economic developments spanning from the 1770s to the 1860s, the century during which artisanal labor, far from becoming simply outmoded, was being usurped for the purposes of capitalist mass production. For a commentator like Engels, that development could elicit a directly stated nostalgia: even as he laments the mental "vegetat[ion]" characteristic of the artisans of the past, Engels expatiates on the healthiness of their occupations and their relative material comfort (51–52). For most Victorians, however, industrialization was a triumph of civilization whose advantages precluded regret. Yet the cases of melancholia that I am examining here do depict a profoundly affecting, if unacknowledged sense of loss: "the medium," as *Middlemarch* explains in commenting on other forms of irrevocable change, for the kind of life that such men both despise and desire is now "for ever gone" (785). The men styled unproductive by Mayhew's categorization of labor suffer their insubstantiality as a form of nostalgia, an affect that had been defined since the second half of the seventeenth century as "a form of melancholia induced by prolonged absence from one's home or locale, . . . the longing for a familiar space."[32] Part of the emotional force of the inodorate misery suffered by these men depends on their rejection of the smelly work done by their forefathers, if not by their actual fathers. The novels in which such melancholics appear suggest that the larger culture is suffering a similar loss.

Although, to revert to Uncle Deane's terms, cheeses continued to be handled throughout the Victorian period, the cases of the male figures that I have been analyzing consign such an activity to an irretrievable past.

The powerful nostalgic pull exerted by trade, by the blandishments of earlier, simpler, precapitalist modes of production, is perhaps best exemplified in *Great Expectations*, even though the message that Pip receives in the course of its action, "DON'T GO HOME" (364), expresses, as Robert Newsom points out, the ironic and unaccountable qualities of the nostalgia that Pip experiences.[33] Such longings are expressed, not directly in Pip's feelings about the forge, but indirectly in the figure of Wemmick, about whom the novel entertains enough ambivalence to render him, in Freud's terms, an object of melancholy regret. Pip finds Wemmick's interest in portable property both vulgar and demeaning. Like his original trade as a wine-cooper, the location of Wemmick's home in Walworth, one of the most infamously smelly of the London suburbs, and his habit of pig-keeping, a practice of both the rural and the urban poor, mark him as a manual laborer.[34] Like the hand-loom weavers whose comfortable ways Engels grudgingly admired, Wemmick is both artisan and farmer, a handicraftsman and a cultivator of his own bit of land. Like many of the artisans who were members of the so-called labor aristocracy, Wemmick is also one of the very small minority of Englishmen who owned the houses that they occupied.[35] Moreover, Wemmick is a wonder of all kinds of artisanal self-sufficiency; as he tells Pip, "I am my own engineer, and my own carpenter, and my own plumber, and my own gardener, and my own Jack of all Trades" (207). Miss Skiffins almost seems to be quoting Locke when she explains that Wemmick's contrivances are "made . . . with his own hands out of his own head" (293), thereby pointing out the attributes of male self-possession that Pip lacks. Wemmick can play all those roles, however, only because he is Jaggers's employee. The "twin Wemmicks" that Pip recognizes (386) are not distinguished from each other so much by a current division between work and home as by the difference between past and present forms of labor,[36] between older modes of production in which the home was the location of one's work and more recent modes that divorce work from domesticity by setting them in their separate, supposedly proper places.

Wemmick enacts his backward-looking ideals through his filial piety. He provides for his father, previously a manual laborer in "warehousing," presumably in Liverpool (291), and now an old man disabled by deafness. An inmate of Wemmick's home, the "aged parent" lives in comfort and contentment, taking his greatest pride in the "beautiful works" of his son's hands (207). Despite Pip's refusal or inability to acknowledge any interest in having such a father for himself,[37] Pip's story is haunted by a lack made more painfully ambivalent by the vulgar, though satisfyingly palpable presence of the Aged P. in Wemmick's life. Like Joe, the other famously dutiful son of *Great Expectations*, the clerk John Wemmick is old enough to be Pip's father—he even carries the Christian name of Dickens's father. To others, Pip, like the majority of sons in the Victorian working and lower-middle classes, appears to have followed the lead of this father by adopting his oc-cupation and becoming a clerk—a lowly status that Pip's earlier compan-ionship with Wemmick has twice granted him, once when Wemmick calls Pip "one of us," one of the lawyer's staff (199), and again when a turnkey in Newgate mistakes the young gentleman for "one of the 'prentices or articled ones of your office" (262), a misidentification that both Wemmick and Pip leave uncorrected. Yet Pip will recognize in neither artisan nor clerk, in neither Joe nor Wemmick, a model for his own affectional or sensual life. Tellingly, the food that Pip rejects at Pumblechook's hands is characterized by that substantial tradesman as "the 'olesome nourishment of your fore-fathers" (471). Pip can look forward to a profession that makes one money; but his work, unlike Wemmick's meals, will never make Pip "warm and greasy" (295). As host to the novel's most memorably filling meals, repasts that join generations around the food provided by the labor of Wemmick's hands, the clerk can play the part of artisan even better than Joe can. As a projection of the pleasures of a condition of labor no longer available to a would-be gentleman, then, Wemmick is less Pip's surrogate parent than he is Pip's double—more so than Orlick, Drummle, or even Herbert. For char-acters like Mr. Pip and his melancholy brethren, Wemmick acts out an un-acknowledged longing to return to a simpler past every time he walks home to join his father in Walworth.

Wemmick's role in *Great Expectations* as the emblem of a nostalgic plentitude is neatly disguised by making him, like Joe, the comic butt of its narrator's need to diminish the stature of any character whose story might have been his own. Yet Wemmick's centrality, not only to Pip's sense of himself but also to an understanding of male melancholia, declares itself in the clerk's pig and the occasions for sensory response that that animal offers Pip. Penned in Wemmick's backyard so close to the house that the would-be gentleman can smell him from the room in which he sleeps when visiting Walworth, that pig becomes an object of introjection, the melancholic im-pulse defined by Freud that might seem least relevant to the case histories that I have been charting. Freud explains that in the melancholic, "the ego wants to incorporate this [lost] object into itself, and, in accordance with the oral or cannibalistic phase of libidinal development in which it is, it wants to do so by devouring it" (14: 249–50). By smelling the odor of Wemmick's pig, Pip can both introject the lost substantiality of artisanal culture and evidence his superiority, his distaste for it. More extreme in his melancholic suffering than Herbert or Evan Harrington, Pip takes such incorporation one step farther: joining Wemmick's Aged P., Pip eats the pig whose odor he has earlier taken into his nostrils. If, as Carolyn Dever has argued, some

Victorian melancholic fictions incorporate as a "disembodied ideal" the mothers excluded from their plots (6), the more materially minded fictions of male melancholy introject the lost object as a sensory stimulus. The things of trade, cheeses and cloth and beer, are incorporated—brought into the body and recognized for their materiality—each time a Victorian melancholic responds to their characteristic smells. Having raised his pig and become adapted to his odor, Wemmick, however, has no need or capacity to smell him. Pip must do so to prove his relatively insubstantial gentility.

Such status is nothing, however, if not uncomfortable, even when it does not threaten one's sanity or life. The impulse evident in *Great Expectations* to save Pip from the extremities to which his disorder can lead explains the uncertain conclusion of his story. As both the most clear-sighted and most evasive depiction of male melancholia in the 1860s, the novel plays with the possibility that all Pip's sufferings will be rewarded and apparently eased by the woman whose unhappiness has, in her words, "bent and broken [her] into a better shape" (480). Now the owner of property in actuality and not in expectation, Estella epitomizes all the potential wives of male melancholics, women who are called on to shore up male insubstantiality with their persons and their property. That Wemmick might require such a mate is never an issue. Unlike Pip or Evan or Herbert, Wemmick can afford to install as the mistress of his castle a woman who is as stiff as a violoncello: Wemmick has no need of yielding female flesh to prove his own substantiality; he can do that whenever he touches the products of his handiwork. That Pip is granted such solace remains in doubt. What it might mean if Estella were not to part from him is made clear in the analysis that I offer in the following chapter of the roles played by women in the lives of Evan Harrington and Arthur Vincent. In making this argument, I add to my account of 1860s melancholics the case histories of a physically robust artisan, two landowners, and two military heroes—additional proof, were any needed, that the affective condition defined by the osmology of high-Victorian fiction has a reach that does not exceed its grasp.

3

Women of Substance

Early in the plot of Charlotte Yonge's *The Clever Woman of the Family*, Rachel
Curtis, the character ironically designated by the novel's title, is sitting qui-
etly at an open drawing-room window with her mother and the young army
officer Alick Keith. They have just dined together. Other guests are grouped
at a distance, talking and playing cards. All the characters in this scene are
engaged in the kind of routine, genteel encounter that occurs often in the
fiction of the 1860s. Suddenly this unremarkable instance of everyday life
gives way to an exchange of quite unexpected physical intimacy, becoming
for Rachel the source of "astonishment and horror." When a daddy long-
legs threatens to annoy Mrs. Curtis by landing nearby on a newspaper, both
Rachel and Alick try to capture it, the former spreading her handkerchief
over the insect as the latter tries to use his hand to detain "the over-limbed
creature." Rachel soon realizes that, as usual, her good intentions have re-
sulted only in "shocking" behavior on her part. Touching one of Alick's
gloves, she discovers in the most visceral of ways that his hand has been
maimed during his service in India:

> To have crushed the fly would have been melancholy; to have come
> down on the young soldier's fingers, awkward; but Rachel did what
> was even more shocking—her hands did descend on, what should
> have been fingers, but they gave way under her—she felt only the
> leather of the glove between her and the newspaper. She jumped and
> very nearly cried out, looking up with an astonishment and horror
> only half reassured by his extremely amused smile. "I beg your
> pardon; I'm so sorry—" she gasped confused.
> "Inferior animals can dispense with a member more or less," he
> replied, giving her the other corner of the paper, on which they bore
> their capture to the window, and shook it till it took wing, with
> various legs streaming behind it. "That venerable animal is apparently
> indifferent to having left a third of two legs behind him," and as he
> spoke he removed the already half drawn-off left-hand glove, and let
> Rachel see for a moment that it had only covered the thumb, forefinger,

two joints of the middle, and one of the third; the little finger was gone, and the whole hand much scarred. She was still so much dismayed that she gasped out the first question she had ever asked him—

"Where————?"

"Not under the handkerchief," he answered, picking it up as if he thought she wanted convincing. "At Delhi, I imagine." (106)

Even when Rachel recovers sufficiently to stop gasping out her apologies and questions, she is haunted by the "unnatural and strangely lasting sensation of the solid giving way" (106). This sensory response records Rachel's relative substantiality by emphasizing the absence of that quality in her future mate: there are no "solid" fingers in the soldier's glove to keep it from giving "way under her." Before this scene Rachel has been sure that she knows exactly what kind of man Captain Keith is. She has thought of him only in the most dismissive of terms: he is a "puppy," an "idler," a "carpet knight" (79–81); he is "almost a boy, slim and light, just of the empty young officer type" (54). At an earlier event she finds him "contemptible" because he wears gloves when she herself knows that the party that they are attending is too "small" to require such formality (57). Now she learns that one of his gloves covers, not fingers, but stubs thereof or even less than that.

Yonge defuses some of the unease that this scene might evoke through the wit displayed by both its creator and its male participant: insects have too many appendages; men, by comparison, make jokes about the loss of theirs. Rachel's discovery also prepares her to learn that Captain Keith is a "Victoria Cross man" (177), a soldier whose selfless act of courage during the Indian "mutiny" fulfills her definition of heroism. Yet, as this scene demonstrates, Alick Keith epitomizes the male insubstantiality that I have defined as the primary symptom of genteel melancholia: languid, sickly, wounded and maimed, he has no physical presence on which one might depend. Moreover, his comparative encounter with a lady testifies to the ambiguous role that women may play in the lives of such men. The pressure of Rachel's hand reveals the absence on his. What he has previously hidden becomes evident during his exchange with her. Alick's amused denial that he has lost his digits under Rachel's handkerchief dismisses even as it entertains the possibility that she has caused the loss that he treats so lightly.

As the outcome of the plot of *The Clever Woman* reveals, novels of the 1860s typically attempt to cast in more positive terms the relations between their respectable men and women. Yet, like vocational uncertainty, restlessness, immobility, and hypersensitivity, an unaccountable need for a particular woman identifies the melancholic as a man forced to depend on the body of his wife, her productive and reproductive potential as the bearer of property— sometimes of children, often of money and land—to give him the substantiality that he lacks.[1] When women in these novels give men their bodies, high-

Victorian fiction represents the role that respectable women of the period undoubtedly played by producing children for their mates. When women in these novels give men their property, this fiction indulges in a fantasy of female ownership that no records of the period confirm as fact. In both instances, the exchanges effected between men and women reveal the vulnerability of the former through the power granted to the latter. Even with—sometimes especially because of—the substance provided by the women in their lives, the representative men of the 1860s threaten to suffer the fate of the figure who presides over the narrative of Trollope's *Nina Balatka*, St. John Nepomucene, the cleric who chooses drowning as the form of his martyrdom, the man for whom a woman presumably could do no good: "a thin, melancholy, half-starved saint, who has had all the life washed out of him by his long immersion" (182).

This chapter focuses on the exchanges between men and women in five novels—Eliot's *Felix Holt*, Meredith's *Evan Harrington*, Oliphant's *Salem Chapel*, as well as, more briefly, Trollope's *Miss Mackenzie* and Yonge's *The Clever Woman of the Family*. In these texts, the physicality that the osmology of high-Victorian fiction recognizes in its marriageable women is acted out in some plots more fully than it is in others. Interestingly, *Felix Holt*, the novel most given to recording odors, and *The Clever Woman*, the one least so, both tell their love stories in terms of explicit references to smells. Some of the heroes of these five novels manage to satisfy their erotic ambitions, while others do not. In that sense, *Great Expectations* seems to contain within its plot the possibilities that these novels explore. Pip exits the grounds of Satis House with no assurance that Estella's friendship will ever be enough to establish for him his own house. Happier outcomes are available for those suffering from less extreme cases of melancholia, as Herbert's union with a purser's daughter testifies. Marriage, however, in all these instances is the prospect that defines women as matter either because they are substance or because they own substance, and I return to the osmology of high-Victorian fiction at the beginning of this chapter to demonstrate how carefully its classification of various kinds of women both measures and conveys their potential as marriage partners. Unlike the men of the Suya people of Brazil, high-Victorian melancholics do not refer to their women as "our rotten-smelling property" (Classen 85). Yet such genteel characters might be tempted to assert their dominance in similarly self-defensive and vitriolic terms if they realized how thoroughly their exchanges with their fragrant-smelling women defined their dependents as their superiors.

Women and Their Scents

In the drawing-room scene during which Rachel Curtis feels the "sensation of the solid giving way" as she touches Alick Keith's gloved hand, her solidity is surprisingly, if only temporarily, almost as questionable as his. At this particular dinner party she is wearing a crown of artificial white roses that her mother has given her earlier in celebration of her twenty-fifth birthday. On the first page of the novel, Rachel and her sister Grace discuss the gift, which Rachel concedes is a beautiful demonstration of "how well nature can be imitated." Because they are not real flowers, the roses that Rachel wears when she encounters Captain Keith give off no sweet odor of marriageable virginity; and he, accordingly, is not represented as perceiving any fragrance when he meets or sits with her. Her earlier conversation with her sister has specified the meaning of Rachel's reluctant agreement to "bedizen" herself with scentless flowers. Rachel announces to her older, also unmarried sibling that her own "young-ladyhood" is now over: "From this moment we are established as the maiden sisters of Avonmouth, husband and wife to one another, as maiden pairs always are." Grace, ready to join this union, responds, "Then thus let me crown our bridal," as she places on Rachel's head the wreath of artificial roses (1). Rachel's unnatural disinclination to marry anyone other than her sister is not an attitude that Yonge will allow to survive the plot of *The Clever Woman of the Family*, but its presentation through odorless flowers conforms to the osmology constituted by the smells in novels of the 1860s: Rachel must learn that she needs the guidance of a good man, and her lack of a scent that a man might perceive reveals how much she has to change before she can become a fit mate.

If a marriageable woman in high-Victorian fiction is not associated with the fragrance of flowers, she may be conforming to the more ancient convention, articulated by Plautus and reiterated by Montaigne, that "the most perfect smell for a woman is to smell of nothing" (Le Guérer 158), but more typically her inodorous state suggests that she will not marry or will fail to do so appropriately. The fact that Estella in *Great Expectations* is never made fragrant by flowers would have warned Pip, had he been a reader of the novels of the 1860s rather than a writer of one of them, that she has, for him, no matrimonial potential at all. The two young ladies of Fullerton's *Mrs. Gerald's Niece* would seem to violate this convention, but they actually prove its force. Ita Flower, a prophetically named adoptee of mysterious birth, marries the gentleman and cleric Edgar Derwent, but she does not smell of flowers. Annie, the heiress who has been Edgar's first fiancée, is properly aromatic. Yet Annie has broken off this engagement to Edgar so that she can encourage him to marry Ita. Annie then becomes wife to the couple by furnishing and managing their house so that they can devote themselves to acts of charity. Telling them, "I mean to be your odd woman" (2: 59), Annie for two years is their housekeeper, head gardener, dairymaid, and benefactor. Since Ita turns out to be the real Annie after all—they were both babes lost at sea— the plot works hard to identify the two women and thus make sense of the olfactory terms in which they are depicted: Edgar, in marrying Ita, actually marries Annie. Less complicated but perhaps even more revealing in this respect is the difference between the opportunities for imaginative olfaction offered in the two short experimental tales that Trollope published in *Blackwood's Magazine* in the 1860s, *Nina Balatka* and *Linda Tressel*: Nina, who will live to marry her supposedly unsuitable suitor, the Jew Anton Trendellsohn, wears clothes that are described as bearing "a sweet scent of last summer's roses" (158), the only smell represented in the story; but Linda, who will die before she can be sacrificed to her socially and politically unfit swain, Ludovic Valcarm, never gives off the faintest scent. In novel after novel, as I point out in the first chapter here, men identify their mates by noticing the floral scents that surround them and make aromatic their promise of fertility. By contrast, women at either extreme of the social scale who are not suitable partners are marked by no such delicate floral scents.

Exuding too much odor reveals a woman's relative social inferiority and, therefore, the impropriety of choosing her as a marriage partner. Working-class characters who should not be romantically appealing give off too grossly natural an odor. Biddy of *Great Expectations* is redolent of "the smell of a black currant bush" (147), exuding, as William A. Cohen has argued, an off-putting *odor di femina* (63); but the eligible lady of Le Fanu's *Uncle Silas* never gives off this scent, even though she spends long hours picking black currants. The title character of Meredith's *Emilia in England*, a poor, half-Italian, half-English cantatrice, is marked as beneath her jealous middle-class suitor when he exclaims that he finds "detestable" the rank smell of the hawthorn blossom that she places "in her bosom" (1: 160). Emilia is also the only woman in this fiction—except presumably Cigarette, the otherwise "scentless and loveless" female army mascot of Ouida's *Under Two Flags* (318)—who smells of smoke, an odor that Emilia's suitor objects to as proof that she has been consorting with working-class men. Isabel Sleaford's compromised status in Braddon's *The Doctor's Wife* is registered when she sits in a garden "where the odour of distant pigsties mingled faintly with the perfume of . . . roses" (23). Oliphant's *Miss Marjoribanks* attests to the fineness of the discriminations that scents can draw. Oliphant's narrator is sure that Barbara Lake, Lucilla Marjoribanks's rival for the attentions of Mr. Cavendish, is "not precisely a lady" (455). When Cavendish strolls down Grove Street where Barbara lives, he finds it filled with the "sweetness of the mignonette" that the residents have just watered, a smell that he associates with the simple pleasures of "love in a cottage" (177). Yet as the plot unfolds, it becomes clear that there is too much aromatic sweetness on Grove Street for Cavendish's good. When he is later caught walking there with Barbara, the street is again redolent with "the fragrance of [its] mignonette," which in this instance becomes an intoxicant that makes him feel as if he, like a better-known victim of a magic spell, has grown "an ass's head on his shoulders." This scene, an "unlooked-for" and "open encounter" (260) that compares the two women to each other, measures Lucilla's lack of a distinctive scent against Barbara's odoriferous excesses, identifying the former as the latter's unquestioned superior.

Similarly, the bodies of women whose social standing is too elevated or whose moral character is too questionable to make them eligible mates also carry on their bodies perceptible odors, though in this case the smell in question is always the fragrance of perfume. The common sense of the 1860s was not as extreme as that of the eighteenth century when matrimonial legislation made possible the prosecution of women who seduced men into marriage by resorting to the use of "scent" and other alluring devices (qtd. Poovey, *Proper* x), yet the logic of the osmology of high-Victorian fiction is equally decisive in distinguishing modes of natural attraction from devious imitations of them: blossoms of cultivated plants are a form of sanctioned seduction, while the perfumes made from them are not, and the women who wear such scents are to be eschewed. In *Salem Chapel*, Lady Western, the charming and wealthy young widow who is beyond the reach of her lower-middle-class admirer, is repeatedly described as existing in a "sweet atmosphere . . . tinged with the perfumy breath which always surrounded Her" (145). Similarly, Helen Rolleston of *Foul Play* fills the air with the artificial scent that she uses, the effect of which, however, is never as "oppressive" as that of the "rich odour" pervasive in Lady Audley's rooms at Audley Court (69). The impropriety of Walter Hartwright's initial attraction to the lady of Collins's *The Woman in White* is recorded when he smells "the perfume of her hair, and the warm fragrance of her breath" (88). In *Our Mutual Friend*, Sophronia, the unfortunate Mrs. Lammle, attempts to convey status beyond her deserts by wearing "scents and essences" (146). Even Lady Corisande in Disraeli's *Lothair*, whose title would make natural her use of artificial aromas, is associated with those of flowers because she is being presented as the future mate of a fellow aristocrat: she allows in her old-fashioned garden "no flowers . . . that have not perfume," and she herself is "a rose" that she bestows on her suitor (463, 467). *Felix Holt* typically elaborates on the odors that identify the material qualities characteristic of different kinds of women. The portrait of the young Mrs. Transome is associated with perfume, the ironically named "odours of paradise" (333). Esther Lyon's initial moral limitations make her, like Rachel Curtis, a slightly anomalous case. When Esther enters the room in which she first meets Felix Holt, her "delicate scent, the faint suggestion of a garden" (60), presents her as eligible, but it is revealed a page later that this subtle effect comes, not from the rose leaves mentioned earlier, but from an artificial source, a bottle of "atta of rose" that would be more conventionally associated with a character like Lady Western or Mrs. Transome or Lady Audley. The artificiality of perfume marks the women who are unfit to be wives of the respectable men of these stories, while flowers, whose subtle scents recall nature in its most refined forms, identify those women who should and do become proper mates.

Perhaps even more telling is the category of women who are represented as having acute, even unnatural sensitivities to the stimuli of floral scents: women who smell of flowers will marry and typically have children, but women who smell flowers almost always do not. Nell Le Strange in Broughton's *Cometh up as a Flower* and Linton's Lizzie Lorton are both presented as characters particularly responsive to such aromas, and the former dies young after marrying badly, and the latter commits suicide after being rejected by the man she loves. Kate, the heroine of Broughton's *Not Wisely but Too Well*, reaches an equally nonreproductive climax to her story, choosing her lover unwisely, as Nell does, but becoming a celibate Sister of Mercy in London's "smoky reeking courts" (356). That outcome is foretold hundreds of pages earlier when she fantasizes about planting poppies: she has not cared for such flowers in the past "because they [have] no smell," but her devotion to a reprobate now allows her to think them the best flowers "in the world" (85). Rose of *Evan Harrington* briefly displays a maritally disqualifying jealousy while sniffing the flowers for which she is named, though her simultaneous gift to Evan of a rose suggests that their story will find a happy ending (fig. 3.1). Dahlia, the fallen sister of *Rhoda Fleming*, another novel by Meredith, conjures up visions of her own death as she imagines smelling her mother's roses. The most elaborate example of this convention, however, is Maggie in Eliot's *The Mill on the Floss*. Going with Stephen Guest into his conservatory, Maggie smells its flowers and confesses, "I think I am quite wicked with roses—I like to gather them and smell them till they have no scent left." As a character more sensual than she should be, Maggie is here reversing what the osmology of the 1860s presents as the order of nature. The narrator remarks on "the large half-opened rose that had attracted" Maggie (388), but it would be more seemly for Maggie to be the object of such attention, not its agent. Good women are flowers whose fragrances are noticed by the good men who should marry them. Women who respond to such olfactory stimuli are evidencing a dangerous or even fatal susceptibility to their own physicality. Each of these categories, however, evaluates female characters according to only one criterion, their capacity to provide the substance that can yield comfort and children. According to this measure, women are property, but as high-Victorian fiction insists, they can also own property.

Female Property

Figuring a woman as a product put up for sale is a consistent practice of Victorian fiction, the most striking instance of which perhaps occurs in *The Newcomes* (1853–1855), when Thackeray depicts "the selling of virgins" by having his young unmarried heroine defiantly place a price tag on her dress

Fig. 3.1 Aromas made palpable: Rose Jocelyn's gift to Evan Harrington. *Evan Harrington* in *Once a Week* 2 (1860): 375. Courtesy of the Beinecke Rare Book and Manuscript Library, Yale University.

(363). "If a lady does but touch any article, no matter how delicate, in the way of trade, she loses caste, and ceases to be a lady," as Sarah Stickney Ellis memorably put it at the beginning of the Victorian period—a prohibition that makes sense because a lady was herself an article in trade. That fact could be celebrated by a conservative like Eliza Lynn Linton; in a comment that gives a new turn to Marx's identification of property and labor, Linton explained: "men have the right to demand from their wives absolute attention to their wishes, because they are their property, their dependent creatures whom they feed and clothe in return for certain services."[2] Conversely, seeing women as possessions might be deplored, as it is by Mill in his frequent comparisons of marriage and slavery in *The Subjection of Women* (1869). The status of women as commodities was the source of considerable anxiety about marriage as a form of prostitution.[3] The fiction of the 1860s often features such fears. When one of Evan Harrington's sisters offers herself to her aristocratic lover in exchange for a position for Evan that would yield him £1,000 a year, he is accused of engaging in "traffic in [his] sister," an idea that undermines his "whole manhood," causing him to sob helplessly (450–51). Elsewhere a woman's dependence is treated less as if it were an instance of potential prostitution than as a matter of simple and unsurprising commodification. Lucilla Marjoribanks is one of her father's "possessions" waiting to be taken up by a husband: she is a "dear production" remarkable only for the costliness of its making (247). Ermine Williams, the disabled though genuinely clever woman of *The Clever Woman of the Family*, dismisses herself as a "helpless commodity" unfit for marriage (78); apparently only helpful products deserve to participate in this market.

Yet as often as the fiction of the 1860s recognizes that women sell themselves to become the property of their mates, it counters that fact with a fantasy of women as property owners. Such characters are not so much objects to be bought as economic agents able to purchase their husbands. The plots of these novels directly contradict what the characters understand about the relations between men and women, the former thought to be all powerful, the latter meekly dependent. It also puts into question the Victorian legal and moral and religious standards that made ownership the test of both identity and mastery, gendering such dominance as male. This point is particularly evident whenever respectable women serve as bearers of property, as agents for the transfer of capital and land. Traffic in women, to use Gayle Rubin's version of Meredith's phrase, is, as fiction of the 1860s understands the process, a matter of a young woman's giving to a man her person along with, not in exchange for, objects of economic value. Instead of a bride-price or bride-wealth, the goods traditionally exchanged for a woman being given in marriage as a way of compensating her kin for the loss of her labor and reproductive potential,[4] the high-Victorian bride gives her price to the man she marries, almost as if what she brings to him is a monetary compensation for his having agreed to take her. In that sense her property becomes what is conventionally called a dowry, but its function would be more tellingly revealed if it were recognized as a groom-price or groom-wealth. Women who participate in such exchanges are therefore practicing a form of prostitution in which the sex-worker pays the john for his willingness to possess her person as his. As humiliating as this role might be for a woman, however, its effect on her partner's manhood may be more demeaning.

The ability of the young female characters of high-Victorian fiction to pay such groom-prices contrasts sharply with the limited economic power of most Victorian women. Since wives during this period could not own the personal property that they had brought into marriage or earned during it, since they could not control the real property or land with whose earnings they endowed their husbands, any marriage of a woman who held property involved a transfer of goods from her to her husband, just as every marriage, according to the principle of *coverture*, absorbed her legal identity into his. Because most property owned by Victorian women was personal—investments, annuities, savings—rather than real, it was governed by common law and was, therefore, absolutely her husband's to do with as he wished. Authority over land, however, was determined according to laws of equity, and its alienation by the spouse of its female owner could be accomplished only with her consent.[5] By one mid-Victorian estimate, the number of women whose families could afford or whose holdings justified the expense of the settlements that protected such real property was approximately 10%—a figure that seems too high since, as another contemporary observer noted, those excluded from such protections were "the whole middle and lower ranks of women, and a certain portion of the upper ranks" (Cobbe, "'Criminals'" 111). Although the possibility of granting women property rights was debated in relation to reforms in divorce law in the late 1850s, even when married women were allowed certain modest forms of ownership by the Married Women's Property Act of 1870, they did not gain the economic freedom of the *feme sole*.[6]

In individual cases, the theoretical rigidities of law may have been tempered in practice by the preferences and self-interest of those men empowered by it.[7] As household managers, many married women were probably given the responsibility of spending their husbands' and in some cases, therefore, their own funds (Langland 46–49). Yet Frances Power Cobbe in 1868 contrasted theory and practice in ways that suggest a different conclusion: even though men were supposed to provide for their wives whose property they had absorbed, the processes of Victorian marriage resembled the devouring of a small tarantula by a larger one, the man being "allowed to eat up the whole of a woman's fortune," the woman thereby becoming "in a very literal manner, 'bone of his bone . . . and flesh of his flesh'" ("'Criminals'" 123, 122). Nor was the death of one's husband an assurance of the relative economic freedom of the *feme sole*. Widows typically inherited their husband's wealth with numerous strings attached—a point made by Lightwood's shocked incredulity in *Our Mutual Friend* when Boffin plans to write a will unconventionally refusing to "bind" Mrs. Boffin to any particular use of his fortune: "Hers freely, to do what she likes with? Hers absolutely?" (98). Even those widows who had been provided for by their husbands were put at a disadvantage by the Dower Act of 1833, which granted them a sometimes uncertain amount of income rather than a third of the property of an estate. More typical still, as Cynthia Curran's archival research has proved, was the poverty of middle-class widows. Forced by their circumstances to beg again and again for small sums from private charities, such women endured the privations and humiliations associated with workers supplicating Poor Law authorities for relief (11–15, 92).

Most directly relevant here, however, is the likelihood that the *feme sole*, the unmarried woman who so often appears in both Victorian and current accounts as enjoying the economic personality that *coverture* denied her married counterpart, was in practice little better off. As analyses by both Susan Staves and Mary Poovey reveal, the nineteenth century inherited a legal system that defined women as bearers of property from one man to another (Staves 229; Poovey, *Proper* 11). To serve that function, a single woman could not control what she legally owned. Typical of middle-class financial arrangements were inheritances granted in trust to unmarried women: "legal ownership" was vested in male trustees, usually brothers or fathers, who had full discretionary power over the property whose income would support its nominal female owner.[8] Even women presumably protected by the law of equity could be exposed to the manipulations, threats, or irresponsibility of their parents, trustees, or guardians. A portion, the part of an estate devised for the provision of a daughter by her parents at their marriage, did not necessarily grant the young woman freedom of choice, even or especially when she came to decide on a marriage partner; and ideals of femininity, which identified as unladylike the handling of practical affairs, would have discouraged the *feme sole* from exercising any economic power that she did have.[9] A woman whose property was given her as protection might be made more vulnerable by its possession than she would have been without it. A well-endowed, single young woman might therefore find herself in the condition of incapacity and powerlessness outlined by Mill in his famous refusal to exercise the marital rights of which he could not divest himself: in terms of her property, if not her person, an unmarried woman was subject to male relations who, like husbands, had "legal power and control over [her] property . . . independent of her own wishes and will" (21: 99). Yet high-Victorian fiction often—more often than not—treats single women of the middle-classes and gentry as if they were subject to no such "power and control."

One novel of the 1860s after another grants unmarried women a remarkable and even fantastic degree of discretion over both money and land. In the earlier fiction of the 1840s and 1850s, penniless heroines, a few of whom do come to enjoy riches, are more typical—Becky Sharp, Amelia Sedley, Esther Summerson, Amy Dorrit, Mary Barton, Ruth Hilton, Agnes Grey, and Lucy Snowe. In their place in the 1860s come a series of already propertied heroines, who are as often the creation of male novelists as of female, as characteristic of plots by Trollope, Dickens, Reade, and Meredith as they are of those by Eliot, Yonge, Oliphant, and Fullerton. Instead of the wide range of female types who appear in the journalism of the period—"'Woman'

. . . as worker, spinster, citizen, moral guide, prostitute" (Hamilton 10)—
the central fictional female character of the 1860s is epitomized by the figures whose stories I consider in this chapter, among whom are Rose Jocelyn,
Esther Lyon, and Rachel Curtis. Yet these characters are not alone in their
ability to control what they own. Miss Havisham can do with the property
that she inherits from her father exactly as she pleases. Annie Derwent, the
presumed heiress of Fullerton's *Mrs. Gerald's Niece*, manages an estate with
an annual income of £12,000, and no male relatives have survived to inter-
fere as her trustees. Mary Marchmont in Braddon's *John Marchmont's Legacy*
is still a "pale-faced girl" when she becomes the "undisputed mistress of
eleven thousand a-year" (185). Alice Vavasor in Trollope's *Can You Forgive Her?* has, despite her father's unhappy presence on the scene, complete
control over her inheritance, the absoluteness of her ownership being adequately expressed only by the repetition of the word *own* when the narrator explains, "Her fortune was her own, and at her own disposal" (1: 351).
Similarly, Margaret Elcombe of *Lizzie Lorton of Greyrigg* can decide on
the day that she turns twenty-one that she will inhabit the manor house in
Cumberland that she has inherited and use the earnings of her estate to do
good for those living near it.

Women depicted in the fiction of the 1860s retain similarly improbable
authority after marriage. Hilda, the seventeen-year-old heiress of Tautphoeus's
At Odds, is unchecked as she gives away money, timber, and livestock—actions made unlikely by the fact that she has both a husband and an uncle,
the latter of whom splutters, "What is the use of my lecturing [on economy]
when I have no power to control? It is monstrous to think that a girl of your
age can make ducks and drakes of such a property" (213). Estella, more re-
alistically perhaps than Hilda, has similar power: at the end of *Great Expectations*, Estella has managed to retain possession of the grounds of Satis
House, even though, as she says, during her marriage "everything else has
gone from me." According to the laws of equity, such an outcome makes
sense, but, as if to underscore the success of the "determined resistance" with
which she has defended her property from her husband's desire for it (479),
the cancelled ending of the novel describes her as remarried to a Shrop-
shire doctor after Drummle's death and living on "her own personal fortune" (481). Not even a bad marriage like Estella's can negate the financial
independence that the novels of the 1860s grant their attractive young
women. Separated from her abusive husband, the heiress Maud Harcourt
in Robinson's *Beyond the Church* manages to regain her father's fortune, and
she lives by herself as a wealthy, if somewhat discontented lady. The plots
of the novels read by respectable Victorian women seem to want to grant
their fictional counterparts what such women rarely had in fact.

More telling than any of these instances is the case of the heroine of *Miss
Mackenzie*. Instead of a trustee empowered to manage the money that she

inherits from one of her brothers, Margaret Mackenzie has to deal only with an executor and a lawyer, neither of whom is interested in advising her about how to invest funds substantial enough to yield approximately £800 a year. As her brother's housekeeper and dependent, Margaret has been the typically disempowered *feme sole*, but the woman who at the age of thirty-five has had "no power of the purse" (25) now has complete charge of a very large purse. Although Trollope commented in his *Autobiography* that this novel was to be one "without any love" since his aging heroine had "money troubles" (188–89), the fact that she has funds sufficient to cause trouble makes a love story inevitable. Everyone wants Margaret's money, including four suitors and her one surviving brother, who has already squandered his inheritance in a unprofitable business making and selling oilcloth. Tellingly, none of Miss Mackenzie's suitors can offer her money; they can provide only different degrees of the respectability associated with the status traditionally granted a married woman. In this comedy of openly acknowledged, commonplace greed, Trollope writes what is arguably his most touching novel—in my view *The Duke's Children* and *An Old Man's Love* vie with it for that title—because Margaret's middle-aged longings for romance are so directly pitted against her clear-eyed recognition that her inheritance has made her "a good thing going in the way of money" (59). Her inheritance, as anyone can see, constitutes a particularly attractive groom-price.

The plot of *Miss Mackenzie* reveals that the substance that a woman has to offer a man inheres in both her property and her body. Trollope's reluctance to sell his heroine to the highest bidder is made evident by a turn of events that improbably but neatly disinherits her so that she no longer has a groom-price to offer. This device, however, merely transfers what had been her money to the most eligible of her suitors, her cousin Sir John Ball, whose renewed proposal she can now accept because it cannot be criticized as an act of greed on his part. Yet the plot also makes clear that his newly gained financial substance would not have been his had not Margaret first inherited her brother's estate: her lawyer is the one who discovers the old deed of gift that proves Sir John to be the rightful heir. Conversely, John Ball never would have considered marrying his cousin if, as his mother crudely thinks of it, "the money [could have] come without the wife" (242). Even after Margaret loses her claim to the monies in question, her story does not escape the nexus of values and responses that I associate with male melancholia. Significantly, Margaret offers her physical presence as the groom-wealth due to Sir John, who is at fifty a failed barrister, a widower whose nine children attest to his previous virility, but one who has become, under the pressures of trying to support them, a man with "the juices of life . . . pressed out of him" (111). Despite his insubstantiality or perhaps because of it, Sir John still can see that Margaret's "arm [is] round and white, and very fair," as he does in a scene between the two that takes place remarkably in her bedroom, long before they are married or even engaged to wed. In view of the relative lack of such physical details in Trollope's fiction, this late-night comparative encounter is doubly significant: what Margaret has to give, what John Ball needs, is fully displayed as the sleeve of her dressing-gown falls from her arm. Uncomfortable and confused, he actually wonders if her dishabille might be a trick to lure him into a "false woman's web" (293). But Margaret is not so much false as willing. Coordinating with the frankness of this scene is her equally open and repeatedly articulated desire to give herself in marriage to her cousin once she has lost her money and may be taken for the "good thing going" without the cash. In the outcome that Margaret's having had money makes inevitable, a lady and her possessions both become a melancholic's property.

Though the plot of *Miss Mackenzie* depends for its resolution on an unmarried woman offering first her property and then her body to a man, it also reveals how unappealing such a spectacle might be. As if to protect Margaret from any tainting suggestions of impropriety, bedroom scene or no, the set piece of the novel compares her behavior to that of less decorous, though supposedly respectable ladies. In Chapter XXVII, "The Negro Soldiers' Orphan Bazaar," during a nasty interlude in the plot while the characters wait for the courts to decide the fate of Margaret's inheritance, the narrator attacks the practice of holding sales for questionable charitable causes, in this case in aid of destitute orphans of the freed slaves who ought to have been back on southern plantations rather than serving in the army of "the Northern invaders" (354). This event, held significantly in a building remaining from the Great Exhibition, reduces to the level of tradesmen the fashionable ladies of London. Margaret, whose story has been widely circulated in the newspaper and has therefore become what the narrator calls "public property" (346), is invited to attend the bazaar, but now that she has almost certainly lost the wherewithal to offer a groom-price, she manages to escape relatively unscathed from a scene of dirt, noise, "riot," and degradation. The participants in the bazaar are overcome by a kind of sexual frenzy: young women run around "begging men to put their hands in lucky bags," men "button . . . up their trouser pockets," and "ugliness and rapacity" turn "young ladies" into "harpies and unclean birds." The narrator gives at full length an encounter between a specific female harpy and her victim, one of the "wether lambs" in the crowd: in a version of post-office, she demands that he put a letter in the "little square hole" that she stands behind and that he pay for both of the mock letters that the two exchange (364–65). In this ugly commentary on the prostitution practiced in the best circles of London's "fashionable society" (356), the narrator raises questions about the bride-price that a young man must pay for the woman he loves if he wishes to marry her. Yet *Miss Mackenzie* confronts a greater horror, the more demeaning implications of a groom-price. Throughout much of the plot,

Margaret has the power to compensate a man for taking her, and it looks as if the only way she can avoid selling herself is by remaining unmarried. Trollope's plot allows her to escape that fate, yet the paying of a groom-price, the humiliation that Miss Mackenzie's lawyer spares her by causing her money to go to her most eligible suitor, is exactly the one that awaits Esther Lyon in *Felix Holt*.

Esther's Estate

Initially the heroine of *Felix Holt* would seem to be the female character in the fiction of the 1860s least likely to become a commodity in a marriage market. Raised by a dissenting preacher, Esther Lyon learns, however, that she is the unfettered owner of the Transome estate, whose income amounts to at least between £5,000 and £6,000 a year. Esther's father is not her father after all, and the nicely discriminating sensibilities that have led her to find noisome the odors of tallow candles and warmed ale simply confirm that her gentility is bred in the bone. Without any restrictions on her ownership or guidance on how to handle her newly discovered wealth—Rufus Lyon declines even to give her advice—Esther eventually decides to renounce her claim to Transome Court in favor of its putative owner, Harold Transome, the man who has proposed to her as a way of holding on to the property that she now owns. Finding appealing neither Harold nor life at Transome Court, she chooses instead to marry the impecunious worker Felix Holt, the man whose moral superiority is presumably worth more than acres or gold. Yet Esther's role as the unrecognized lady of *Felix Holt* and the elaborate legal contortions that allow her to possess entirely the estate that she chooses to give up are, like the plot devices of *Great Expectations*, unlikely versions of a state of affairs that high-Victorian fiction takes to be decidedly normal.

Like so many other female characters attached to melancholics in the fiction of the 1860s, Esther is presented as securing both Felix and Harold against the worst effects of the insubstantiality from which they suffer by offering them either the physical presence of her body or the ownership of property or both. That the cure constituted by Esther's substance is not strong enough is also made evident by her effect on her two suitors and, later, on the one she chooses to become her husband. Like many of the other exchanges of bodies and funds and land enacted in novels of the 1860s, Esther's gifts to Harold and Felix simply witness to their recipients' inadequacies and impotence. If these men must await a woman's coming to their aid, they must be frail indeed. From this perspective, Felix and Harold, the two radicals of *Felix Holt*, become its odd couple, male melancholics who, as masters of their separate fates, are less than impressive. As the outcomes of their stories are linked to the will of the same female character, they reveal the doubtful boon that loving a woman may become. Moreover, as if to confirm that physical substance is the central issue here, the story of their pursuit of Esther is largely rendered through representations of odors and, therefore, explicitly in terms of the values conveyed by the osmology of high-Victorian fiction. Specifying the extent to which the ending of *Felix Holt* allows Esther to play the heiress provides a context for examining how those smells confirm a diagnosis of the melancholia suffered by its heroes.

Although the plot of *Miss Mackenzie* turns away from the payment of a groom-price in monetary terms, Margaret's physical attractions being payment enough, *Felix Holt* offers an instance of such an exchange, presenting its outcome as a literal redistribution of "wealth." Like Esther in the role of property-owner, Felix Holt seems a character less in need of a woman's substance than anyone else in the novel. As he announces both early and late, Felix intends to remain true to his working-class "heritage" and to the "blood [he has in him] of a line of handicraftsmen" (224): "My father was a weaver first of all. It would have been better for him if he had remained a weaver. . . . I mean to stick to the class I belong to" (57). Yet the conclusion of the novel has other plans for Felix. Esther's love for him makes him worthy of her groom-wealth. Having magically, like Miss Mackenzie, gained full control of the Transome estate—no male trustees need apply—she gives it up. But not quite all of it. In the penultimate chapter of the novel, Esther reveals to Felix that she will accept—"if you approve"—a tiny portion of her inheritance as heir to the Transome estate:

> I think of having some wealth. . . . I think even of two pounds a-week;
> one needn't live up to the splendour of all that, you know; we must
> live as simply as you liked: there would be money to spare, and you
> could do wonders, and be obliged to work too, only not if sickness
> came. And then I think of a little income for your mother, enough for
> her to live as she has been used to live; and a little income for my
> father, to save him from being dependent when he is no longer able to
> preach. (397)

Though Esther here uses the word *wealth* playfully, even ironically, that word is quite appropriate when one considers that weavers during the early 1830s, the time at which the action of the novel is set, were earning only six shillings a week (Mathias 184). Added together, the sums that Esther will be able to offer not only Felix, but also his mother and her father, will put at her command something like £200 a year. That is as much as a quite well-paid clerk would earn annually. It is more, in fact, than Harmon supposedly has to spend when he proposes to marry Bella Wilfer on £150 a year, an income that gives them, according to Bella, "all we want, and more" (663);

more than Mrs. Lammle's annuity of £115 a year in *Our Mutual Friend*; and much more than the thirty shillings a week that the narrator of Wright's *Johnny Robinson* claims will support a working-class family of five if the wife is a good manager (1: 26). To enjoy a steady income by having an annuity or collecting rent from property or interest on investments is not to be working class at all. As any reader of the autobiographies written by Victorian workers must know, the fact of contingency, of one's dependence on the health of one's body and on the health of the market, defines the material conditions of working-class life. As Esther, however, explains, she will provide enough security so that Felix will not have to work at all: she appeals to his pride by claiming that he will be "obliged" to work, then counters that point by adding, "only not if sickness came." She offers her substance to Felix, pays him her groom-price, as a way of acknowledging the moral superiority she has seen in him from their first meeting, but there is more at work here than the simple exchange of a steady income for enlightenment, goods for good.

This outcome would not be possible if Felix had not already demonstrated how thoroughly he suffers from genteel melancholia and how little aligned, therefore, he is with the working-class heritage to which he purports to be so committed. Much as Felix claims his status as a working man, the novel in which he appears conjoins its representations of odors, food, and trade to demonstrate his need of a lady's substance. Unlike Arthur Vincent of *Salem Chapel* or Evan Harrington, characters desperately longing for genteel respectability, Felix Holt, the Radical, as the full title of the novel calls him, judges such desires to be conducive to neither dignity nor happiness. The futility of social ambitions in *Felix Holt* is epitomized by the tradesmen of Treby Magna, who are more prosperous than the shopkeepers featured in *Salem Chapel*, but whose appetites are quite similar to those of Tozer, Brown, and Pigeon. Headed by "Wace & Co., brewers of the celebrated Treby beer" (40), the tradesmen of *Felix Holt* are characterized by their consumption, not of things, but of food and drink: "Such people naturally took tea and supped together frequently; and as there was no professional man or tradesman in Treby who was not connected by business, if not by blood, with the farmers of the district, the richer sort of these were much invited, and gave invitations in their turn. They played at whist, ate and drank generously" (41). Similarly, the renowned market dinners available at "that excellent inn" the Marquis of Granby (40) draw together the "substantial townsmen" of the district, including Mr. Wace, the brewer, and a wealthy butcher from Leek Malton (177); there such men engage in the "serious business" of eating dinner followed by the consumption of "wine, spirits, and tobacco [that raise] mere satisfaction into beatitude," as the narrator condescendingly notes (178). Like the work of the shopkeepers of *Salem Chapel*, the "business" of the leading men of Treby Magna, both their social and their professional business, involves the making of food and drink as well as their consumption of both.

Felix Holt will have nothing to do with such eating and drinking. He has rejected for moral and political reasons both trade and the clerkly, lower-middle-class pretensions to gentility that he denounces as characteristic of a "pence-counting, parcel-tying generation" (59). As his mother endlessly laments, Felix, like Evan Harrington, has given up his inheritance, his father's business as the producer and distributor of Holt's Cathartic Pills, Holt's Elixir, and the Cancer Cure. Mrs. Holt's discourse on the value of those commodities, as evidenced by the demand for them, is enough to make both Harold Transome and his clergyman uncle "explode" in laughter (348), but she makes the serious point that Felix's refusal to sell such wares has taken from them the source of a relatively secure income. Felix comes to have a reputation among the townspeople of Treby as someone who has "spoken ill of respectable tradespeople. He had put a stop to the making of saleable drugs, contrary to the nature of buying and selling" (299), a fact that both they and Mrs. Holt view as an insult to the Providential dispensations of commercial life. Despite his being, in his mother's words, a "low working man" (348), Felix, like Joe Gargery, another middle-class idealization of working-class life, is vocal on the subject of his contentment with his lot. Yet the odors evoked in the novel, which are typical of the osmology characteristic of high-Victorian fiction, tell a different story.

Again like Joe Gargery, Felix does not smell in the sense of giving off odors. Unlike Joe, however, who presumably wields a heavy hammer over a hot fire, Felix, as a watchmaker's journeyman and a teacher of young boys, would have little occasion to sweat. Again unlike Joe, Felix, as I stress in the first chapter of this study, is depicted as a character who perceives others and the values that they represent through odors. As such, he is the inodorate superior who can recognize the inferiority of those marked by the traces of perfume or gin or rose leaves. Such sensibility, like Pip's olfactory responses to the artisans he encounters, identifies Felix, not as a middle-class idealization of working-class character, but as an unmarked man who already enjoys a good measure of gentility. Felix Holt's occupations suggest that he straddles the border between middle and working classes: he is both an artisan and a teacher, the position that *Our Mutual Friend* characterizes in the desperate and painful lower-middle-class respectability of Bradley Headstone. Yet Felix's susceptibility to smells indicates that he has already overcome the physicality that would identify him as working class.[10]

Felix ultimately does rise above his origins—not merely by virtue of his olfactory sensitivities, but through a plot whose patent absurdities turn him into a full-fledged melancholic. During the time that he is being attracted to Esther Lyon, Felix tries to establish his influence over the workers of Treby Magna and the miners in an outlying village. Even though he devotes him-

self to two specific occupations, he suffers the same lack of vocational direction that afflicts Arthur Vincent, Pip, and Evan Harrington. Willing in good
Carlylean fashion "to do small work close at hand," Felix is also "preparing
for" the advent of "speculative chances at heroism" (245). This passive open-
ness, this dependency on the arrival of his great expectations, makes pathetic
the ambiguous role that Felix plays during an election riot. When he tries to
control the violence of the mob by becoming its leader, the results are predictably disastrous: he kills a constable, Felix himself is shot by the military
forces come to restore order, and he is tried for manslaughter and sentenced
to four years' imprisonment. From this fate he is released only because Esther
speaks for him at his trial and moves the gentry of Treby Magna and its
environs to present a memorial pleading for his pardon. The unlikeliness of
this constellation of events seems to emphasize the extremes to which the
plot must go to free its worker from his supposed class position; but as they
contribute to a portrait of melancholia, Felix's actions make perfect sense.
Put in the center of a rioting crowd whose unruliness turns him into a murderer rather than a savior, Felix presents the image of a physically impressive manhood ironically powerful only to defeat its own intentions. More
important, the effect of these events on Felix Holt is precisely that of the
plot of *Salem Chapel* on Mr. Vincent: Felix undergoes a process of dematerialization, of disembodiment, that will ultimately align him with those unmarked male members of the gentry and middle classes whose sensitivities
to smell he already shares.

Felix enters the novel as a large man—*massive* is the word repeatedly used
to describe him—notable for his physical strength. Rufus Lyon first sees him
as a "shaggy-headed, large-eyed, strong-limbed person" (54), and the reader
hears often that Felix has a muscular arm, an impressively large head and
prominent, cool grey eyes. In the aftermath of the election riot, Felix still
has his "great Gothic head," but his "person" becomes only "somewhat
massive" (367). He is more ghostlike than substantial. Wounded by a rifle
shot, having had "little food during the day," this strong man "faint[s], and
reviving, . . . faint[s] again" (271). In prison for committing an act of the kind
of working-class violence that typically attended Victorian elections, Felix
embraces the melancholic's preferred condition of disembodiment. Earlier in
the novel, Esther has talked with him at length about what she labels his melancholy, what he calls his sense of the "negations" in him: "I'm not up to the
level of what I see to be best. I am often a hungry discontented fellow"
(220–21); but as the plot of the novel demonstrates, Felix's hunger is purely
figurative. Imprisoned, he welcomes failure even more eagerly than his previous conversation with Esther might suggest he would. In their meeting before his trial, Felix, now "very pale," calls her a thrush sent, like a raven, to
"croak 'failure' in [his] ears" (363–64). At the trial, the man who has often been
described as "abstracted," becomes inanimate: "Felix might have come from

the hands of a sculptor in the later Roman period, when the plastic impulse was stirred by the grandeur of barbaric forms" (373). His massiveness is now immobilized, statuesque, except when he trembles to see Esther take the stand. Testifying at his trial to his "very melancholy" mood on the morning of the riot (376), Esther recognizes the class status that has been his all along and to which she will give substance in her last act in the novel.

Felix's acceptance of Esther's "wealth" turns the character whose participation in election rioting might have evoked fears about working-class physicality and working-class numbers into a man hanging from his wife's apron strings. In a final attempt to establish for Felix the working-class credentials that are rightfully not his, the narrator represents his acceptance of Esther's proposal and his adoption of the relative security of a middle-class income as an embrace of an incongruously material discursivity: "Why," he tells Esther, "I shall be able to set up a great library, and lend the books to be dog's-eared and marked with bread-crumbs" (397). Even before marriage he can imagine himself as the owner of property that workers will damage. Although the narrator tries to mark Felix's trail here with the bread crumbs that might lead to conviction about his working-class identity, the ploy does not succeed. Instead of making and selling drugs, Felix will now be lending, presumably without charge, the books that Esther's inheritance will provide. Felix's disappearance from Treby Magna to a "secret" location that the narrator will not reveal (399) is the final disembodiment into genteel melancholia of a character who ought to be called, not Felix Holt the Radical— much less Felix Holt the Killer, as Judith Wilt argues—but, more accurately, Felix Holt the Librarian.

When Esther announces her supposedly unconventional acceptance of her lot as Felix Holt's wife, which he mistakenly describes as "shar[ing] the life of a poor man," she does so in the olfactory terms that the fiction of the 1860s establishes as quite conventional. It will be a "very bare and simple life," he warns her, and she agrees, "Yes—without atta of roses" (396). Such artificially produced essences are not, as these novels demonstrate, the odors that mark middle-class women as potentially productive wives and mothers. Here Esther recognizes that she is about to become, not the "fine lady" whose allure is signaled by her "atta-of-rose fascinations" (60, 224), but the respectable woman whose "delicate" scent is reminiscent of a garden.[11] As such, she will be the perfectly appropriate partner for the man whose sensitivity to odors has identified him from the beginning of the novel as the unmarked, the source of value, the ultimately disembodied ideal, not of working-class life, but of middle-class manhood. Felix's rejection of trade in the form of his father's doubtfully curative drugs foretells his grumbling acceptance of the substantive property that Esther brings him along with the son, the "young Felix," that her body will later provide (399). When Felix leaves Treby Magna, he has accepted both financial and biological dependence on his wife.

That a woman's effect on her man might not be as restorative as was claimed by those upholding the pieties of Victorian domesticity is made clear not only in Felix's case but also in Harold Transome's. His journey into melancholy is prepared for by his confrontation with his father, Harold's earlier interview with whom has "shocked" his "sense of mastery" (281); but the revelation of Esther's claim to Transome Court, which Harold initially thinks he can easily defeat by marrying her, puts him under "the yoke of [a] mighty resistless destiny" (386). Women's opinions, according to Harold's earlier formulation, do not matter because women "are not called upon to judge or to act" (36). Yet Esther's opinions come to matter to him more than anyone else's. On her rejection or acceptance of his proposal, Harold thinks, rest not only whether he will suffer the "humiliating loss" of his family's estate (305) but also whether the shame of his publicly declared illegitimacy will be made "more bearable" by her love and loyalty (389). As Esther is endowed with the power to determine Harold's fate, he loses in narrative substantiality what he gains in property. If Felix is erased from Treby Magna in the archly toned "Epilogue" to the novel, Harold's disappearance is even more strikingly complete. After the narrator records Esther's rejection of Harold, an event his reaction to which is not represented, he is mentioned only once again when Felix refers to him as the man whom Esther has chosen not to marry. Harold appears in the epilogue only as an unnamed member of "the Transome family" traveling to unnamed destinations (399). Endowed with the income and acres that Esther's generosity grants him, Harold is nonetheless sent on his melancholic way by her refusal to marry him. Once again Esther has demonstrated that a woman who supposedly cannot "make her own lot" (342) has it within her power to make or break a man's.

Like Felix, Harold is an unlikely candidate for melancholia. Yet because he undergoes a process of dematerialization as thorough as that experienced by the eponymous hero of the novel, Harold proves, like Pip and Evan as well as Felix, that the gentility of the melancholic is established by the marks of those doing the kind of work no longer done by men of his class, that a retreat from production and exchange is central to this process. As the younger son of the Transome family, Harold has made a "fortune . . . in trade" in Smyrna (282); but as the prospective inheritor of the Transome estate after the death of his older brother, he is a member of the gentry, thus typifying the transition from commerce to land-owning that it took most tradesmen's families several generations fully to accomplish. Yet Harold, tainted by his too-recent commercial transactions in Smyrna, cannot easily embody the gentility that characterizes the infirm elder Mr. Transome, his supposed father, who is a "waxen image" of a man (348). Harold, by contrast, is fat—a point that he makes about himself no fewer than four times (17, 295, 344, 353); and as Esther notes, he is a man much too fond of his sauces. Harold's girth identifies him not only with his unacknowledged father Jermyn but also with the fat hands of the tradesmen of Treby Magna, to whose concerns he, as the owner of Transome Court, thinks himself superior. Jermyn himself is part of this realm of trade, less because he is a professional man serving its interests than because he buys and sells, he trades on the estate he manages by speculating illicitly in mortgages and annuities drawn against its value. Harold's uncle, a rector notable for his obtuseness, does not recognize the resemblance between his nephew and Jermyn, whom he describes as "a fat-handed, glib-tongued fellow, with a scented cambric handkerchief; one of your educated low-bred fellows . . . one of your middle-class upstarts who want to rank with gentlemen, and think they'll do it with kid gloves and new furniture" (30). According to the tenets of the osmology of high-Victorian fiction, Jermyn's perfumed handkerchief immediately marks him as a participant in trade and commerce.

If Harold is not to join his father among the "low-bred," he, like Felix Holt, must give up his substantial bodily presence, and that is precisely what happens to Harold after Jermyn announces the fact of his fatherhood to him. This proud, stout, florid man, tanned by Eastern suns, presumably coddled in exotic culinary and sexual pleasures by the slave wife whom he has purchased—this man must learn to turn pale and go without dinner. At the meeting just before Jermyn announces their relationship, Harold "look[s] brilliant . . . his blood . . . flowing prosperously": "He had just that amount of flush which indicates that life is more enjoyable than usual" (381–82). After hearing Jermyn reveal his humiliating secret, Harold turns "white" and sees himself reflected, along with Jermyn, in the two dimensions of a mirror (382). Harold returns in the "pale English sunshine" to Transome Court, where he refuses to eat dinner and decides that he must assert "his character" as a "gentleman" through his actions (383), but there is nothing that he can do except confront his mother to confirm his illegitimacy and reveal in vague hints to Esther that he has been dishonored. So thoroughly does Harold retreat into genteel discursivity that his mother sees him as a piece of writing: when he enters her room, she thinks, "It was as if a long-expected letter, with a black seal, had come at last" (384). Harold reacts the next morning to Esther's entreaty on his mother's behalf with an uncharacteristically nervous response: like Arthur Vincent or Pip or Evan, Harold becomes all nerves, "a painful thrill . . . show[ing] itself in his face with that pale rapid flash which can never be painted" (394). Formerly stolid and imperturbable in his self-satisfaction, Harold is now sensitive to emotions that strike like lightning, emotions that could not be represented in the material medium of paint.

In a novel so concerned with the mastery that men exert over women, with Felix Holt's dominance of his mother and Harold's of Mrs. Transome, the requirements of gentility seem to master both of the radicals portrayed in its pages. From this perspective, therefore, it is possible to agree with Alison Booth's claim that *Felix Holt* conveys a "muted" feminist message ("Not

All" 158). The osmology that the novel so insistently and self-consciously invokes ultimately finds acceptable the substance that women possess, as it rejects the similarly substantial making and selling of odorous things. If both Felix and Harold are fully to give up trade, they must lose the fleshly existence associated with it. Brothers in their melancholic sense of failure, pale versions of their former selves, they disappear from Treby Magna but only after their melancholia has been both treated and exacerbated by the woman central to both their stories, a lady whose characteristic odor of gentility establishes her as the appropriate arbiter of a man's fate.

The Cost of a Groom-Price

Among the female characters of her decade, Esther Lyon, it turns out, is a fairly typical heiress. In Harold's flattering terms, she is "empress of [her] own fortunes—and more besides" (325). *Felix Holt* grants Esther such power through testamentary machinations so complex that its author had to seek professional advice on their legality, but the plot of *Evan Harrington* takes such female property-owning as its simple assumption. As this novel clarifies the connection between the tactility of trade and the melancholic's rejection of it, it also, more directly than any of the others that I discuss, confronts the possibility that the transfer of property may cost a man his manhood. In Evan's earlier removal to the Continent, his sisters have played the role of the Parcae in his life (26). Now destiny takes over in the shape of Rose Jocelyn, the Three Fates rolled into one. Rose, an heiress already worth £10,000 and potentially the owner of the estate where her family lives, represents the financial independence that Evan's sister the countess has been looking for on his behalf. Although the narrator plays up the ironies involved in Rose's inheritance's having been made in the grocery trade, the basic outline of the novel's complicated plot is clear: poor boy loves rich girl, and they marry to live happily ever after. This story requires, however, a turning away from trade, a rejection that has untoward consequences. A man can leave the shop behind, he can rise "Above Buttons," but he may leave his manhood there as well. The novel literally marks its women—with brands and the disfigurements of deformed limbs or skin disease and even the bruises of marital abuse—so that their bodily forms become more and more evident. Yet at crucial points in the plot, Evan threatens, like St. John Nepomucene, to disappear altogether. In the end Evan does vanish, not simply because his story is over, but because *Evan Harrington* is remarkably frank in its definition of Rose as a producer both of property and of children.

The threat that Evan's love poses to his manhood is made clear halfway through the novel when Rose and he become engaged to each other. She now

knows that he is the son of a tailor, even that his name is on the door of his
father's shop at 193 Main Street, Lymport-on-the-Sea. Evan is without income or prospects, except those provided by the shop and its debts; and he
has avoided the few months of training as a tailor that a friend of the family
has offered him, feeling no doubt, as the countess does, that he cannot touch
cloth or a gentleman's leg. In this crisis Rose takes over. Becoming the "general" of a domestic campaign meant to ensure their marriage, she leads her
beloved as they go to confront her mother, whom she, Rose, will inform of
the engagement. In one of the most significant of the comparative encounters in the novel, the two discuss this plan, and Evan's response makes it
clear that a crucial exchange has taken place: Rose is the superior, the "First"
here; Evan, her inferior, "second fiddle." She articulates his discomfort—
he cannot even speak for himself—and the narrator adds a long paragraph
outlining the effect of this turn of events on Evan:

> At the library door Rose turned to him, and with her chin archly
> lifted sideways, said:
> "I know what you feel; you feel foolish."
> Now the sense of honour, and of the necessity of acting the part it
> imposes on him, may be very strong in a young man; but certainly, as
> a rule, the sense of ridicule is more poignant, and Evan was suffering
> horrid pangs. We none of us like to play second fiddle. To play
> second fiddle to a woman is an abomination to us all. But to have to
> perform upon that instrument to the darling of our hearts—would we
> not rather die? nay, almost rather end the duet precipitately and with
> violence. . . . There could be no doubt that he was playing second
> fiddle to Rose. And what was he about to do? Oh, horror! to stand like
> a criminal, and say, or worse, have said for him, things to tip the ears
> with fire! To tell the young lady's mother that he had won her
> daughter's love, and meant—what did he mean? He knew not. Alas!
> he was second fiddle; he could only mean what she meant. Evan loved
> Rose deeply and completely, but noble manhood was strong in him.
> You may sneer at us, if you please, ladies. We have been educated in a
> theory, that when you lead off with the bow, the order of Nature is
> reversed, and it is no wonder, therefore, that, having stript us of one
> attribute, our fine feathers moult, and the majestic cock-like march
> which distinguishes us degenerates. You unsex us, if I may dare to say
> so. Ceasing to be men, what are we? If we are to please you rightly,
> always allow us to play First. (312)

If there were any doubt that Evan's manhood is at issue here, the final references to the "unsexing" loss of feathers and cocklike walk would clarify the
point. Rising in crescendos of mock-amusement, the voice of the narrator,

whose "we" presumably announces the manly consciousness that he embodies, intones the possibilities: death, end of love, criminality, reversals of
nature, and, finally, emasculation. Not surprisingly, the outcome of this confrontation between Evan and Rose—between, as the narrator later puts it,
"the niggard spirit of the beggarly receiver, and the high bloom of the exalted giver" (316)—is that Rose decides that she will face her mother alone
while Evan waits outside on the grounds to hear his fate. Rose here becomes
as psychologically dominant in her relation to Evan as she is visually so in
Charles Keene's depiction of her as she sits with her suitor Ferdinand Laxley:
so substantial is Rose in this wood engraving that the size and shape of even
her dress can put a man in the background (fig. 3.2). Like Ferdinand, Evan,
who wants his "noble manhood" to be "strong," becomes repeatedly "only
second fiddle."

During this chapter Evan has cried out to Rose in his humiliation, "Why
must I owe everything to you?" (316), and the ending of the novel confirms
his indebtedness as its convoluted plot determines the ownership of Beckley
Court, which first passes from Rose's grandmother to Rose's cousin Juliana.
Smitten, like her cousin, with the would-be gentleman, Juliana wills the estate
to Evan, by whom it is immediately transferred to Rose's ne'er-do-well
brother Harry "in reversion" from his mother (497). Depicted as a pathetic,
sickly, and deformed nonentity open to the manipulations of even the countess, Juliana, like most propertied young women in high-Victorian fiction,
nonetheless has improbably complete discretion over the estate. Both she
and her grandmother before her can will it away apparently without objection from the many male relations around them, and Evan in turn disposes
of it in a way that emphasizes the link between women and property: the
estate is not to go directly to Harry, but to him through his mother. The
plot requires that women serve repeatedly as the bearers of Beckley Court,
and the traffic in those women benefits the men who neither desire nor deserve the profits it brings them. The novel's staging of the reengagement of
Evan and Rose makes this point directly. The two lovers have been separated by false reports of Evan's having forged an anonymous letter and by
Rose's having accepted a proposal of marriage from Evan's titled rival, but
they are reunited in a scene in which Evan is once again the undisputed second fiddle. In an act of what appears to his relatives to be simply senseless
renunciation, he has given up his claim to Beckley Court and has withdrawn
to the shop that is the location of both his work and his home, having accepted the fate that has made him a tailor. En masse Rose and her family
descend on the shop, and in the penultimate chapter of the novel, mistitled
"A Lovers' Parting," Rose makes love to Evan. Her mother has been called
by one of Evan's relations, "the staunchest piece of woman-goods I ever
————" (431); and Rose becomes a piece of goods here, the "recompense"
that the Jocelyns offer Evan in exchange for the estate (514).

Fig. 3.2 A young lady's substance: Rose Jocelyn and her genteel suitor, Ferdinand Laxley. *Evan Harrington* in *Once a Week* 3 (1860): 337. Courtesy of the Beinecke Rare Book and Manuscript Library, Yale University.

In "A Lovers' Parting," Evan confesses his love to Rose by linking it directly to a proposed rejection of his trade as a tailor: "Rose, I will leave [the shop]. I will accept any assistance that your father—that any man will give me. Beloved—noble girl! I see my falseness to you, though I little thought it at the time—fool that I was! Be my help, my guide—as the soul of my body! Be mine!" Evan's renunciation of trade is cast in the cloying language of erotic identification, with Rose as the soul of Evan's body, but the effect here is more like that of the worker's heart beating in the chest of Marx's capitalist. Another exchange, however, results from the final encounter of the young lovers: by turning from his manual trade, Evan becomes soul, and Rose's body becomes his property and the assurance of a livelihood in the future. When Rose offers Evan her hand, when he takes from her "her hand and her whole shape, [as] she with closed eyes let him strain her to his breast" (513), he is embracing the property that will define him as a gentleman. At issue here is not just Rose's £10,000, but, remarkably, the financial gain that will attach to her reproductive potential. The fairy godfather of the novel, Tom Cogglesby, the brother of Evan's brother-in-law, has promised £1,000 a year to the couple should they marry and another £1,000 a year once Rose produces her first child. As the other characters assume, this groom-price will be augmented by the Jocelyn family when they settle Evan's father's debts, the "great Mel's" princely losses in trade. Rose is a staunch piece of goods after all.

The plotting about the money that ensures this outcome, however, occurs behind the backs of Evan and Rose so that they can remain innocent of the implications of the financial arrangements toward which the action of the novel directly insists on pointing. Like *Great Expectations*, *Evan Harrington* does not want to make too openly the bargain between love and property. Yet the end of the novel confirms the suspicion that Evan, in taking Rose as a cash-endowed substitute for both the estate and the tailor's shop, has diminished himself. Evan's fate as Rose's spouse allows him to sustain his melancholic condition rather than be liberated from it. If his rejection of trade entails a manhood that can be secured only by the possession of his wife and children—as both the source of his income and his identity—he is further defined by his willing acceptance of a profession wed to discursivity, the relatively immaterial realm of writing. He has served as a private secretary; now he enlists in the genteel ranks of the foreign service, in which writing and talking are the central activities. One can imagine Evan as he works in Naples, doing his bit for his country as he polishes his history of Portugal or begins another on Italy, while Rose sits by his side, perhaps encouraging yet new acts of generosity by Tom Cogglesby as she produces one child after another.

As if to emphasize the leading role that Rose plays in the denouement of the novel, Evan appears in its final chapter only in the countess's contemptuous epistolary account of him: "I will talk of Evan first. . . . Attaché to the Naples embassy, sounds tol-lol. In such a position I can rejoice to see him, for it permits me to acknowledge him. I am not sure that, *spiritually*, Rose will be his most fitting helpmate. However, it is done" (517). In the last sentence of *Evan Harrington*, the countess casts doubt on Evan's gentility in terms that identify him as insubstantial: as far as "being the *real* gentleman [goes,] . . . whatever Evan may think of himself, or Rose think of him, I *know the thing*"(519). And Evan is not it. Underlining both the terms that indicate substantiality—*real* and *thing*—the countess marks the distance of the British attaché in Naples from the material reality to which he is connected only through his wife's reproductive powers. Though this loss in *Evan Harrington* is construed as a gain—its characters and narrator cannot forget that a tailor is but one-ninth a man—Evan's exit from the novel as the dependent of the Jocelyns' patronage and Tom Cogglesby's wealth suggests that the countess may have a point in her final dismissive comment on her brother. To the extent that he becomes the gentleman that he would be, Evan ceases to be the man whom "*the thing[s]*" of the tailor's shop would make him.

Bodily Substance

Evan Harrington's fading into insubstantiality brings my argument full circle to the case with which I began in the previous chapter. If there is any melancholic in the fiction of the 1860s who conclusively demonstrates the extent of a man's impotence through his dependence on a woman, that character is Arthur Vincent. The hero of *Salem Chapel* embraces a self-definition of discursivity that offers him only a "posthumous and nameless life" (439), but taking renunciation of the flesh and its comforts to its logical outcome—death, the annihilation of the race—is not a development that a high-Victorian novel can readily countenance. The last chapter of *Salem Chapel*, which recounts events two or three years after the occurrence of the main action, gives Vincent a second chance at substantiality. This opportunity is depicted as a glorious and unexpected gift granted by the materiality of middle-class women, their bodies offering him sensuous perceptions that prove that he has sensory organs—eyes, ears, skin—able to feel in physical terms their physical presence. In this coda to *Salem Chapel*, Vincent prepares to welcome his mother and his sister Susan as they return from the Continent, where they have retreated to avoid the shame and notoriety attendant upon Susan's near seduction by the villain Colonel Mildmay. The two Vincent women bring back with them the villain's daughter, Alice Mildmay, the slightly retarded but preternaturally beautiful young woman who has been kept from her father by his estranged wife and who has been abducted with Susan when Colonel Mildmay tricks her into leaving her home. The effect that these two young women have on Vincent is revolutionary: as "unexpected apparitions," they "transformed life itself and everything in it." Within a day, however, Vincent becomes convinced that these "apparitions" are "real creatures" (460).

In the lengthiest and most stunning of the novel's many encounters, Susan and Alice, now living in Vincent's house, allow him to exchange abstraction for physicality, granting him in the bargain a metaphoric rise in social status that all his passionate preachings and grand ambitions have not afforded him: "The Nonconformist went back to his little home with the sensation of an enchanted prince in a fairy tale. Instead of a mud-coloured existence, what a glowing, brilliant firmament! Life became glorious again under their touch. . . . Seeing these two as they went about the house, hearing their voices as they talked in perpetual sweet accord, with sweeter jars of difference, surprised the young man's life out of its shadows;—one of them his sister— the other—" (460–61). This unfinished thought, the penultimate sentence of the novel, hints at a future in which the sensations of seeing and hearing will be augmented by a further physical consummation between Vincent and Alice. For the benefit of his congregation, Vincent has earlier defined the relation between men and their families as a matter of simple possession: "you secure a certain woman to yourself to make your hearth bright, and to be yours for ever; . . . you have children who are yours, to perpetuate your name and your tastes and feelings" (452). But the preparation for the resolution to which *Salem Chapel* looks in the distance beyond its last paragraph suggests that women are the source not only of existence in perpetuity but also of a man's ability to have sensations in the present.

The repeated evocations of the sweet murmurings of Susan and Alice as they move gracefully about Vincent's London home indicate both their importance as objects of Vincent's perceptions and the sexual complications required to make possible a happy resolution of the novel's action. Crucial to the emergence of this outcome is the figure of Susan—her identity as a material mass as well as a person. The knots of incestuous and homosocial desire that link the various plots of *Salem Chapel* into what Vincent calls "strange bonds" (413) are bizarrely wrought: Colonel Mildmay, the half-brother of Lady Western, the lady whom Vincent loves, tries to seduce Vincent's sister Susan, and Vincent presumably ends up married to the would-be seducer's daughter, who is named for Lady Western and is also her physical image, while Lady Western marries the man whose name her brother has used to woo Vincent's sister. More striking, however, than even this concatenation of relations is what happens to Susan's physical form once she leaves her mother's house in Lonsdale in the company of Colonel Mildmay: his failed seduction of her unaccountably changes her body into an object that provides Vincent with the woman who may become his marriage partner. Although Susan has not been sexually violated by Mildmay, as the text specifically and repeatedly insists, her brush with vice transforms her from a "frank, fair Saxon girl" of eighteen (222) into an almost monstrous physical presence of gigantic proportions. Only a few days after leaving her mother's house, she finds her way to her brother's lodgings in Carlingford, but she has by then become swollen into insensitivity, a comatose giant made of "white marble" (343). Engorged by the "frightful, tropical blaze of passion" (289) that she has not experienced, she becomes pure physicality to Vincent's pure discursivity.

It would be hard to exaggerate the excesses of the narrator's descriptions of "the grandeur of [Susan's] stricken form, the features sublimed and elevated, the majestic proportions" of the previously "fair-haired girl" (289). Most telling is the view of her given through the eyes of the doctor who attends her in her illness. Looking at her, he thinks her capable of killing her seducer, the crime of which she is briefly suspected:

> The doctor, who has never seen the fair Saxon girl who was
> Mrs Vincent's daughter a week ago, thought in his heart that this
> full developed form and face, rapt to grandeur by the extremity of
> woe, gave no contradiction to the accusation he had just heard with
> so much horror. That week had obliterated Susan's soft girlish
> innocence and the simplicity of her eighteen years. She was a grand
> form as she lay there upon that bed—might have loved to despera-
> tion—fallen—killed. Unconsciously he uttered aloud the thought in
> his heart—"Perhaps it would be better she should die!" (267–68)

Susan is no murderer, however, and she does not die. Yet the body that she later brings back from the Continent to Vincent's house, "that grand figure, large and calm and noble like a Roman woman" (458), continues to be presented as the result of "fiery sorrow and passion [that] had acted like some tropical tempestuous sun upon [her] youth" (460).

But a force considerably less exotic than a tropical sun is at work here. Vincent has earlier been presented as feeling sexual jealousy when he hears that his sister is being courted, no man he knows except himself being good enough to enjoy "the simple graces of his pretty sister" (51). The young and mentally challenged Alice has also become enthralled by Susan's charms; as Alice's voluble governess puts it, "Girls of that age, if you will not think it strange of me to say so, very often fall in love with a girl older than themselves—quite fall in love, though it is a strange thing to say" (410). Focusing the desires felt by both brother and younger girl on Susan's sexually inexperienced body becomes a way of allowing that phantasmatic object to produce a conventionally acceptable marriage. Taken off but untouched by Mildmay, Susan, accompanied by his child, gives birth to that child as a marriageable woman.[12] Susan is saved from death by Alice's cries, her demands that Susan take care of her. When they retreat to the Continent, where Alice provides an "occupation" as well as a "little income" for Susan (446), Alice's feeble mind is strengthened by its proximity to Susan's great body. Susan herself sees the connection between the two events: "I was little and Alice was foolish when we went away. At least I was little in Lonsdale, where nobody minded me. Somehow most people mind me now, because I am so big, I suppose: and Alice, instead of being foolish, is a little wise woman" (459). Existing in a state that resembles a perpetual pregnancy, Susan secures not only her brother's physicality but also his future wife's mental abilities. For all the Roman grandeur attributed to Susan's form, then, it bears a more commonplace impress. In her role as a surrogate mother, Susan produces for a man the wife and presumably the children whom he can possess—"a certain woman . . . to be yours for ever . . . children who are yours" (452). Such possessions grant Vincent existence in the present and the future, but only at the cost of his having had to depend on his sister for his resurrection.

Smelling Substance

In *The Clever Woman of the Family*, as in *Salem Chapel* and *Evan Harrington* and *Felix Holt*, a wife and her children serve as the possessions that allot to the genteel melancholic a physical identity not easily secured in his own person. Filling *The Clever Woman* with disease, death, and the suffering of the innocent as Yonge characteristically does, she also proposes happy endings for the characters who manage to survive her plot, outcomes based not only on faith but also on a lady's sometimes reluctant acceptance of the role of wife and mother. This statement holds true for both the putative and the genuine holders of the designation offered in the title of the novel—Rachel Curtis, the would-be clever woman, and Ermine Williams, the one so named in its last line. One has a head too strong, and the other, a body too weak; but they still manage to grant their men access to the materiality that they would otherwise lack. In a kind of efflorescence of needy men, the conclusion of the novel brings together four such figures: a blind clergyman, a wounded and dying Scottish lord, and two ailing soldiers, not to mention Ermine's brother, a "wreck of a man, stunned and crushed, and never thoroughly alive" (329). The two military men, Captain Alick Keith and his older distant relative Colonel Colin Keith, are, however, saved by their women, Rachel and Ermine, respectively. Through its conjoined representations of smells, substance, and offspring, the ending of *The Clever Woman* confirms the patterns evident in the novels that I discuss in this study. Because Yonge grants her male characters a secure gentility based on their status as men well beyond economic want—no women need function here as bearers of estates that they blithely give away to the men who, like Evan and Felix and Harold, all too obviously lack them. Even so Rachel is the "joint heiress" of an estate worth, as the narrator casually puts it, "some three or four thousand a year" (5). Any distinctions between Yonge's story and those told by Trollope and Meredith and Eliot, however, simply make more evident the power

of melancholia to define the form of respectable manhood characteristic of
the 1860s.

Remarkably, Colin Keith uses his nose both to realize that Ermine, from
whom he has been long separated, is still alive and to recognize the home
that she eventually makes for him. Now a retired soldier on the half pay that
he hardly needs since his colonial adventures have been predictably lucrative, he had gone off twelve years earlier to his military assignments in India
and Australia, leaving behind Ermine, the clergyman's daughter who was
presumably on her deathbed after she had been injured in a fire. Not knowing whether she has survived, Colin identifies her as the author of periodical essays written by "the Invalid" when he reads one that refers to "the scent
of the thyme," a reference that triggers in him an olfactory memory of her
father's parsonage. Telling Ermine about this episode, Colin connects reading and meeting: "Well it might give me the sense of meeting you! And in
other papers of the series I traced your old self more ripened" (62). Even
when Colin finally convinces Ermine to marry him, they are separated again
when he must set off within hours of the wedding to tend his dying elder
brother. When Colin returns to the home he has prepared for Ermine, he
discovers that she has transformed it with her presence, and he articulates
his pleasure by referring to a smell: "And the room has exactly the old geranium scent!" Ermine explains that after great effort she has been able to find
a new incarnation of "the old oak-leaf geranium" that was in her father's
conservatory, a plant from which Colin was wont to gather from time to time
an aromatic leaf. As if speaking of Ermine and not of the plant, he responds,
"I have been wondering where the fragrance came from that made the like-
ness [to the parsonage] complete. I have smelt nothing like it since!" He then
holds in his hand the plant that reminds him of his wife, who coos, "There,
now you have a leaf in your fingers, I think you do feel at home" (361).

Yet Colin Keith cannot quite accept that his long-cherished "dream" of
life with Ermine has been turned from "vision" to "reality" (361–62). Like
his younger relative, Alick Keith, Colin is himself anything but substantial.
"Worn and altered," so disabled by the bullet still lodged in his chest that
he cannot live through a northern winter or venture outdoors after sunset
on a cold day, Colin, like the good melancholic he is, has defined his life as
a quest for one woman: marrying Ermine, he tells her, has been "the one
object and thought of my life, the only hope I have had all these years" (77).
In this instance, however, even the scents of thyme and geranium are not
enough to convince him that she is his. Nor is Ermine the kind of substantial presence whose body could provide such proof. She is still not sufficiently
recovered from her injuries to be able to walk. Yet her good sense and her
previous care of her niece Rose have convinced Colin's brother that she
should become on his death the foster mother of his child, Colin's nephew,
the heir to the Scottish estate of Gowanbrae. The will whereby Colin and

Ermine become the infant's guardians also grants Colin a portion of the family lands that he has not expected or wanted to inherit. When Colin protests that he "can hardly feel" that his "vision" is a "reality," Ermine promptly offers a chapter-closing response when she turns to call a servant to bring in the orphaned child to whom she is now mother: "Then I shall ring. Tibbie [the housekeeper] and the poor little Lord up-stairs are substantial witnesses to the cares and troubles of real life" (361–62). Presumably unable to give birth herself, Ermine has managed to connect her husband to the materiality that such maternity would ensure. As the "little Lord" exclaims in the coda to the novel when he has grown old enough to say so, "You are mother!" (365). Earlier the narrator has pointed out that the "restoration" to Colin of Ermine's "real substantial self" has blinded him to "her helpless state" (74). At the end of the novel, the terms *real* and *substantial* reappear to define what Ermine possesses and what she can present to her mate.

In the final chapter of *The Clever Woman*, the action of which takes place several years after Colin returns to his new home, Ermine again uses the word *substantial*, applying it this time, not to her husband, but to the other Mrs. Keith. Speaking of the transformation that Rachel has wrought in Alick Keith, Ermine remarks, "I am glad to see him looking so much stronger and more substantial" (365). Throughout the novel, Alick's missing fingers have not been the only evidence of what he lacks. Unlike Pip and Evan and Felix and Vincent, Alick has a secure profession, finding in his devotion to his "hereditary family," his regiment of the Highlanders, the work that he unquestionably wants to do. Yet the profession that he has adopted does require that he continue on a global scale the wandering that issues from the melancholic's restlessness, and he never completely overcomes an insubstantiality that is presented as both physical and temperamental. "Almost shattered to pieces" by his injuries in India (61), he has returned to England in a "miserably sensitive condition of shattered nerves" (190). Having lain for a year upon a sofa, he is unaccountably disengaged from the activities around him, so much so that Colin Keith cannot decide if Alick is "the coolest or the most sensitive fellow living" (262). Subject still to fits of an "old Indian fever," Alick suffers "a failure of the physical powers" every third day whenever a crisis brings on his illness, which is often so severe that the intervening days are spent in exhaustion and depression (314–15). Even after marrying Rachel, his characteristic posture, which he again assumes in the last chapter of the novel, is reclining with his eyes half closed—almost as if he were one of Pip's five brothers lying on his back in his grave. Yet in the last scene of the novel, Alick, more "substantial" than he has been, is also more energetic. Holding in his arms his son, the second child whom Rachel has given him, he discourses on the futures faced by his children in "one of the effusions which sometimes broke through his phlegmatic temperament." If Alick has not needed Rachel to give him a groom-price—he himself has more than the £5,000 settled on her at her marriage—if he has not found in her the work he wants to do or the permanent home that might be wreathed with the scents of flowers in honor of her maternity, he has depended on her to give him children. Significantly, concern for their welfare overcomes his usual, effete indolence, rousing him to a patriarchal manhood that Rachel knows will "keep" not only her but also her children "in order" (367). In Yonge's world no story could come to a happier conclusion.

Despite the resolutions reached by the love trials of the two Keiths in *The Clever Woman*, high-Victorian novels as often as not represent women as possessions and possessors who might alleviate genteel male insubstantiality only also to testify that applying such treatment may exacerbate the disease. When Rachel Curtis first touches Alick Keith's glove and has the "sensation of the solid giving way" under her hand, she experiences in physical terms what many of her fellow heroines discover about the men to whom they give way. Some of the sturdiest of the male characters in the fiction of the 1860s declare that they are dying for or cannot live without the love of a particular woman—Squire Gilmore in Trollope's *The Vicar of Bullhampton*, Harry in Hughes's *Tom Brown at Oxford*, the heroes of Trollope's *The Belton Estate* and Blackmore's *Lorna Doone*, John Fordyce in Robinson's *Beyond the Church*—but requited love, as the tales of melancholics reveal, can have equally deleterious effects. Men ailing from melancholia, like Alick Keith ailing from fever, go to their women for a cure. Even when treatment is available, as it is for Evan and Felix, the result may be as little invigorating as when there is faint hope of recovery. In *Our Mutual Friend*, the novel to which I now turn, Dickens offers an extreme instance of a now-familiar pattern: the male melancholic, the living dead, having repudiated the father tainted by trade, is given birth by his wife through the property she grants him and the child whom she bears for him. Yet this happy ending, represented as a consummation of erotic desire devoutly to be wished, has untoward effects, and John Harmon's fate therefore suggests the extent to which manhood may depend on forms of support beyond those offered by a woman. Comparative encounters between male melancholics and their physically vibrant and often well-heeled women, ineffective as the resulting exchanges frequently are in making men of their male participants, demonstrate that solutions outside the home might have to be sought if such men are not to become, in Magwitch's telling phrase, "molloncholly-mad sheep" (329).

4

Treating the Melancholic of
Our Mutual Friend

The last smell represented in the last of Dickens's completed novels evokes
the warm comfort of a tradesman's workplace, which in this instance is
conventionally, if more weirdly than usual, also his home. Silas Wegg, the
minor villain of *Our Mutual Friend*, goes to consult with his supposed fellow
conspirator, the embalmer and articulator of skeletons, Mr. Venus. Entering the shop, Wegg, in a characteristic gesture, sniffs the air. Since he has
been exposed to long hours of cold work as he has watched the Harmon dust
mounds being carted away, Wegg is not in good humor. Venus, however,
has been sitting cozily at his fire, and Wegg comments on the aroma that
attends him:

> "Why, you smell rather comfortable here!" said Wegg, . . .
> stopping and sniffing as he entered.
> "I *am* rather comfortable, sir," said Venus.
> "You don't use lemon in your business, do you?" asked Wegg,
> sniffing again.
> "No, Mr. Wegg," said Venus. "When I use it at all, I mostly use it
> in cobblers' punch."
> "What do you call cobblers' punch?" demanded Wegg, in a worse
> humour than before.
> "It's difficult to impart the receipt for it, sir," returned Venus,
> "because, however particular you may be in allotting your materials,
> so much will still depend upon the individual gifts, and there being a
> feeling thrown into it. But the groundwork is gin." (760)

In portraying this olfactory encounter, Dickens is having good fun with the
values that the osmology of high-Victorian fiction invokes whenever the
odors of tradesmen's food and drink are made representationally sensible:
based on the vulgar "groundwork" of gin, elaborated by fantastic pretensions to artistic talent and expressiveness, cobblers' punch "smell[s] rather

comfortable," its aroma promising sustenance and ease. Significantly, in this scene Venus recognizes that Wegg has grown so thin that the "kivering upon" his "bones" is "weazen and yellow." Venus, however, previously described as "a haggard melancholy man," has now grown "fat" (85, 761) like the tradesmen of Broughton's *Cometh up as a Flower* and Trollope's *The Struggles of Brown, Jones, and Robinson*.

Coming as it does before the scene in which both Wegg and Venus repair to the supremely inodorate realm of gentility in *Our Mutual Friend*, the mansion that John Harmon and his wife Bella and the Boffins inhabit together, this reference to a smell does more than simply identify the two conspirators as tradesmen, the kind of men from whom the male melancholic of the 1860s must distance himself if he is to maintain his status. The olfactory register of this encounter, like that of similar scenes in *Salem Chapel* and *Felix Holt*, grants even Venus a substantiality that the primary melancholic of the novel, John Harmon, characteristically lacks. As such, the aroma of Venus's aptly named cobblers' punch prepares for the exchange that takes place in the second half of this chapter when Harmon performs his most physically impressive action in *Our Mutual Friend*. Punishing the lowly street-seller Wegg for plotting to blackmail their mutual benefactor Boffin, Harmon exhibits an energy and even a taste for violence that might seem unaccountable. In a moment and for a moment, everything that Harmon has become is transformed. As J. Hillis Miller remarked long ago, in *Our Mutual Friend* "characters from all levels constantly meet and interact with each other"; unlike such events in *Bleak House*, "here there are dozens of encounters which change both persons."[1] What it means in Dickens's last novel when a comparative encounter effects, not simply change, but an exchange is the question that this chapter addresses.

The man who served as Dickens's office boy when *Our Mutual Friend* was being written later recalled that his employer "lived a lot by his nose. He seemed to be always smelling things" (Van Dyke 50). The roughly thirty odors represented in this novel confirm that observation, their number and variety giving Dickens claim to the title of the most attentive and inventive of high-Victorian novelists in his treatment of olfactory responses. Yet these representations also reveal the extent to which Dickens conforms to the conventions of the osmology that he shares with his fellow novelists, using it as a structure of sensations to ratify the common sense of his culture, conveying values that might more typically remain unacknowledged. Examining Dickens's elaborate and sometimes wonderfully implausible representations of olfactory impressions in this novel once again raises the subjects of male melancholia and female substantiality. As Esther Lyon becomes the typical heiress of the fiction of the 1860s, John Harmon functions as its archetypal melancholic. Along with other characters whom I treat briefly later in this chapter—the hero of Linton's *Lizzie Lorton of Greyrigg* and two gentlemen in Charles Reade's novels *Hard Cash* and *Put Yourself in His Place*—Harmon demonstrates the extent to which conceptions of respectable Victorian manhood depend on incorporating rather than rejecting working-class physicality. By representing the significance of bodily strength, such figures provide a perspective on the preeminent political issues of the 1860s and, therefore, on the argument to which this chapter leads.

Problematic Plots

In treating "these times of ours" (13), as *Our Mutual Friend* announces in its first sentence, the novel deals with characterizations and plot elements typical of the 1860s, but it exaggerates their effects by placing them in the context of a commodity culture that is openly reviled. *Our Mutual Friend* extends the pattern evident in *Evan Harrington, Miss Mackenzie, Salem Chapel,* and *Felix Holt* by envisioning the profits of trade as refuse, disinheritance as death, women as subjects of legacies or promissory notes, and the ownership of property as rebirth. No longer depicting the past that in *Great Expectations* makes appropriate fantasies of idealized artisanal labor, *Our Mutual Friend* describes a culture that encourages a market in orphans, adulates misers whose sisters make pies of dead sheep, and puts on sale only the debris left over from industrialized production—bits of cloth and crockery and coal. In this realm of getting and spending, even nostalgia seems set at too high a price: the pauper Betty Higden puts into practice Joe Gargery's principles of self-reliant industry and contentment with her lot only to end up dying in the performance of them. Yet in this world, dirtier and sloppier than even the London that Pip first sees, Dickens conjures up a plot that grants its main character what Pip's story denies him, a plot in which a man's great expectations of a fortune are as completely realized as his desire for a flawlessly loving and trusting woman. John Harmon's story, however, takes this process one step further, acting out the unease that a woman's salvation of her man might engender. In one sense, then, Harmon recapitulates the stories of Evan Harrington and Felix Holt and Philip Pip. Harmon, like them, has risen above his working-class background, which is constituted in his case by his having turned sailor at fourteen years, the traditional age at which working-class youths began their apprenticeships. Yet Harmon also reverses the pattern of worker-turned-melancholic when, at least in his confrontation with Wegg, he demonstrates that he knows how to use his own strong hand.

The reading of *Our Mutual Friend* that I offer here therefore privileges its central plot, the story of John Harmon, the man whom Boffin identifies as the eponymous hero of the novel when he is known only as Mr. Rokesmith (115). The Harmon plot has not been a favorite among critics of the novel,[2]

Stephen Gill memorably calling it "the albatross about Dickens's neck" (22). Yet this story does accomplish the strenuous work that Dickens sets for it through a series of complicated substitutions, even more complicated than its perpetual play with disguises and self-consciously assumed theatrical roles might suggest. After having run off from his father's London home and gone to sea, John Harmon returns some fourteen years later to claim his father's fortune. Old Harmon, the dust contractor, has left it to his son on condition that he marry Bella Wilfer, now a young woman of not yet twenty, whom the old man has apparently chosen for his son because she has been an extremely, even violently willful and selfish child. The younger Harmon, taking on the disguise of a seaman whom he resembles, is robbed and left for dead, afloat in the Thames. Emerging from the river and adopting two more false identities—first as Julius Handford and then as John Rokesmith—Harmon sets in motion a plot that allows Boffin, the old man's foreman and alternate heir to his fortune, to become the young Harmon's substitute father after employing him as his secretary. Both Mr. and Mrs. Boffin become Bella's surrogate parents when she is brought into their house in reparation for her loss of the potential husband who is now presumed dead, with Boffin offering to provide for her a marriage portion, a groom-price. Like Esther Lyon, who must sacrifice an estate gained through trade, Bella must be convinced to deny herself any part of the profits made from the household refuse collected in the dust heaps. Bella, who has been left to Harmon, as she accurately explains, "like a dozen of spoons," must be completely transformed into what Boffin calls her "true golden gold at heart" (45, 752). The plotting of the characters is so ornate and so apparently important to the outcome of the novel that it must, famously, dupe even its readers if it is to accomplish its goal of turning a bad and miserly father into a wholly good and generous benefactor and a bad girl into a perfectly good and self-denying mate, thus ending in the happy marriage of Bella and John, a triumphant substitute for the misery that old Harmon had apparently planned for them.

As this account suggests, *Our Mutual Friend* is the most extreme instance of the nexus of values toward which the osmology of high-Victorian fiction points because it strives to be the most fully literalized enactment of it. The premium placed on the reformulated gentility acted out in Harmon's story is evident, for example, in the way in which Eugene Wrayburn is physically beaten, his arms broken and his body crushed, into a chastised and presumably hard-working, self-denying manhood. The excesses of Dickens's last completed novel result from its drive to materialize—to represent as substantive—both anxieties about respectable manliness and the concomitant fantasy of salvation through the possession of a woman's body as the bearer of property and the site of reproduction.[3] In treating the novel as a materialized depiction of a vitiated manhood and of the fulfillments it seeks, I try to take seriously the terms in which the novel proposes to understand the dilemmas and solutions that it provides, not objecting more often than I can help to the cloying sentimentality with which it surrounds its central female character, Bella Wilfer, and the sheer mindlessness with which it comes to endow her. In *Our Mutual Friend*, even more than in other fictions of the 1860s, excessive literalization is often confirmed and countered by excessive idealization, whose power to serve important cultural purposes should not be overlooked (cf. Kucich, *Repression* 226–27). When John and Bella reveal their love for each other, the narrator reports obsessively on her disappearances into his embrace: first, she "seem[s] to shrink to next to nothing in the clasp of his arms" (592); later on, she simply is "vanishing" in one "disappearance" after another (593, 595, 596), as she does again repeatedly on wedding John (652, 655). Although this device grows old quickly, perhaps as early as its first repetition, Dickens here is rendering in physical terms the effects of the doctrine of *coverture*. As a married woman, Bella's legal identity is subsumed in her husband's status as a person. The supposedly delightful cuteness with which Bella acts out her own erasure strains to make attractive what might be seen as an uncomfortable outcome to her story. Understanding the point of this scene and gauging the full extent of Bella's significance in *Our Mutual Friend* depend on recognizing how the osmology of high-Victorian fiction both grants her positive values and acknowledges their limitations.

Expurgating the Smell of Trade

In telling the entangled stories of *Our Mutual Friend*, Dickens invokes the conventions of the osmology that I have identified, and he also extends the implications of its discriminations. As they are in so many novels of the 1860s, trade and those involved in it are marked in *Our Mutual Friend* by smells, principally those associated with Venus's shop and "the drug-flavoured region of Mincing Lane," where Veneering's firm has its counting house, a neighborhood that makes Bella feel on a visit to it "the sensation of having just opened a drawer in a chemist's shop" (589). Significantly, Bella is also the character who imagines that trading with China must involve dealing in "odd-smelling silks" as well as tea and rice and "tight-eyed people . . . painted on transparent porcelain" (665). In relation to trade in *Our Mutual Friend*, Bella is the unmarked agent sensitive to the olfactory evidence of its materiality, just as she is the character forced to undergo a series of unsettling encounters with men beneath her status—a police inspector, a ship's steward and his mate—so that she can prove her faith in her husband's innocence. As in both *Salem Chapel* and *Felix Holt*, business, including the business of Society that is based on profits from trade, seems to depend on eating and drinking, activities particularly evident at the perpetual dinners given by the Veneerings. Once again smells give away the game. The Veneerings, "bran-new people in a bran-new house in a bran-new quarter of London" (17), are trying to rise above trade on the fabulous profits of Chicksey, Veneering, and Stobbles. Yet the telltale odors given off by both the Veneerings's furniture and their food reveal that they still have far to rise: "the surface smelt a little too much of the workshop" (17), and their meals become aerated into "mutton vapour-bath" flavored with sweets and coffee (134), "volatilized," as Alexander Bain would say (158), into an odor in which the guests arriving after dinner have a chance merely to swim. Like the magenta paint used to adorn the retail store in *The Struggles of Brown, Jones, and Robinson* or the warm meat in a butcher's shop in *Eleanor's Victory*, items related to buying and selling mark those associated with them as the inferiors of those who perceive their odors.

In more lowly settings, however, food and drink give off the aromas of comfort, as Wegg's grudging response to the odor of Venus's punch testifies. Like this "comfortable" smell, the "fragrant" odors of Fledgeby's coffee and Venus's tea (419, 491) identify drinks enjoyed by characters marked by their involvement in questionable trades, the first in "queer" bills, the second in body parts; but they also stand as emblems for the gustatory pleasures of the plenty enjoyed by those below the genteel middle classes, Fledgeby's apparent social acceptability notwithstanding. Other examples make the same point. Harmon's payment of his rent to the Wilfers provides the family with an unusually hearty meal, after which Rumpty Wilfer enjoys a rum whose "perfume . . . diffuse[s] itself throughout the room" (50). Similarly, although Wrayburn and Lightwood have a kitchen in their chambers, they never intend to have food cooked there, but the burned sherry that they drink while slumming at the Six Jolly Fellowship-Porters "steam[s] forth a delicious perfume" (163). Wegg is brought on stage for another olfactory demonstration of this point when he calls on the Boffins, newly enriched by the Harmon fortune. The couple has divided the sitting room into two realms, one for "Fashion" and the other for "Comfort," one furnished with "expensive articles of drawing-room furniture" and the other outfitted like an "amateur tap-room" (62–63). The proof that Comfort wins this contest is Boffin's open display of the food that will make his visitor feel at home. Acting like the stereotypical fat tradesman that he is, Boffin asks Wegg to name the comestibles that he wants to consume as if he were a customer at an inn, and Wegg pretends to sniff out an apple pie: "*Have* I lost my smell for fruits, or is it a apple pie, sir?" (65). This ruse allows him to hint at what he actually wants, the meat pie in plain sight. Dickens grants another lower-class character similarly acute olfactory capacities. When Betty Higden is wandering toward her death and looking into the shops that she passes, she wonders "whether their masters and mistresses taking tea in a perspective of back-parlour—

not so far within but that the flavour of tea and toast came out, mingled with the glow of light, into the street—ate or drank or wore what they sold, with the greater relish because they dealt in it" (497). This unconventional attribution of a positive olfactory response to a character at the bottom of the social scale in *Our Mutual Friend* simply makes the point conveyed by similar references in novels like *Salem Chapel* and *Felix Holt*: not merely comfortable, trade is the realm of substance, a removal from which threatens existence itself.

Although these olfactory images confirm what one would expect from a novel of the 1860s in so far as its osmology conveys both the conventional high-Victorian distaste for trade and a covert recognition of its substantial values, they do not identify two distinctive qualities of *Our Mutual Friend*: first, its ambivalent rejection, not only of the distribution but also of the manufacture of products from raw materials; and second, its impulse to turn the refuse of old commodities into a literal estate, an inheritance of a mansion and the funds sufficient to support it, possessions that guarantee the genteel status of a middle-class man.

More insistently than in other novels of the decade, there are in *Our Mutual Friend* no smells of things being manufactured. The drugs that Bella perceives as odors mark a counting house, not a factory. In a novel that began publication only a year after the worst of the widely publicized crises of the Cotton Famine, Dickens seems to be imagining a world in which not only industrial manufacture but also artisanal forms of production have come to a similar halt. The workers of *Our Mutual Friend* are, rather, those who trade in every conceivable kind of commodity—from dolls and soggy gingerbread and shares to orphans and marriage partners and amputated limbs. The only characters who make anything at all in the novel are Venus and Jenny Wren, both of whom fashion their creations from the scraps and detritus of previous acts of, respectively, procreation and manufacture.[4] Lizzie Hexam, the character who might be expected to work with her hands, never does so except when she is seen rowing on the river or sewing in her father's house. Later, when she works for a "seaman's outfitter," she oversees his stock-room (222). Even later in the plot, when she ends up at a paper mill, whose notoriously noisome processes are presented unaccountably as issuing in a "sweet, fresh, empty store-room" (508; cf. David 82–84), she again supervises the work of others: having quickly risen to a "place of confidence" at the mill, she notes that her hands, "which were coarse, and cracked, and hard, and brown when [she] rowed on the river with her father," have been "softened and made supple by this new work" (509, 519). Part of the studied unreality of *Our Mutual Friend* inheres in the fact that no one in its world needs to make anything from scratch, perhaps not even its author, who, in what Henry James called the "intensely written" qualities of this "manufacture of fiction," is recycling old stories and revisiting old wounds.[5] Commodities can make identities, and they have done so in the case of Mr. Boots and Mr. Brewer. As Mayhew explains, men, according to a practice "common in all mechanical or commercial callings," are known by the things they make or sell: thus, one of Mayhew's informants says of another, "Oh, yes, I know him—he's a sweet stuff" (1: 158). But commodities serve this purpose in the novel because they are already made, already in circulation by the time that its action begins.

Our Mutual Friend eradicates production by not representing its characteristic smells, and in that sense the novel shares with most of the other instances of high-Victorian fiction that I have surveyed the impulse to banish smells from its narrative territory. Like *Salem Chapel* and *Felix Holt*, *Our Mutual Friend* presents fewer and fewer smells as the story progresses, with three times as many references to odors in its first half as in its second. Yet in more specific and more unconventional terms, the novel turns its nose from the obviously unpleasant. The fantastic features of the osmology of *Our Mutual Friend* accomplish this end in two ways—by creating imaginary smells and by ignoring obvious odorants.

Chief among the former scents are those of the flowers that Jenny Wren perceives as she works to turn scraps of fabric and straw into fashionable dolls. Jenny describes her fanciful olfactory sensations in the presence of Eugene Wrayburn; and that "commonplace individual," as he calls himself, responds in a commonsensical fashion, "you smell flowers because you *do* smell flowers." Jenny counters by explaining that hers is not a "flowery neighbourhood": "It is anything but that. And yet as I sit at work, I smell miles of flowers. I smell roses, till I think I see the rose-leaves lying in heaps, bushels, on the floor. I smell fallen leaves, till I put down my hand—so—and expect to make them rustle. I smell the white and pink May in the hedges, and all sorts of flowers that I was never among. For I have seen very few flowers indeed, in my life" (237–38). Imagined olfaction is so unusually powerful here that it creates sense impressions in other modalities, sight and touch. In view of the belief held by Victorian psychophysiologists that the idea of a smell may create an actual physical sensation, however, this passage is less remarkable than it might at first seem. Jenny is here simply experiencing an elaborate form of mentally induced sensory impressions called "suggested feelings" by Grant Allen and "sensory representations" by Henry Maudsley. Similarly, when Rose in *Evan Harrington* returns by sea to her homeland, she declares, "I smell England" long before she sees its shores (27).

Jenny's ability to smell flowers when they are not present is typical in other ways. Like her fiction about the "him" who is coming to rescue her from poverty and loneliness, her investment in olfactory experience marks her, like Maggie Tulliver, as an unlikely candidate for marriage, Sloppy's waiting in the wings for her at the end of the novel notwithstanding. More important, the aroma of flowers comes to Jenny when she is at work, as her visions of angelic children attend her when she is in pain. According to both Victorian science and high-Victorian fiction, smell is the sensory modality most closely associated with labor: like a man at work smoking a cigar or a woman surrounded with the flowers that announce her potential fertility, Jenny is attended by aromas, the olfactory evidence of her work, though in her case those scents are created by her thinking of them. Her fantastically delicious perceptions also enact the typical high-Victorian disinclination to register bad smells or the material reality from which they arise. Compared to the countess's blunt assertion in *Evan Harrington* that "the shop smells!" (395), Jenny's responses to imaginary flowers attempt to turn her arduous and unending work into a pleasurable activity. Such aromas have, therefore, much the same effect as Dickens's representations of the Harmon dust heaps, the chief example of the second category of the weirdly conventional smells of *Our Mutual Friend*, those that are not, against all expectations, perceived at all.

Mounds of refuse—as Lightwood describes their contents, "coal-dust, vegetable-dust, bone-dust, crockery dust, rough dust and sifted dust,— all manner of Dust" (24)—the dust heaps never smell.[6] Unlike the river Thames, which is once represented as having an "ill-savoured tide" and near which accumulates the "scum of humanity . . . like so much moral sewage" (33, 30), the dust heaps are simply inodorous. No one who comes into contact with the mounds is ever represented as responding to them as if they might provide olfactory offense—not Rokesmith, Venus, Wegg, Boffin, or the narrator. In Boffin's case, that fact might certainly be explained by the physiological process of adaptation, which was well understood by both Victorian scientists and other, less learned contemporary commentators. Like the workers in Mayhew's *London Labour and the London Poor*, men who are "all used to the smell and don't complain about it" (2: 175), Boffin has spent his life among the dust heaps, and he therefore does not notice the odor of the refuse whose collection and sifting he has overseen and next to which he has also lived. According to one of the dustmen interviewed by Mayhew, "The smells nothink at all, ven you gits used to it. Lor' bless you! you'd think nothink on it in a week's time,—no, no more nor I do" (2: 178). But such testimony will not suffice to explain the cases of Venus and Rokesmith, the former of whom visits the dust mounds only occasionally, the latter of whom has been long distant from them. These characters are, in the lack of their previous or recent exposure to such odorants, more in the position of Mayhew than in that of his informants; and Mayhew bluntly recognizes the "stench of the dust-heap" and the "effluvia most offensive" that such a site exhales (2: 175). In placing much of the action of the novel at the mounds, Dickens deals with a materiality that in a novel of the 1840s would give off the rank odor of decay, if not death. Yet in a manner typical of the 1860s, garbage causes no olfactory discomfort.

Even that negative representation, however, cannot match in its daring unlikelihood the flight of fancy in which Boffin engages as he conjures up the pleasures offered by the dust yard, pleasures equal to those provided by Jenny's imaginary flowers. He expatiates on such delights for the benefit of Wegg, whom he has just employed to read to him of an evening at the "Bower," the renamed Harmony Jail where the dust heaps are located, and who has offered to recite poetry occasionally as a friendly gift to his new patron. As Boffin tells Wegg, "This is a charming spot, is the Bower. . . . There's a serpentining walk up each of the mounds, that gives you the yard and neighbourhood changing every moment. When you get to the top, there's a view of the neighbouring premises, not to be surpassed. . . . And the top of the High Mound is crowned with a lattice-work Arbour, in which, if you don't read out loud many a book in the summer, ay, and as a friend, drop into poetry too, it shan't be my fault" (64). The pleasure that Boffin attributes to sitting on a dust heap, particularly during the summer when the heat of the day would no doubt activate the decay of any organic matter in it, simply emphasizes how thoroughly these piles of refuse have been sifted and withdrawn from the smelly arenas of manufacture. Only in the endnotes to recent editions of *Our Mutual Friend* do the mounds figure in the work that would turn them into raw material for new forms of production,[7] as Mayhew also specifies, for use as agricultural landfill or in the creation of bricks (2: 170).

The dust heaps in *Our Mutual Friend* are anomalous in other ways. Unlike contemporary depictions of dust mounds, Dickens's verbal image of the heaps includes no workers, no women and children sifting through the debris that old Harmon has gathered, no men bringing in new supplies of refuse. Both the text describing and the illustration depicting a dust yard in Mayhew's *London Labour and the London Poor* swarm with activity:

> The whole yard seems alive, some sifting and others shovelling the sifted soil on to the heap, while every now and then the dustcarts return to discharge their loads, and proceed again on their rounds for a fresh supply. Cocks and hens keep up a continual scratching and cackling among the heaps, and numerous pigs seem to find great delight in rooting incessantly about after the garbage and offal collected from the houses and markets. (2: 171; cf. illustration facing 2: 173)

The drawings and text from the *Penny Illustrated Paper* of 1866 and from the *Illustrated London News* of 1873 similarly emphasize the numbers of workers present in dust yards "alive" with activity.[8] Marcus Stone's typically inept drawing in the illustrations of *Our Mutual Friend* actually works well to make Dickens's point when it comes to the mounds.[9] Stone's literally flat rendering of the Harmon dust heaps, with Boffin standing at night on the top of one of the mounds as Wegg and Venus look on, corresponds nicely to Dickens's verbal depiction of their inactivity. The mounds present, as Catherine Gallagher notes, "an image of peculiar fixity," which "de-emphasizes the circulation of debris in the dust trade," serving instead as a kind of "self-burying" or grave for old Harmon's miserly accumulation of refuse ("Bioeconomics" 55). The dust heaps stand idle, as if their value could not decrease; as Boffin tells John Rokesmith, they "take no harm by standing where they do" (186).

Boffin's homely pride in the delights of the dust heaps is, of course, a comic revelation of his limitations, but his treatment of mounds as if they were a country estate to which he is introducing a genteel tourist foretells what will happen to them in the course of the novel and what to a large extent has already happened: they become real estate. In *Our Mutual Friend*, fantastically, such property requires no work, not even supervision, as Lightwood explains to Boffin when he is thought to have inherited the Harmon wealth: "And what is particularly eligible in the property Mr. Boffin, is, that it involves no trouble. There are no estates to manage, no rents to return so much per cent. upon in bad times . . . no voters to become parboiled in hot water with, no agents to take the cream off the milk before it comes to table. You could put the whole in a cash-box to-morrow morning, and take it with you to—say, to the Rocky Mountains" (94). Old Harmon has left at death a substantial fortune—to how many millions would his £100,000 now be equivalent?—but the dust heaps are a physical embodiment of only a small portion of that wealth. As Mayhew explains in *London Labour and the London Poor*, the income earned by dust contractors came principally by the early 1850s from arrangements with parishes for the removal of household debris, not from the sale of the rubbish itself, although twenty-five years before that time, when old Harmon was presumably making his fortune, the sale of refuse was so lucrative that dust contractors paid parishes for the privilege of carting it away instead of being paid by them to do so (2: 167, 173).[10] That the dust heaps of *Our Mutual Friend* never give off the least unpleasant odor suggests that by the opening of the novel, they have already begun the transformation that they will undergo from the detritus of commodities into money, the most cleanly form of commerce, and then into property, trade's antithesis.

As Eve Kosofsky Sedgwick has explained, the critics who find in Dickens's treatment of the dust heaps a simple moral lesson about the filthiness of lucre underestimate the complexities of *Our Mutual Friend*.[11] Dickens seems to be offering in his depiction of the mounds a literalized version of the point that Marx makes in the first volume of *Capital* when he recalls the reply of the Roman emperor chided for taxing public toilets, "*Non olet*"—money "has no smell" (205). Trollope, who liked to compare the work of the novelist to that of a shoemaker or pastry-cook, was particularly fond of this saying since it distinguishes between odorous labors and their inodorate effect as cash. In both *Can You Forgive Her?* and *He Knew He Was Right*, the narrator cites the concept when dealing with the profits of frankly smelly work. Cheesacre, the wealthy farmer of the first Palliser novel, is a "man of substance" whose "heaps of manure" and "muck" are ironically cast as inoffensive because, as one character notes, "money's never dirty . . . nor yet what makes money" (*Can* 1: 139–40). Similarly, the appropriately if cruelly named Mr. Outhouse, a London clergymen serving the poor in a parish in the East End, mutters "*Non olet*" to himself as he accepts the annual charitable donation of the owners of a "large commercial establishment for turning the carcasses of horses into manure," the inescapably noisome effects of which Mr. Outhouse finds "less objectionable" only with time and adaptation (*He Knew* 246). Even more pertinent here is Marx's formulation that, although commodities may smell, they are material forms waiting to be cashed in as money, and they are therefore always already inodorous: "The capitalist knows that all commodities, however tattered they may look, or however badly they may smell, are in faith and in truth money, are by nature circumcised Jews, and, what is more, a wonderful means of making still more money out of money" (256). If even the positive stereotypes of Jews in *Our Mutual Friend* conform to the casual slur in this passage from *Capital*, if both texts confirm the osmology that conveys the values of high-Victorian culture, Dickens's novel parts company with Marx's analysis by declining to see money as capital, as, like usury, a means of making more money from money. There are no "valuables" to be found in the heaps of *Our Mutual Friend* as they are carted off at the end of the story. The dust has already been "coined . . . into money" by the "hard old jailer of Harmony Jail." Significantly, the "purchasers of the Mounds" are inexplicably other "dust contractors," not farmers or manufacturers (759)—as if to imply that the mounds will stand idle again, as they have at Harmony Jail, once they have been moved to the yards of other dustmen.

More important than any use to which the mounds might or might not be put, therefore, is the fact that they are cleared away to prepare for the life of leisure that John Harmon and his bride Bella take up as they, magically on the same day that the last heap disappears from the Bower, join Mr. and Mrs. Boffin in the "Eminently Aristocratic Mansion," as the advertising hype has it, that Boffin has previously purchased with old Harmon's fortune (182, 194). Like Dickens himself, bent on owning Gad's Hill Place, Harmon comes to inhabit a gentlemanly residence. He has remarked earlier, when he has planned to give up to the Boffins his title to his father's estate, that he is turning it into "a machine in such working order" that even they will be able to "keep it going" (367). Long before his entry into the supposedly carefree leisure that he himself has made possible, however, John Harmon is associated with the ownership of property rather than with trade when Lightwood introduces him as a "small proprietor, farmer, grower—whatever you like to call it" (25), the *whatever* being here limited to forms of land-owning and agricultural production. Similarly, the narrator explains that Harmon is returning to London with more than £700, the proceeds from the "forced sale of his little landed property" (39). The profits of his "little" estate at the Cape are lost to prepare the way for his gain of the much greater "HARMON ES-TATE," as it is designated on the iron box in Lightwood's office (93). Dickens seems to be proposing that residence in a large house near Cavendish Square in the West End of London constitutes membership in a kind of urban gentry, even if the mansion in question is a "great dingy house" comparable in its gloom only to Harmony Jail itself (53, 184).[12]

Coined into money that does not smell, therefore, the dust heaps contribute to Harmon's eventual homeownership, a status that points to and further confuses the class positions in the novel in ways that, in Williams's terms, "promote superficial comparisons and . . . prevent real ones" (*Country* 54). Outright purchase of a home, like Wemmick's possession of his castle, was relatively rare in the mid-Victorian period: perhaps only 10% of the population, almost all of whom were members of "the upper working classes," were owner-occupiers (F. M. L. Thompson, *Rise* 168). The oddity of Harmon's ownership of his house stresses the extent to which his status at the end of the novel is dependent on Boffin's early decisions about how to spend the Harmon wealth. Harmon's position is thus as anomalous as the cleanliness of the dust heaps. Because he inhabits a house for which and in which he does not have to work, he becomes the social superior not only of Podsnap and Veneering but also of the proprietor of Gad's Hill. Yet to achieve this status, Harmon must tacitly accept Boffin's characteristically working-class notion of owning one's home as a form of self-respecting independence.[13]

Through such evasions and indirections, *Our Mutual Friend* works hard to make John Harmon the unmarked social superior of its plot. As such a figure, he is not smelled by any of its other characters, but he also fails to fulfill the requirements of his role as their superior because he does not smell any of them. Harmon is not, after all, either Wrayburn or Lightwood, gentlemen born and bred, whose olfactory sensitivities occasion the only visual representation of a smell that I know of in the illustrated fiction of the 1860s, the engraving of Wrayburn holding out pastilles to fumigate Mr. Dolls (fig. 4.1). Harmon explains that he has "through a series of strange fatalities, faded out of [his] place in life" (513), but the man who has been raised for the first seven years of his life next to dust mounds has no place out of which to "fade." Yet John Harmon acts as if his dip in the "unsavoury" waters of the Thames has cleansed him of any association with his childhood as a dust contractor's son. When Boffin first encounters Harmon in Fleet Street, the narrator calls the would-be secretary "a man of genteel appearance" (99). When he becomes Boffin's employee, the narrator sardonically describes as "wonderful" the "swiftness with which the lodger had lost caste in the Secretary" (207). More Boffin's equal than either the narrator or he will acknowledge, however, Harmon indulges in the fantasy of having

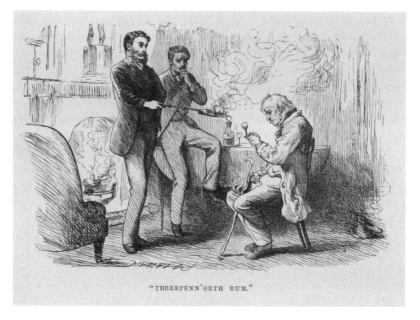

"THREEPENN'ORTH RUM."

Fig. 4.1 Odors made visible. *Our Mutual Friend*, no. 13 (May 1865). Courtesy of the Beinecke Rare Book and Manuscript Library, Yale University.

a status that he can lose. To a great extent, I argue, that status is dependent on his identification as a melancholic.

Wealth as Property, Wife as Mother

Throughout the action of *Our Mutual Friend*, Harmon is a "living-dead man" (367), the high-Victorian melancholic par excellence. His first words in the novel are "I am lost!" (32). When he is introduced to the Wilfers, he appears as a "dark gentleman," handsome, but "in the last degree constrained, reserved, diffident, troubled" (46). He exists under a "nameless cloud," harboring a secret that may involve his having been imprisoned or having committed murder (193). The chapter called "A Solo and a Duett" is given over to explaining the "shrinking" and "mistrust" that he feels even before he has been presumed drowned. As Harmon tells himself, "I came back [to England], timid, divided in my mind, afraid of myself and everybody here, knowing of nothing but wretchedness that my father's wealth had ever brought about" (360). After being caught up in a plot that steals from him almost all his money, he also, like Pip in his fever, loses all sense of his own identity: "There was no such thing as I, within my knowledge" (363). Self-

divided, doubting, and insubstantial, Harmon in Hamlet-like fashion acts
out the "longing for disembodied discursivity" that Paul Morrison defines
as central to nineteenth-century fictional characterization. A "Ghost,"
Harmon serves as Boffin's "haunting Secretary" (207), managing papers with
exemplary skill and living in a room that expresses a version of discursivity
so extreme that it includes written proof of his own death: "There were
shelves and shelves of books . . . and in a portfolio on the writing-table there
were sheets upon sheets of memoranda and calculations in figures, evidently
referring to the Boffin property," and "carefully backed with canvas, var-
nished, mounted, and rolled like a map, . . . the placard descriptive of the
murdered man" (446). Classically melancholic, Harmon wanders from place
to place between his lodgings at the Wilfers and the Boffins's two residences,
uncertain of what he will do in the future, awaiting contingencies to determine his fate. The images that dominate his memories of the attack upon
him—"a wall, a dark doorway, a flight of stairs, and a room" (359)—are
symptoms of both hyperaesthesia and anaesthesia: Harmon cannot escape
their haunting presence in his mind, but they are insufficient to explain what
has happened to him. Like Evan Harrington, the diplomatic attaché, Harmon
is identified by his writing and his speech—as Wegg puts it, Harmon, alias
Rokesmith, is "the talking-over stranger" (302).

    The source of Harmon's melancholia, at least according to him, is nei-
ther overwork nor occupational worry, the chief causes identified by alienists in the 1860s, even though the novel purports to tell a story of the early
years of that decade. Rather, the fear and sadness without cause traditionally associated with melancholia are given sources here in domestic and erotic
losses, the results of the family "disagreements and misfortunes" to whose
untoward effects the disguised Harmon alludes in explaining his reticence
to the curious Inspector (34). More specifically, however, Harmon, like Evan
and Pip and Felix, is fleeing the family business. Harmon's childhood unhappiness, like his later attachment to Bella, serves as a blind for the more
directly economic concerns that might, but do not apparently, motivate him.
Lightwood, in recounting Harmon's childhood, makes much of the mean-
ness and cruelty of his "anathematizing" father, who has cursed and expelled
from the Harmony Jail first his wife, then his daughter, then finally his son
John, the third of these expulsions having occurred when John has ques-
tioned his father's treatment of his sister, whom his father has rejected because she will not marry the mate of his choice. When Lightwood says that
this arranged marriage would "make Dust of her heart and Dust of her life—
in short, would set her up, on a very extensive scale, in her father's business" (24), he hints that her father has tried to force her to marry into the
family of another dust contractor. At fourteen, returning from the cheap
school in Brussels where he has been sent, John has confronted his father
and challenged his determination to bend his daughter to his will, his desire

presumably to sell her in marriage. Differing little from the kind of rejection with which Charley Hexam treats his obviously disreputable father, John Harmon's departure from England is a judgment rendered against old Harmon; and as Gaffer Hexam recognizes, Charley's self-exile from his house brands him a "man as ain't good enough for his own son" (81). John Harmon, however, remains untainted by any suspicion that he has engaged in the kind of social climbing that convicts Charley of self-serving ingratitude. Harmon's flight from his father and, more to the point, from his father's trade occurs in the service of a sister and not, as Charley's does, in the betrayal of one.

Tellingly and typically, Harmon, like the culture whose values he epitomizes, can both reject trade and profit from it. The byzantine intricacies of the plot of *Our Mutual Friend*, comparable to Pip's schemes to establish Herbert in business, are calculated to release Harmon from his melancholia by granting him his father's wealth once it is cleansed of its taint, but those intricacies can easily obscure the fact that the central cleansing agent in this story is not Boffin, but Bella Wilfer. Not possessing his father's property but still managing it, Harmon vows in the second book of the novel, "John Harmon shall come back no more" (367). Yet even after Bella scornfully rejects his first proposal, he remains on the scene, passively leaving open the option of declaring himself alive so that he can collect his legacy. But he cannot do so while Bella remains an object dispensed to him by his father's will. If he married her in accordance with the terms of that will, he would become like Harold Transome in *Felix Holt* in his relation to his Turkish wife; as Harmon reflects, "I should have purchased her . . . as a Sultan buys a slave" (367). After all the complicated play with the old Harmon's three wills—the last of which is finally abrogated by Boffin's insistence on giving the bulk of the estate to John Harmon—it is Bella's love for John that gives him a reason to come back from the dead and claim his inheritance.[14] If Harmon, under the guise of Rokesmith, had not proposed prematurely to Bella, Mrs. Boffin would not have recognized him. Until that moment, as Mrs. Boffin explains, he "had fully meant never to come to life, but to leave the property as our wrongful inheritance for ever and a day" (752). Moreover, the failed proposal moves Boffin to invent his "pious fraud," his adoption of the miser's role to test the extent of Bella's desire for wealth (751). Yet Bella's turning into "true golden gold" is a necessary but not sufficient cause for the happy outcome of the story. Not even love is enough to transform dust heaps into property. If Harmon has prematurely sought to "possess [Bella's] heart"—to which Boffin scoffingly responds with his famous "Mew, Quack-quack, Bow-wow!" (583)—such affective ownership is not ownership enough to make Harmon, in Boffin's words, a "man of property" who knows "the duties of property" (457).

That transformation can occur only when Bella becomes a mother. This point explains one of the critical puzzles of *Our Mutual Friend*: Why does

Harmon wait until long after they are married to reveal to Bella, who has repeatedly proved her devotion to and trust in him, that he is the man whom his father's first will intends her to marry?[15] Harmon hesitates, of course, because, like Hamlet, he doubts. Yet Harmon also hesitates because he can, because his possession of Bella is absolute, because in Simmel's terms she is "an unconditionally complying object" (qtd. Nunokawa 77). The way in which Harmon expresses his indecision is telling: over and over he has told the Boffins, "I can't afford to be rich yet. I must wait a little longer" (753). What groom-price is it that Bella has still to offer him even though they are already married? The answer is simple: a child. The conclusion to the revelation scene in Book the Fourth, Chapter XIII makes the point explicitly: John has, through Mrs. Boffin's narration of his story, revealed his identity as Harmon, not Rokesmith. As an antidote to the shock of that revelation, the baby-Bella, "the Inexhaustible," has been placed on her mother's lap (735, 757); and Bella has then been shown the house that old Harmon's money has bought. The final illustration featuring Bella in the novel (fig. 4.2)—whose subject Marcus Stone chose, though Dickens supplied the caption (*Letters* 11: 87, 88, 95)—offers a visual impression of the scene that Mr. and Mrs. Boffin see when Bella retires to the nursery to breast-feed her crying child:

> "Come and look in, Noddy!" said Mrs. Boffin to Mr. Boffin.
>
> Mr. Boffin, submitting to be led on tiptoe to the nursery door, looked in with immense satisfaction, although there was nothing to see but Bella in a musing state of happiness, seated in a little low chair upon the hearth, with her child in her fair young arms, and her soft eyelashes shading her eyes from the fire.
>
> "It looks as if the old man's spirit had found rest at last; don't it?" said Mrs. Boffin.
>
> "Yes, old lady."
>
> "And as if his money had turned bright again, after a long long rust in the dark, and was at last a beginning to sparkle in the sunlight?"
>
> "Yes, old lady."
>
> "And it makes a pretty and a promising picter; don't it?"
>
> "Yes, old lady." (757)

Boffin subsequently puts in the last word here, punctuating the cloying submissiveness of his repeated affirmatives with a final ambiguous "Mew, Quack quack, Bow-wow!" (759). Yet the image of Bella mindlessly abstracted in the physicality of suckling her child in the house where she and John and their surrogate parents, Mr. and Mrs. Boffin, will live together does bring to full circle the story of an angry father who could not make his daughter do his bidding.

MR. BOFFIN DOES THE HONOURS OF THE NURSERY DOOR.

Fig. 4.2 Bella dispensing her substance. *Our Mutual Friend*, nos. 19 and 20 (November 1865). Courtesy of the Beinecke Rare Book and Manuscript Library, Yale University.

Yet if Old Harmon has envisioned a marriage that would bring back to Harmony Jail his wandering son, the plot of the novel, which insists on the procreative potential of his return, takes that vision to its weirdly logical extreme. "Baby," the word that Dickens twice emphasized with triple underlining in his plans for the final double number of the novel,[16] is the final resolution that Harmon's story seeks. In one sense, this child, as the embodiment of the riches that his father can now "afford," functions as conventionally as do the prospective progeny of Arthur Vincent in *Salem Chapel* or the money-bearing offspring of Rose and Evan Harrington: as the product of a female body, the baby gives substance to her male parent. Yet in a fashion equally typical of the materializations to which *Our Mutual Friend* treats such plot elements, the baby must be born so that Bella can become the sister whom Harmon has lost. Strikingly, Bella's maternity is less an opportunity for maturation on her part than an occasion for regression. In an uncomfortable parody of Jenny Wren's work, which is directly evoked in the scene in which Bella sews baby clothes during her pregnancy (724), the baby-Bella becomes a doll that her mother dresses and undresses to no obvious purpose. Bella's "cherubic father" even remarks that "the baby seemed to make [his daughter] younger than before, reminding him of the days when she had a pet doll and used to talk to it as she carried it about" (736). By transforming Bella into a prepubescent girl, her maternity turns her into a substitute for John's older sister: by being reborn in the form of another woman who is becoming younger, that sister can marry her brother and inherit the wealth that her father has unfairly denied her, and she can have the child who allows "the old man's spirit" to rest. "Among the first words" that the baby-Bella hears, in a worldly form of baptism, is a duet of her parents crooning over their affectional wealth. Her father asks, as he has done repeatedly before, "Would you not like to be rich *now*, my darling?" Her mother responds, "Am I not rich?" (735), the baby becoming the only kind of wealth that either one can afford to acknowledge.

The timing of apparently fortuitous incidents in the novel highlights the way in which Bella's role as mother explains the otherwise unaccountable delays that the plot involves. Harmon reveals his identity after he has been recognized by Lightwood, but that can happen only "two or three months" after the baby is born (736) when Bella, at the end of her period of confinement, can be seen on the streets again, meeting her husband in London after doing errands there, turning the corner where together they encounter Lightwood. This point is confirmed by an earlier chapter, the fifth in the fourth book, when Harmon is apparently ready to reveal his identity to Bella but does not do so, first because her father interrupts their conversation and then because Bella reveals, in her predictably coy fashion, that "a little baby" is coming "in a ship upon the ocean" to join them (672). Just before Bella makes this announcement, Harmon says to her, "And now I am brought to a little piece of news, my dearest, that I might have told you earlier in the evening. I have strong reason for confidently believing that we shall never be in the receipt of a smaller income than our present income" (671). That Bella forgets to ask John what his "little piece of news" might be, the fact that they have been rich throughout their idyll in a cottage at Blackheath, simply allows the plot to materialize her maternal potential, as Stone's illustration does, before they enter the Eminently Aristocratic Mansion that will be theirs. As a product, a thing already made and now out of circulation because she is married, Bella fulfills only part of her role.[17] As the product capable of reproduction, the mother of the Inexhaustible baby, her work is complete.

Yet the effect on John Harmon of Bella's treatment of his ills is not wholly positive. In *Our Mutual Friend*, it is more difficult than its plot imagines to shake off the potentially emasculating condition of melancholia.[18] Now that Bella has produced something, Harmon can afford—and this is another of those luxuries that he "cannot afford" earlier in his marriage—to produce nothing. Like Herbert and Evan, melancholics provided for by others, Harmon becomes another of Mayhew's unproductive men because he makes nothing. He is not even what Mayhew calls an "auxiliary" worker. Before John reveals his identity to Bella, throughout the time that they have been married and become parents, he has been going off each day to work in the City, where he is "'in a China house'" (665), a phrase put in quotation marks to emphasize its status as a fiction since John is going, not to the City, but to the Boffins's mansion near Cavendish Square to manage his own money. When he tells Bella that "the China house is broken up and abolished" (746), he is putting an end to an occupation that has never existed. Moreover, during this time he suffers from the particular form of melancholia that some mad-doctors of the 1860s identified as monomania. Having supposedly given up money, he can talk of nothing else. As Bella recognizes, Harmon is always "still harping on that notion of their being rich" (736). Even more tellingly, as one might expect from the tendency of *Our Mutual Friend* to render as material whatever conditions it depicts, Bella, who is the "bright light" of the cottage that she has shared with John (667), is also able to make "light" of her husband in a literal fashion. The man who is first introduced as "extremely pale" and who becomes "white," as Bella says, with his longing for her is, at the end of the novel, a kind of Cheshire cat. The only expression that his face can convey is the "radiant look" of "kindling triumph" that it repeatedly reveals as Bella successfully passes one test after another to prove her "perfect faith" in him (512, 740, 739). As Brian Cheadle aptly notes when discussing Harmon's relation to work, the character is "unappealingly colourless" ("Work" 328), a quality that Dickens renders in uncompromisingly physical terms.

The work that John Harmon does do in the final book of the novel further unmans him. Asking Bella what kind of house she imagines for herself and her child, he becomes an interior decorator, a role that for nonprofessionals in Victorian culture was gendered distinctively female.[19] Harmon manages to materialize Bella's desires in a magical single day between her expression of them and their satisfaction: he provides the house with a rainbow-colored nursery, a staircase adorned with flowers, which oddly recalls Jenny Wren's fantasy of "long bright slanting rows" of white-chad children lifting her up to be made "light" (238), an aviary full of tropical birds, and a dressing room with an ivory casket filled with precious gems. In the house that he has "tastefully ornamented" for Bella (748), John does the only work of which he seems capable when she turns to him and says, "John dear . . . you're a good nurse; will you please hold baby?" (754). Like the two Keiths of *The Clever Woman of the Family*, John in his role as husband displays ladylike tastes and abilities: he reincarnates Colin Keith, who redecorates a house for Ermine when he spreads throughout it the souvenirs that he has been gathering for the twelve previous years of his military career; and like Alick Keith, whose year of invalidism has made him the best nurse whom wife or ailing kinsman could require, John is good with babies. Venus complains that he has been a "haggard melancholy man" since his first meeting with the woman he hopelessly loves, the desire for whom has permanently unmanned him: "I have never since been the man I was. My very bones is rendered flabby by brooding over it" (85, 492). Yet Harmon's requited love has a similar effect.

Along with Venus, the characters in *Our Mutual Friend* consistently associated with the word *melancholy* are Twemlow, Eugene, and Mortimer. Eugene even finds "lugubrious" the "little old song" that declares, "Away with melancholy" (292). Wrayburn and Lightwood, the genteel idlers who lounge about their chambers and talk and accomplish nothing, are reminiscent of Pip and Herbert, unproductive men made guilty and miserable by their inactivity. Even when Wrayburn and Lightwood move to new digs, any suggestion that they might be getting down to work is unacceptable, the fresh paint on their door smelling too much like trade (281). Marriage seems to hold out the only hope for curing their sadness without cause, as Boffin notes when he says of his mate, "I should go melancholy mad without Mrs. Boffin" (63). Yet Twemlow and Mortimer remain unmarried, finding ease from their conditions in gumption and work, respectively. Playing with class positions as it characteristically does, the novel grants Venus the title of melancholic and then offers him substance, literally fat on his bones, when a woman agrees to be his wife. Like the hero of *Framley Parsonage*, who profits from the transformation of the sweet "aroma" of his fiancée's virginity into the "solid comfort" of his wife (522), Venus is made solid by the prospect of wedded bliss. Harmon, however, even after his marriage keeps his place in the ranks of the melancholic, as he fades into contented uxoriousness at the end of the novel.

The Worker's Hand

Harmon, however, unlike Felix and Harold and Evan, does not fade away without a fight—or not, at least, without a final exchange that allows him to enact the values that his culture, like the novel in which he appears, often attempts to obscure. Before coming to dispense the sums of money that he gives away in the penultimate chapter of the novel—remarkably like the baby-Bella, Harmon's funds are "Inexhaustible"—he deals with Wegg. In "Checkmate to the Friendly Move," the chapter that follows the depiction of Bella as a nursing mother, after the scene in which Venus treats Wegg to cobblers' punch, the two men visit Boffin in what has become John Harmon's mansion. There the former street-seller, who has now been installed as reader and resident overseer at the Bower, expects to collect the blackmail from Boffin that will keep him quiet about the Harmon will that apparently turns the entire fortune over to the state. Venus quickly reveals what even the reader has not been allowed to know. Far from aiding Wegg in their "friendly move," the "trick" (*OED*) that they have planned to play on Boffin, Venus has joined a counterconspiracy against Wegg, who remains unfazed by this revelation. Even before this point in the scene, however, Wegg should know that his comparative encounter with the inhabitants of the Eminently Aristocratic Mansion will undermine his supposed superiority to them. Refusing to call Boffin "Mr." and sitting down in the dustman's presence with his hat on, Wegg is given a lesson in due deference: "Mr. Wegg instantly underwent the remarkable experience of having his hat twitched off his head and thrown out of a window, which was opened and shut for the purpose" (764). Only in the next paragraph is Harmon identified as "the owner of the hand which had done this" (764), an impersonalizing rhetoric reminiscent of the "hands" of *Hard Times*, workers reduced to appendages capable of labor. Harmon has finally found the work to which he is ready to turn his hand.

As this scene goes on—and it does go on and on—the violence of which the grasp of that hand is capable increases as Harmon's denunciations of Wegg mount. Harmon explains the murderous desires that the very sight of Wegg arouses in him, specifically in terms of the last will that his father had drawn, which has been found earlier in a Dutch bottle:

> . . . to his boundless amazement, [Wegg] found himself gripped by
> the cravat, shaken until his teeth chattered; shoved back, staggering,
> into a corner of the room; and pinned there.

"You scoundrel!" said John Harmon, whose seafaring hold was like that of a vice.

"You're knocking my head against the wall," urged Silas faintly.

"I mean to knock your head against the wall," returned John Harmon, suiting his action to his words, with the heartiest good will; "and I'd give a thousand pounds for leave to knock your brains out. Listen, you scoundrel, and look at that Dutch bottle. . . . That Dutch bottle, scoundrel, contained the latest will of the many wills made by my unhappy self-tormenting father. That will gives everything absolutely to my noble benefactor and yours, Mr. Boffin, excluding and reviling me, and my sister (then already dead of a broken heart), by name. . . . Consequently, the paper now rattling in your hand as I shake you—and I should like to shake the life out of you—is worth less than the rotten cork of the Dutch bottle, do you understand?" . . .

"Now, scoundrel, said John Harmon, taking another sailor-like turn on his cravat and holding [Wegg] in his corner at arms' length, "I shall make two more short speeches to you, because I hope they will torment you." (766–67)

Concluding his angry excoriation, Harmon gives a final "very ugly turn indeed on Wegg's cravat," adding "through clenched teeth, 'The wonder is . . . that I didn't try to twist your head off, and fling *that* out of window!'" (768). Sloppy, who has been adopted by the Boffins to replace the first orphan chosen to reincarnate the John Harmon whom they have thought is dead, now takes over Harmon's role in the scene. Acting "in the manner of a porter or heaver who is about to lift a sack of flour or coals," Sloppy, here gentrified as "Mr. Sloppy," approaches Wegg, who has been trying "with a melancholy air" to convince Boffin at least to give him sufficient funds to set up a new street stall. At a gesture from John Harmon, a lifted finger, Sloppy throws out the last piece of human "scum" in the novel so that it lands "with a prodigious splash" in a streetcleaner's cart (768–70). Sloppy, who in disguise has overseen the removal of the dust heaps from the Bower, here removes Wegg from circulation, at least within the precincts of the Eminently Aristocratic Mansion.

In this scene, the only one that puts in question Harmon's status as a confirmed melancholic, he reverts to his previous working-class status as a seaman by exhibiting the violence with which members of the Victorian working classes were almost invariably associated, just as Bradley Headstone reverts to form during his murderous pursuit of Wrayburn, even wearing the clothes that imitate the dress of the waterman Rogue Riderhood. Twice in this scene the narrator explicitly evokes Harmon's past as a seaman by referring to his "seafaring hold . . . like that of a vice" and the "sailor-like turn" that he gives to Wegg's cravat. Sailors during the mid-Victorian period were legendarily drunken, improvident, and profligate, and Harmon's identification as one of their number would seem odd were it not for the fact that sailors were even better known for their physical strength and dexterity, and it is on the latter qualities that this scene focuses. Seamen, taller and more robust and more agile than landlubbers, were notoriously careless and daring because of their physical prowess. Sailors in the Royal Navy, who typically also served in the merchant marine, did not at midcentury constitute a standing force of military men, about the uses of which the British public were traditionally suspicious, and they were therefore often valued as relatively unthreatening embodiments of manliness. They might have been a "rough, illiterate, muscular lot," but they were "real men."[20]

Dickens prepares for Harmon's apotheosis as a seafaring man in an earlier scene when, disguised as the sailor who has plotted to kill him, he visits the shop run by Pleasant Riderhood. Attentive to identities since she knows that sailors are easy prey, Pleasant immediately recognizes that Harmon actually is the sailor he is pretending to be:

> His manner was the manner of a sailor, and his hands were the hands of a sailor, except that they were smooth. Pleasant had an eye for sailors, and she noticed the unused colour and texture of the hands, sunburnt though they were, as sharply as she noticed their unmistakable looseness and suppleness, as he sat himself down with his left arm carelessly thrown across his left leg a little above the knee, and the right arm as carelessly thrown over the elbow of the wooden chair, with the hand curved, half open and half shut, as if it had just let go a rope. (347)

As Rosemarie Bodenheimer points out, this scene is remarkable because it conceives of Harmon as manly because he has put on another man's clothes, exchanging his identity for a working-class physicality made evident in his rough jacket and enormous beard; and this disguise allows Harmon to "act out a manhood that seems an essential precondition of his appearance onstage as himself" when in the next chapter he tries to sort out, for the reader's benefit as well as his own, exactly who he is and what he wants.[21] Headstone's case is also pertinent here: the schoolmaster becomes himself, looks like himself, only when he wears an outfit that imitates Riderhood's dress, clothes that allow their wearer to revert to his working-class origins. Significantly, Harmon, by disguising his current identity and acknowledging his past class status, comes to inhabit a body with which he is totally at ease because it is the working-man's body in which he has formerly lived. He also gains control over that body, whose "formidable appearance" later in this scene ensures his mastery of both Riderhood and his daughter (348). Earlier during Harmon's introduction to the Wilfers, the narrator has remarked twice on the melancholic's "hesitating hand" (46), but appearing in a seaman's outfit steadies his grip. Similarly, but more extensively, at the end of the novel when he confronts Wegg, Harmon regains the power of his hand to deal Wegg the punishment that that conspirator supposedly deserves.

Harmon's Counterparts

Much has been made of the doubling and redoubling of characters in *Our Mutual Friend*, though John Harmon is not often invited to join in this critical exchange.[22] For my purposes, the linking of Harmon and Headstone is the most significant of these analogical relationships: both are violent men with working-class pasts, and both suppress themselves in their attempts to rise to a higher status. Early in the novel the narrator explicitly links them, remarking that if Headstone as a "pauper lad" had been "told off for the sea," he would have risen high in the ranks of the ship's crew (218). As my identification of Harmon as a melancholic also suggests, however, he finds many more and, perhaps, more telling doubles among male characters in novels by writers other than Dickens. In donning a seafarer's dress and exerting the pressure of a sailor's vicelike grip, Harmon is also enacting, making physically and literally manifest, yet another conventional characterization prominent in the fiction of the 1860s. Positive representations of working-class strength appear with some frequency in such fiction. As Herbert Sussman notes in another context, "muscle envy" often typifies Victorian depictions of workers (41, cf. 144–46). As a writer for the *Cornhill* explained in 1860, many a Victorian gentleman "looked wistfully" at the brickmakers who worked on a "manlier scale" than did men of leisure reduced to mending the toys broken by their children ("Work" 603). Such physically competent and hardy workers are relatively rare in the fiction of the 1860s, but the ideal that they represent is more pervasively evident. Setting Harmon against the working-class men who do figure in high-Victorian fiction and their more genteel doubles reveals the extent to which Dickens in this one character embodies all the varied and bizarre forms that gentility can take when endowed with physical strength. That perspective, in turn, suggests why Harmon is represented as returning to his working-class past, whose significance the telling of the story of *Our Mutual Friend* tries so insistently to obscure.

Even after the apparent evanescence of physical-force Chartism in the late 1840s, working-class muscles could be seen as a threat, particularly if they were flexed in the cause of working-class politics. High-Victorian fiction routinely guards against such fears whenever it explicitly recognizes them. Thus, Joe Gargery is "a sort of Hercules in strength, and also in weakness," whose illiteracy is cast as a disinclination to "rise" ("like a sort of rebel") against the "government" over him that he grants to Mrs. Joe (8, 50). When Joe does learn to read and write, his otherwise "great good hand" wields a pen as if it were a sledgehammer or crowbar, and he quickly becomes a ludicrous figure of comedy covered in ink (460–61), a depiction that makes sense of Dickens's conviction that the comic actor J. L. Toole should play the role of Joe if the novel were to be adapted for the stage (Guiliano and Collins 851n1). Similarly, the soldier turned apprentice farmer in Meredith's *Rhoda Fleming* is strong when he is needed to save one of his betters from drowning, but he is completely unmanned by the "comparisons" that he draws when he visits a church full of gentry: "crest-fallen," he exhibits the "trembling sensitiveness of a woman" in love (2: 121). In some instances, a worker's physicality is actually turned against him: James Duke, the foundling of Gilbert's *De Profundis: A Tale of the Social Deposits*, would be a giant of a man, the size of a grenadier, if it were not for the deformity of his legs, a feature that ensures that they, as if subjected to Venus's ministrations, will become "specimens of morbid anatomy" worthy of inclusion in a museum (84). Strength among workers is acceptable, but only if it appears in conjunction with other, more powerfully debilitating forms of weakness. Not a grotesque as Gilbert's Duke is, Harmon, like the former soldier of *Rhoda Fleming*, has such strength, although throughout much of the plot of *Our Mutual Friend*, he trembles as if he were a woman.

One of the most characteristic and apparently effective ways in which workers' physical prowess might be seen as contained within the existing social hierarchy is to depict it as an attribute of a worker who is also "one of nature's gentlemen,"[23] an idea that Twemlow at the end of *Our Mutual Friend* refers to when he specifies that the status of a gentleman can "be attained by any man" (796). This is the containment to which Joe Gargery is subjected when he is judged by Pip to be, not quite a gentleman, but a "gentle Christian man" (459). Similarly, Harry Winburn, the agricultural laborer who has been Tom Brown's boyhood friend, is a man "tall and lithe, full of nervous strength"; a stay in jail and entrance into the army are necessary to turn him into a color-sergeant in India and "a gentleman at heart," whose "manners and speech" are, like Magwitch's, magically "improve[d]" (Hughes 2: 282, 342). The historical setting of Blackmore's *Lorna Doone* justifies a more meteoric rise: its hero, John Ridd, ascends to a knighthood and gentlemanly ease, thereby satisfying the desire to see all such social mobility as the reward of unthreatening simplicity.[24] The fantasy that men who lived by manual labor might be morally and even almost socially genteel was a powerful one at the Victorian midcentury, as powerful as the fantasy of rising above one's station to attain gentility for oneself or one's children; and novels like *Evan Harrington*, *Felix Holt*, and *Great Expectations* perpetuate, more or less explicitly, both of these ways of adapting to what Bagehot called the "*removable inequalities*" of Victorian culture. Typically, Harmon acts out both plots:

as a dustman's son, he rises by his work in the colonies and returns home to display the effects of the good breeding with which his rise, as if by magic, endows him. Another fully elaborated instance of the joining of such stories occurs in Eliza Lynn Linton's *Lizzie Lorton of Greyrigg*, whose narrator is even more interested than that of *Our Mutual Friend* in what constitutes a "representative man," the title that Dickens's narrator ironically applies to both Podsnap and Veneering (132, 243). Figuring forth the values revealed by the osmology of high-Victorian fiction, Linton's story contains all the elements of the melancholic's ills by portraying a man doubtfully cured by his wife's substance. Moreover, an analytic encounter between *Lizzie Lorton* and *Our Mutual Friend* illustrates the contrast between male violence and male gentility that the ending of Dickens's novel attempts to transform at least temporarily into an identification.

The hero of *Lizzie Lorton* is Ainslie Forbes, the new superintendent of the recently opened mines at Haverbrack Fells, located in a remote region of the Lake District. Unlike the other "representative men" of the novel (27), a "womanish" rector and an effete London gentleman (6), Forbes is manly. He first appears during a scene that would be comic if it were not also sad, when he rescues the rector, who has fallen into the unusually calm waters of the lake on which Lizzie Linton, Hexam-like, has been rowing him: "Tall, powerful, bronzed, black-bearded, [Forbes] dwarfed [the rector] to the dimensions of a boy, and made him look weaker and less masculine than many a girl; not so much by mere superiority of size as by the superiority of power which his whole bearing expressed" (30). According to one of his rivals, Ainslie Forbes is a "good-looking ruffian," clearly "not a 'gentleman'" (104, 42). Like Headstone, he resembles "a navvy or a blacksmith in his Sunday clothes" (107). As Dickens points out in one of his *Uncommercial Traveller* essays, *ruffian* in Victorian parlance was a strong word, indicating men known for "violence and plunder"; navvies were also among the "troublesome" and "disorderly classes of men" (302). Yet, like Harmon's past as a sailor, Forbes's physical prowess is both tempered by the events to which the plot subjects him and given a role to play in it. As is the case in *Felix Holt*, a lady and her groom-price subject a strong man to melancholia. Margaret Elcombe, homely and unconventional enough to want to shun London so that she can settle down in Cumberland and do good with her inheritance among its primitive folk, is yet another example of a young lady fully in control of her own destiny and her own property, which in this case includes real estate yielding £700 a year. Margaret has "her life in her own hands" (69). And she gives it freely, along with her wealth, to Ainslie Forbes, to whom she proposes marriage. Their conjugal life together, however, is not allowed to commence until Forbes joins the ranks of the melancholic. He has accidentally killed a man, throwing him off a cliff as they grapple in a way that recalls the similar struggle of Headstone and Riderhood. Accused of a capital crime, imprisoned as Felix

Holt is for an act of violence, Forbes must be tried; and, again like both Felix and John Harmon as well as Blackmore's John Ridd, he suffers a kind of ritual death. "Quivering, tortured, humbled" when he must watch as Lizzie publicly declares her dishonor to save his life, Forbes is exonerated and returned to Margaret's arms, "as one risen from the dead" (165–66).

Lizzie Lorton is unconventional in its casting of a woman's inheritance on a man before he suffers from melancholia, before he is rendered insubstantial by his unconfessed crime. Yet the novel is wholly conventional in its acting out of a fantasy of male violence, entitlement, and privilege. No matter how many inadequacies a man may have, there is always a woman willing to offer him whatever he needs. In this case, two "real lad[ies]" (165–66), Margaret Elcombe and Lizzie Lorton, are ready to supply what Forbes lacks: female body, purpose, property, groom-price—in short, everything he could desire. Yet in *Lizzie Lorton* what qualifies the hero for that reward is not so much his need for it as his physical strength. The only male arms within which "a real lady" would want to come to rest are those of a man "of not too elevated social position," one who has had, as he says, "a thorough training in all athletic sports and exercises" (38, 37). The physicality that Harmon briefly regains at the end of *Our Mutual Friend* is the basis for Forbes's ability to become at the conclusion of his story Margaret's kept man, but only the act of killing another man can prove his strength. Forbes becomes a gentleman or, at least, more nearly approximates being one because he is strong. Like Harmon, he has had no "place" in society to lose, but a woman's love can endow him with one that will render his melancholia a permanent condition. The fantasy enacted in *Our Mutual Friend* therefore goes beyond that imagined in *Lizzie Lorton*: according to Dickens's novel, a man who is as respectable as Harmon is assumed to be can have all the accoutrements of gentility—wife, fine house, leisure—without giving up the physical strength that his relatively lowly status in the past has granted him as his birthright.

Yet Harmon finds his brothers not only among figures like Evan and Felix and Pip and Ainslie Forbes, variants of whose stories become intertwined in the telling of his, but also in two other characters of the 1860s, men who render working-class strength unthreatening by making it an attribute of their genteel bodies and therefore of respectable manhood. The most striking instances of such a pattern appear in the heroes of two of Charles Reade's crusading novels of the 1860s, *Hard Cash* and *Put Yourself in His Place*, which feature, improbably and respectively, a gentleman fallen on hard times who chooses to become a fireman and a Sheffield saw-grinder trying to escape his lineage as the nephew and heir of a squire. Each man is the product of a "misalliance" (*Hard* 1), a union between a lady and a man slightly her social inferior; and both men have mothers who are oddly ready, once misfortune impoverishes them, to work as manual laborers, polishing knives in the case of *Put Yourself in His Place* or making dresses, a trade that earns the mother of *Hard Cash* the surprisingly liberal income of £500 a year. Yet these mothers object strenuously when their sons give way to their tastes for working-class physical labor, refusing to be the gentlemen they so obviously already are. The strangeness of Reade's fiction, if less imaginatively satisfying than that of Dickens's novels, can be equally effective in conveying his culture's common sense. In their different ways, Reade's muscular gentlemen reveal what Dickens is doing when he has Harmon exert his sailor's grip on Wegg's cravat.

The impulse to idealize as well as to contain working-class strength is prominent in both these stories. Edward Dodd of *Hard Cash* evidences his penchant for lower-class physicality, even when he is a student at Oxford. Son of a captain in the merchant marine, Edward has the strength of a Joe Gargery, and he is also a would-be artisan, displaying an unsettling fondness for his "lathe and tool-box," from which he "would make you in a trice a chair, a table, a doll, a nutcracker" (2). Later Edward "disguise[s] himself as a common workman" to sell the things made by his hands, but he finds a more satisfying "business in which physical strength goes further than intellectual attainments" (417) when he saves a man from a burning building by using his expertise as a "practised gymnast," deciding therefore to become a fireman. Legendary for his "Herculean arm" and "hands of iron" (421–22), Edward closely resembles Henry Little, the hero of the later novel *Put Yourself in His Place*. Depicting a thinly disguised fictional version of Sheffield, notorious in the 1860s for the violence of its union members, Reade unconventionally creates a locale whose work is rank with odors, its streams overflowing with "ink, stink, and malaria" (1). The son of a lady cast off by her brother because, as he notes on the reverse of her portrait, she has "GONE INTO TRADE" (12), Henry becomes first a tool-maker, then a saw-grinder. Exhibiting the kind of pride that Edward Dodd feels in his manly work as a fireman, Little declares, "I'm a British workman, and worth a dozen [gentlemen]—useless scum!" (17). His uncle, the squire in an outlying parish, however, is one of those "scum," and every comparative encounter in which Henry engages reveals that, despite his clothes and his work, he is his uncle's social equal. Henry quickly changes his mind about his working-class loyalties when he meets and falls in love with a lady: predictably he concedes, "I'd soon be a gentleman for her sake" (123). Betrayed by another gentleman and violently harassed by the unions of brickmakers and sawgrinders, Little emerges as a successful inventor living near the hall of his uncle, with whom he is quickly reconciled, just as Edward Dodd gives up his fireman's role to become a respectable banker.

The hybrid heroes of both *Hard Cash* and *Put Yourself in His Place* demonstrate that manhood inheres in physicality. When Dodd's womenfolk object to his career as a fireman, he silently rejects their feminine "idea of a Man" as "a tall, strong, ornamental creature, whom the women were to

cocker up, and pet, and slave for" (423). In their various careers, Ainslie
Forbes, Edward Dodd, Henry Little, and John Harmon also argue against a
feminized version of manhood, acting out their superiority in encounters that
reveal the strength of their arms and the power of their hands. Yet, as the
outcomes of their stories all demonstrate, a manhood that is both physically
impressive and genteel is an ideal that can be only temporarily sustained. By
combining in one male character, variously named Harmon and Handford and
Rokesmith, every possible permutation of male class identities—worker turned
gentleman, worker as gentleman, gentleman degenerating into worker—
Dickens demonstrates the full appeal of such exchanges.

Why Wegg?

Yet John Harmon seems to render doubtful an idealization of working-class
strength when he treats Wegg to the kind of murderous violence more typical of Sheffield saw-grinders than of gentle giants like James Duke and Joe
Gargery. More perplexing still is the identity of the object on which Harmon
chooses to expend such energy. Why does the happy possessor of a fortune
and a West-End address even notice Wegg's existence? Like the action in
the following chapter when Headstone kills Riderhood by toppling with him
into a river lock, Harmon's punishment of Wegg emphasizes Harmon's
physical superiority, but again as it is in the following chapter, this outcome
depends on a disconcerting physical intimacy between the man exacting
revenge and the man suffering its effects.[25] If Harmon's hold on Wegg is not
the death embrace with which Headstone confines Riderhood, it seems almost odder. Why should Harmon touch Wegg at all? Although it was acceptable for a respectable Victorian gentleman to box against a lower-class
professional—according to the convention that makes both plausible and
comic Pip's match with Herbert when they are boys—there are no formal
rules of fisticuffs operating here to make palatable such physical contact. How
can the genteel melancholic touch pitch and not be defiled?

The scene makes sense as a necessary conclusion to the Harmon plot, I
think, because it turns a comparative encounter into an exchange. Here the
working-class physicality evidenced in Harmon's grasp becomes moralized
as a virtuous power that, like the long and arduous removal of the dust heaps,
finally eradicates the last trace of trade from the mansion that he inhabits.
Although Harmon is the most elaborate example in the fiction of the 1860s
of a character whose manhood is put in question by his rejection of trade,
sensuous contact with things still has not been satisfactorily banished from
the home he will inhabit, even when his father's profits have been cleansed
by Boffin's generosity and Bella's adoration. Like the dark stain on the bot-

tom of Gaffer Hexam's boat, the taint of trade must reappear at the end of the story, as if in hopes that it might finally be eradicated; and that taint is embodied in Silas Wegg. No wonder that a confirmed melancholic like John Harmon would offer a thousand pounds for the shaking out of the street seller's brains.

Bringing together in his less-than-complete body two subjects that *Our Mutual Friend* consistently treats with scorn, commodification and social climbing,[26] Wegg demonstrates the connection between them. Although he proudly calls himself "a Man" who is "worth [his] price" (766), he enacts the tendency of the men who knew only the price of an item to become themselves commodities in the market where social distinction is bought and sold. Finding his identity—his "I" (84)—in the dead, fleshless bone of his amputated leg, the lowly vendor tries to buy himself so that he can prepare to raise himself: as Wegg explains to Venus, "I have a prospect of getting on in life and elevating myself by my own independent exertions . . . and I should . . . wish to collect myself as a genteel person" (88). As both Headstone and Charley demonstrate, however, the desire to rise marks the most unpleasant and unattractive figures in the novel, and Harmon specifically denounces Wegg as "a mud-worm [who] presume[s] to rise in this house against this noble soul," Boffin (768). In one sense, then, Wegg reappears at the end of the novel so that Harmon can mete out to him the punishment that he so richly deserves for wanting the property that Harmon effortlessly manages to keep. Yet Wegg is simply trying to climb more openly to the social eminence that Harmon achieves on the strength of old Harmon's money, and that connection between the would-be blackmailer and his attacker reveals the most significant source of the latter's animus: Wegg, despite his lowly disreputability or perhaps because of it, becomes in this scene a second self for both John Harmon and his father.

That doubled identification is stressed in a number of ways. Wegg has imaginatively inhabited the mansion he calls "Our House," and he is actually the one to determine where the newly enriched Harmon will live by suggesting that Boffin buy or let the Eminently Aristocratic Mansion in which he "has an interest" (182). Wegg is defined, like John Harmon, by his relation to books and by his service to Boffin since Wegg sells the dustman his expertise, his literacy: if Harmon is a secretary, a man who, as Jonathan Arac points out, "'write[s] for another'" (*Commissioned* 186), Wegg is Harmon's complement, one who reads for another. Harmon is also linked to Wegg through the word *move*, the term in *Our Mutual Friend* that repeatedly defines the deceptions or tricks typical of the conspiracies that the novel portrays. Wegg and Venus engage in a "friendly move," but the Inspector, learning that Harmon has lived in London long after he is thought dead, thinks that "he never did know such a move" (743), a word that Fledgeby also uses to define that supposed epitome of commercial shrewdness, Riah

(419). Openly acting out his covetousness for Boffin's wealth, an impulse that Harmon cannot allow himself to acknowledge even when it might be disguised as a function of his love for Bella, Wegg is also a reincarnation of old Harmon. As Wegg observes the removal of the dust heaps, his "rapacious eyes" are directly identified with those "no less rapacious" of the old man who had "watched the growth of the Mounds in years bygone, and had vigilantly sifted the dust of which they were composed" (759). Yet Wegg is old Harmon in a minor key, the pettiest of the small tradesmen in *Our Mutual Friend*, originally a purveyor of ballads and hard nuts and soft gingerbread, only to be transformed into a dealer, like Fledgeby, in bad paper, in this case a superseded will. Mayhew's categorization of street sellers reveals the lowliness of Wegg's position: he sells gingerbread, a commodity that was "formerly in much greater demand than it is now," and the way in which he sells ballads puts him among the men who "have generally been mechanics, porters, or servants, and [who are now] reduced to struggle for a living as 'pinners-up'" (1: 160, 272). Only in such a diminished form is Harmon's father allowed to haunt his son.

Wegg's role as John Harmon's double, evident most obviously in his inability to know his proper place, is most meaningfully represented in the olfactory sensitivities that Wegg puts to use when he first visits Venus's shop. Such genteel susceptibilities are wholly absent, by contrast, when the Journeyman Engineer of Wright's *Johnny Robinson*, whose working-class credentials and disinclination to rise are not open to doubt, records his visits to the kitchen where Tim the Tinman and his wife do their work. As the fiction of the 1860s demonstrates, the ability to perceive the smells of working and eating is the distinction of the unmarked. In the scene that prepares for the one in "Checkmate to the Friendly Move," Wegg sniffs out the various odors that he encounters in Venus's shop when asked to take tea there: "Mr. Wegg sits down on a box in front of the fire, and inhales a warm and comfortable smell which is not the smell of the shop. 'For that,' Mr. Wegg inwardly decides, as he takes a corrective sniff or two, 'is musty, leathery, feathery, cellary, gluey, gummy, and,' with another sniff, 'as it might be, strong of old pairs of bellows'" (84). Wegg can use his nose to tell the difference between the aromas of food and the odors of products in the making, be they stuffed birds or articulated skeletons. Yet Wegg, like Harmon, makes nothing.

The final comparative encounter between these two characters in "Checkmate to the Friendly Move" issues, therefore, in a complicated exchange. Based on the unlikely attributions of class identity previously established in *Our Mutual Friend* and the language used to depict this encounter, Harmon is the seafaring worker, and Wegg, the melancholic gentleman. "Worn . . . down to skin and bone," speaking with a "melancholy air" when he contemplates the pleasures he has lost when he gave up selling gingerbread and ballads (759, 769), Wegg acts out not only Harmon's interest in his father's estate but also the olfactory delicacy that Harmon should but never does evidence; and Harmon takes on the physicality associated with working-class men so that he can demonstrate what the former street seller lacks, the bodily strength as well as the literal will that would allow him to secure the property for which he longs. If my technically correct use here of pronouns *he* and *him* has become as complicated as the narrator's studied indeterminacy in his account of the final encounter between Headstone and Riderhood, such grammatical cross-references testify to the impulse in *Our Mutual Friend* to make palpable the effects of comparative encounters that enable exchanges— exchanges in values as well as in class positions.

Once again trade is the specific material reality that such maneuvers attempt to evade: since Harmon's violence does not allow Boffin to compensate Wegg for the loss of his wares, he will need presumably to find other ways to make a living. In the odd, fantastic but ultimately quite conventional symbolic economy of *Our Mutual Friend*, those involved with trade cannot be allowed to continue, and Wegg is only the first among equals when it comes to the cleansing to which commerce is subjected in this novel. Riah closes up Pubsey and Co. on the orders of a badly beaten and well-chastised Fledgeby. Wilfer leaves Veneering's counting house so that he can be "appointed Secretary" to his wife's son (783). Boffin and his wife go back to the walks that they used to take on Sundays when he worked; now they can spend all their time looking in shops. A week after the action in the final chapter of the novel, Veneering will be entered in "the Books of the Insolvent Fates," going bankrupt, taking the Chiltern Hundreds, and retiring to live on the Continent (792). Even those only metaphorically associated with trade are banished. The fictive lime merchants disappear as Lightwood and Wrayburn take up their genteel legal professions. Headstone, who on his introduction in the novel is cruelly represented as a man of slow intellect superintending his "wholesale warehouse" of painfully acquired knowledge (218), is put out of business by his self-inflicted death.[27] Betty Higden, who must travel to sell her wares only to purchase her death, is perhaps the most telling case. When Sloppy is chosen to be the new John Harmon without that name, Betty decides that she must leave London so that he will take advantage of his good luck. In two contiguous paragraphs, Mrs. Boffin plans "to set Betty up in trade," and Harmon, hearing from Betty that Sloppy "would have made a wonderful cabinet-maker . . . if there had been the money to put him to it," concludes that "it will not be hard to find a trade for him" (378). Here bad trade meets good trade, selling comes face to face with making: Betty cannot live on her version of trade; Sloppy will prosper on his. He may even marry on the strength of what it can give him and Jenny Wren. In their final scene in the novel and their first scene together, Sloppy proposes, as Joe Gargery offers Pip's labor in a similar situation, to make all kinds of things to amuse and please Jenny, doll "nests" and drawers and crutch handles

(788). In *Our Mutual Friend*, artisanal trade finally wins out over shopkeeping trade. Yet even handicrafts are ultimately not for sale: like Harmon dispensing charity from his "Inexhaustible" inheritance, Sloppy proposes to give the work of his hands to Jenny. Significantly, Dickens in his postscript to the novel identifies himself as "the story-weaver at his loom" (798), a weaver who is pointedly not preparing cloth for the market but, rather, allowing his readers to glimpse its emerging patterns as he creates them.

On that self-deluding and nostalgic note, *Our Mutual Friend* concludes its attempts to deal with the anxieties about respectable manhood so evident in novels like *Lizzie Lorton* and *Hard Cash*, not to mention *Felix Holt* and *Salem Chapel* and *Evan Harrington* and *Great Expectations*. Like those works, Dickens's last novel presents the olfactory encounters of everyday life in a way that both expresses and manages these anxieties. Meetings in the fiction of the 1860s overturn conventional conceptions of some of the most prized values in Victorian culture. Constituting an osmology that explains more than the modesty of an individual reference to a smell might suggest, this representational code conveys a cultural common sense, a series of interrelated, self-evident truths. Women—even ladies, especially ladies—are valued as matter and the procreationists of matter, less angels in the house than they are open-handed possessors of houses. Such materially defined women are identified with the world of trade from which they cannot be distanced: women are, of course, objects of commerce; but they are also, more importantly, its agents, conferring on men the things that they lack. Trade, the smelly realm of buying and selling, becomes a cultural scapegoat, allowing gentility to distance itself from a substantiality on which it is based and without which it cannot exist. Respectable men are relatively disembodied arbiters of moral worth, figures who not only represent the virtues of insubstantiality but who also serve as moral guides for wayward women like Esther Lyon and Bella Wilfer. The power of a strong hand, which such men typically lack, is so highly prized that it becomes the instrument of virtue both in the person of John Harmon and in the actions of Charles Reade's oddly hybrid heroes. *Our Mutual Friend* differs from other novels of the 1860s only in the extent to which it makes literal such exchanges of value by having them acted out in terms of traded clothing and consciously adopted disguises, therefore materializing a middle-class manhood reinvigorated by working-class physicality. This constellation of values has demonstrable political implications, the subject to which I now briefly and finally turn.

AFTERWORD

If John Harmon had actually lived in the 1860s rather than in one of its novels, the passage of the Second Reform Act in 1867 would have enfranchised him whether or not he managed to marry a woman with a heart of gold. The well-rewarded hero of *Our Mutual Friend*, however, becomes entitled to vote through a different and decidedly apolitical process. As a single man lodging in first the Wilfers's house and then the Boffins's, Harmon does not come within the pale of British Constitution, but his devotion to his wife, by giving him a motive for accepting his father's fortune, allows him more than to meet the property qualifications for the franchise that had obtained since 1832. He does not need, therefore, to wait until the members of Parliament decide to confer the right to vote, as they did in 1867, on numbers of both householders and lodgers. The same is true of the strong man made melancholic by the plot of *Lizzie Lorton of Greyrigg*: marriage to a woman offers a man not only his groom-price but also his ability to qualify as an elector.

In this literal sense, then, there is a precise political point to the complex interrelations of trade, substance, and gender constituted by the osmology of high-Victorian fiction: domesticity can accomplish what politicians might or might not be trusted to do. Such a conclusion suggests that the odors recorded in novels of the 1860s simply confirm, if in a more material fashion than usually adduced, the conception of the Victorian period that has remained influential since the late 1980s, when Nancy Armstrong and Mary Poovey published *Desire and Domestic Fiction* and *Uneven Developments*, respectively: the realm of the domestic is cordoned off from the public sphere so that the political problems of the latter may be fantastically and often satisfyingly solved in the former. The explanatory power of this analysis I would be the last to deny. Yet I want to stress that exactly the opposite of such a process occurs during some olfactory encounters: the anxieties inherent in Victorian conceptions of male respectability cannot be fully assuaged in domestic terms, even in novels that insistently privilege home and love over work and public life.

Bella's willingness to play the roles of wife and mother may contribute to the property-owning status that confers the vote on her husband, but his eagerness to exercise his strong hand against Wegg suggests that the enfranchisement entailed by the possession of "Our House" is not the only one that he seeks. *Our Mutual Friend*, depending on the osmology that it shares with other novels of the 1860s, represents encounters that constitute a politics of daily life by which people are governed and govern others, but like other high-Victorian fictions, it also provides a perspective on the formal parliamentary politics of the 1860s, which from the middle of the decade on were largely dominated by debates about the possibility of extending the franchise. In the realm of constitutional questions, the relations between melancholics and their male inferiors, between an inodorate character like Pip and a survival of smelly artisanal life like Wemmick, extend to its logical conclusion the effect of the meetings characteristic of daily life: by identifying in the low the values lacking in the high, such olfactory encounters justify exchanges of political power. *Middlemarch*, the novel that Eliot began writing in the middle of 1869, provides the best fictional evidence for such an argument. My desire to claim this "home epic" (779) for the 1860s might fairly be dismissed as an attempt to make my chosen decade greater in achievement that it was. Yet as a post-reform novel, *Middlemarch* offers the occasion for the final words of this study because its plot reveals the connections between political change and the issues of male melancholia, female property, and physical strength. Although *Felix Holt*, the novel that preceded *Middlemarch*, and the "Address to Working Men, by Felix Holt," which Eliot's publisher John Blackwood badgered her into writing, are often taken as her fullest response to reform politics, engaging these three texts in an analytic encounter offers, I think, a better way of understanding how fiction in the 1860s both elucidates the impulses behind the Second Reform Act and, in the case of *Middlemarch*, reflects its effects.[1]

Crucial to the differences between *Felix Holt* and *Middlemarch* is a simple matter of dating, which distinguishes between the circumstances not only of their publication but also of their composition. In 1864 Gladstone surprised his parliamentary colleagues by defending a limited extension of the suffrage based on the kind of moral eligibility for the vote that Lancashire factory operatives had displayed during the Cotton Famine: facing privations that extended month after month, then year after year, such men had evidenced admirable "self-command, self-control, respect for order, patience under suffering, confidence in the law, regard for superiors" (*Hansard* 175: 325). The early months of the following year saw the founding of the Reform League. Yet the event that made reform a genuine possibility, rather than the dead issue it had been for over twenty years, was the change in parliamentary leadership occasioned by the death of Palmerston in October of 1865 (Hoppen 242). By that time, Eliot had been at work on *Felix Holt* for over six months. Moreover, when Gladstone introduced his reform measure in March of 1866, she had nearly finished the second volume of the novel

(Haight 381; *Letters* 4: 189, 236n3). Eliot's assessment of the state of British politics at that time was as dyspeptic as the state of her health. In the same letter that she told her friend Barbara Bodichon that she was "finishing a book, which has been growing slowly like a sickly child, because of my own ailments," Eliot complained that the politics of "the English world" were more "trivial and insincere" than even polite conversation.[2] "Sickly" though its author thought it was, *Felix Holt* appeared in June of 1866 as Gladstone and the Russell government, unable to gather sufficient support for their bill, resigned and gave way to the Conservative ministry of Lord Derby and Benjamin Disraeli. During the late summer of 1866, reform was the central topic of political debate, with the so-called Hyde Park riots occurring a month after Eliot published in *Felix Holt* her account of an earlier election riot; throughout late 1866 and into the spring of 1867, "monster meetings" in support of reform took place in London and the cities of the industrial north and Scotland. In this context, three months before the passage of a reform bill dealing with England and Wales in July of 1867, Eliot told her publisher that she was entertaining "private projects" about a new "English novel," the work that would become *Middlemarch* (*Letters* 4: 355). Now more engaged than disgusted by politics, Eliot evaluated the contributions of various speakers to the parliamentary debates then taking place, finding Mill's advocacy of female suffrage "sober and judicious" (*Letters* 4: 366). The writing of *Middlemarch* did not begin for another two years as Eliot made herself miserable revising *The Spanish Gypsy*; but when she was ready to start work on the novel, she commented, "The various elements of the story have been soliciting my mind for years" (*Letters* 5: 16). Her "English novel," the action of which she set in the years just before the passage of the First Reform Act, therefore offers a revealing perspective on the results of what contemporaries called "the English measure" of 1867.

Under Disraeli's leadership in the House of Commons, a complex series of parliamentary maneuvers eventually made that act three times more inclusive and presumably more liberal than the bill of 1866: the law that passed nearly doubled the number of those eligible to vote, enfranchising for the first time the majority of the men of the urban working classes (Cowling 46). In many ways the 1867 act ratified the value placed on domesticity in the fiction of the 1860s by making householding, even as practiced in its most modest forms by lodgers, the test of citizenship. As a number of historians have recently argued, the 1867 act altered the symbolic basis for citizenship when it changed the qualifications for the borough franchise. The Reform Act of 1832 had identified the ownership of property as the standard for that suffrage. By contrast, in its final form, the 1867 measure took as its central qualification male householding, thereby including only those men who could prove their stability and independence by having dependents, by being, as Gladstone in 1866 specified, "fathers of families," male heads of house.[3]

Like genteel women in high-Victorian fiction, working-class men were to be valued and rewarded for their procreative capacities. In 1866 and 1867, manhood suffrage became the watchword of the most radical of those championing reform, but even among them the term *manhood* indicated that only a particular kind of man would be deemed worthy of the vote (R. Harrison 117, Biagini 273–75); it specifically excluded, as the radical M.P. John Bright explained, the "residuum," disreputable inhabitants of the boroughs, those characterized by their "almost hopeless poverty and dependence" (*Hansard* 186: 636–37). Evaluating workers according to a specific definition of manhood became a way of testing political eligibility. What the fiction of the 1860s further reveals, I think, is why the passing of the 1867 bill might have been as much about conceptions of genteel manhood as it was about the manly independence of working-class householders.

More specifically, the values revealed by the osmology of high-Victorian fiction helped to make possible franchise reform in 1867. Commentators at the time debated whether the credit for the passage of the bill belonged to Gladstone, who initiated the process, or to Disraeli, who saw it through; many also speculated whether the popular agitation of monster meetings or the maneuverings of parliamentary parties were decisive. In the 1872 introduction to the second edition of *The English Constitution*, Bagehot pointed to the passing away of Palmerston's generation of politicians, the aged "pre-'32 statesmen," as the great change that opened the way for franchise reform (5: 167). More recent accounts propose still other factors as contributing to the outcome of debates over the 1867 bill, including the pressures of empire and the unrest fueled by the reappearance of cholera and the economic downturn of the mid-1860s.[4] Passage of the bill is now also frequently attributed to the "class collaboration" that marked the mid-Victorian period and the adoption by the members of the working classes of middle-class standards of respectability, self-discipline, and self-improvement.[5] Yet the encounters and exchanges represented in fiction of the 1860s define "class collaboration" as a process by which members of the middle classes and gentry come to recognize among working-class men values quite other than the moral virtues of self-restraint and self-help.[6]

Such issues might seem far distant from *Middlemarch*, whose action begins in 1829, when some workers did have the franchise, a right that they would lose in the so-called progress of the Reform Act of 1832. Yet in her novel of the First Reform Act, Eliot offers a political analysis attuned more to the issues of the 1860s than to those of the 1830s. Conventionally linking the subjects of male melancholia, trade, and female substance, Eliot emphasizes in the career of Will Ladislaw the political implications of such conjunctions. Two of the most highly prized characters in *Middlemarch*, Dorothea Brooke and the clergyman Farebrother, laugh about insects holding reformed parliaments; and the narrator makes wryly self-satisfied comments about the folly of the great expectations that the prospect of reform engenders in drunken or foolish agricultural laborers. Yet the plot of *Middlemarch* seems to want to go beyond such jejune sarcasms to suggest that post-reform politics constitute an arena of manly endeavor to which the enfranchisement of working men has contributed.

In both *Felix Holt* and the "Address" that Eliot published in *Blackwood's* in January of 1868, the character Felix Holt rejects the idea that an extension of the franchise is a political good. As he is depicted in the novel named for him, Felix is hardly an argument for reform: his condescending contempt for his superiors and the murderous outcome of his leadership of an unruly crowd are the reverse of the characteristics that Gladstone had earlier identified as reasons to give workers the vote. Felix's later speech to his fellow workers does reveal, however, the lessons pertinent to reform that comparative encounters teach. An orgy of imagined working-class self-loathing, Felix Holt's commentary on members of the working classes can envision only the sorts of everyday meetings with workers that prove their shortcomings: "To us who . . . often walk abroad, it is plain that we can never get into a bit of a crowd but we must rub clothes with a set of Roughs . . . who are gamblers, sots, libertines, knaves, or else mere sensual simpletons and victims" (417). In such a passage, the tone of Felix's argument against political change approaches that characteristic of Carlyle's intemperate *Shooting Niagara: and After?* which uses the odors characteristic of the fiction of the 1840s to convey how thoroughly its author despises the "Plebs," the "wild horse" dragging its betters through "malodorous quagmires" (54–55). Yet at one point Felix's address offers a different account of the issues central to the 1867 act. In defining workers as members of "a class whose wants have been of a common sort" and their betters as the "classes who hold the treasures of knowledge," Eliot, speaking as Felix, describes working-class "wants" in material terms as food and shelter, while the immaterial advantages of their betters are "the treasure of refined needs" (419). What the holders of such treasure might lack is made clear in *Middlemarch*.

In its imaginative evocation of smells, *Middlemarch* conforms to the osmology of high-Victorian fiction, consistently offering the kinds of representations and values that I have identified as typical of the 1860s. As a novel dealing with the past, it includes more references to the pleasant smells of country life than most novels of the decade; as a novel by George Eliot, it also offers more metaphors based on odors, but its osmology is predictably conventional. Rosamond, like Esther Lyon or the poseur Wegg, exhibits her gentility in her olfactory delicacy; she objects strenuously to her brother's taste for herrings and grilled bone for breakfast, and she opines that the "scent of rose-leaves" characterizes the "wide corridors" of the best of the county homes outside Middlemarch (275). Rosamond and Dorothea are both associated with the aromas of flowers: the former, herself the "flower of Middlemarch," sits among "the summer scents of the garden" (275, 328); the latter, her better, is wreathed with the fragrance of "sweet hedges" (406). Trade is odorous and distastefully so. When Brooke takes up politics, the narrator trenchantly explains the dissatisfaction felt by his Tory friends and relations: "The result had oozed forth gradually, like the discovery that your neighbour has set up an unpleasant kind of manufacture which will be permanently under your nostrils without legal remedy" (337). Like Trollope's characters Mr. Outhouse and Mrs. Tappitt, Brooke's associates recognize trade as a source of olfactory offense, a manufacture that smells, as does the petty doctoring of the surgeon named Gambit, whose "satisfactory practice [is] much pervaded by the smells of retail trading" (419). Equally conventional, however, is the positive value attributed to the work of tradesmen when it is made evident in the good smells of their food. The aroma of Featherstone's ham ironically represents the substance that his would-be heirs hover like vultures to devour, but the scents associated with Caleb Garth—the odors of apples and quinces that pervade his attic and of the fruit that his daughters gather in his garden—idealize a life-giving substance longed for by Fred Vincy and the Rev. Mr. Farebrother, the men who perceive such aromas. Garth, the land agent, is the narrator's ideal of a manly man because he is in touch with material realities, whose physicality is subtly represented in the odors that attach to him as he works. Looking down upon other sorts of occupations—"politics, preaching, learning, and amusement"—Garth values activities that offer him "such close contact with 'business' as to get often honourably decorated with marks of dust and mortar, the damp of the engine, or the sweet soil of the woods and fields" (236). Garth is a member of a class of men not above physical labor, marked by dust and made odorous by sweet-smelling soil. As such, his food smells good, promising substance to those who lack it.

Fred and Farebrother are not, however, the only insubstantial men in *Middlemarch*. The novel is awash with forlorn figures of dissatisfaction and of more or less openly recognized loss. One of its epigraphs invokes Burton's *Anatomy of Melancholy* to explain that Casaubon has been made "lean, dry, ill-coloured" by "hard" study (39). Yet *Middlemarch* is, far more than this confined reference would suggest, a female-chauvinist festival of male impotence, most instances of which are cast in domestic and professional, not political terms. Brooke flees home once his role as a rotten landlord has been revealed. Lydgate recognizes Rosamond as his master, one who makes him fear both her and himself. Featherstone, in his last moments, cannot bend a woman to his will, and he therefore cannot distribute his property according to his last wishes. Casaubon dies in a similar state of frustrated dependency on a woman who will not do his bidding. Bulstrode's only moment of redemption comes when he looks up at the wife who stands over him. Fred is made a man by Mary, and Farebrother remains incomplete through his lack of her, though the cleric is literally granted a living by another woman, Dorothea, whom his mother likens to a Fate. In such a context, one would not expect Will Ladislaw to escape the diminutions to which the plot of *Middlemarch* subjects his fellow male characters, and to a great extent he does not. But like Bella Wilfer, whose apparent descent into the idiocy of marital acquiescence can be seen as culturally productive, Will is endowed with qualities and narrative possibilities whose functions need to be taken seriously. Will, like Fred Vincy, becomes at the end of the novel a recovering melancholic, and the light that their stories cast on their shared condition defines Will as a man conceived in the post-1867 reform period.

Not as fully defined by discursivity as Casaubon, the character to whom the term *melancholy* is frequently attached, Fred and Will are the young men in *Middlemarch* who suffer from the specific condition that I have defined as male melancholia. They are the ones who most resemble Philip Pip and Evan Harrington in their linked romantic longings and vocational uncertainties. Like so many other men of the 1860s, Fred and Will wander from place to place as they mope, unsure of how they should spend their time or prepare for their futures, both defined by their love for women who, in either social or moral terms, are portrayed as beyond their grasp. Will traverses the Continent looking for a future, settling in Middlemarch, leaving it, and then returning. Like Herbert Pocket's, his unfocused energies make him suffer melancholically. Eliot's characterization of Will literalizes and feminizes his uncertainties: he so much resembles the portrait of his grandmother that Dorothea looks at that miniature only to watch as its womanly features are transformed into those of the man she will come to love. At odds with himself and his future, Fred travels to a horse fair at which he so worsens his financial problems that he sickens with a fever, an illness that, like Pip's, materializes his inadequacies. Recovered, Fred is then again sent to Oxford to try for the degree for which he sees no use. In depicting the town of Middlemarch and its environs, George Eliot stresses the number and variety of the kinds of work that a man might do: preaching, lawyering, banking, collecting, selling, supervising, farming, inventing, improving, diagnosing and curing, managing land, and manufacturing goods. Remarkably but typically for the melancholic of the 1860s, neither Fred nor Will can imagine doing anything if it is not done in service of his devotion to a particular woman. In one of the few novels of the 1860s that tries but fails to reject the concept that a man's identity inheres solely in his love for a woman, Tom Brown thinks of romance as a "bed . . . too narrow for a man to stretch himself on" (Hughes 2: 312). For Fred and Will in *Middlemarch*, romance is the only bed upon which they can imagine lying.

Unlike many characters in the 1860s, however, Fred and Will are granted relief from their melancholia. Mary accepts Fred's marriage proposal, giving him a goal for which to work. Not coincidentally, through her father she also offers Fred "close contact" with the materiality from which his fine education has divorced him. The morning on which he finds his vocation by assisting Caleb Garth is appropriately one that exhales "the scent of the earth" (522); and on that occasion Fred physically challenges and defeats, albeit on horseback, a group of unruly farm workers. Not inheriting Featherstone's land, Fred is nonetheless granted residence on it since his aunt Bulstrode, like Dorothea, has a living in her gift. In Will's case, female substance similarly shores up male insubstantiality. Dorothea, herself prey to "languid melancholy" and "Hamlet-like raving" (724, 730), is unable to bear separation from Will, and she reveals to him that she is not dependent on Casaubon's fortune. Through her parents she has her own £700 a year. As Brooke explains, she is the typical heiress of the 1860s, fantastically empowered to do as she pleases: "She can act as she likes, you know" (765). More important, however, is the vocation that Dorothea's substance grants Will. On that income, literally a fortune in the 1830s, Will can devote himself to politics without having to prostitute himself as "a mere pen and mouthpiece" (762): "Will became an ardent public man, working well in those times when reforms were begun with a young hopefulness of immediate good which has been much checked in our days, and getting at last returned to Parliament by a constituency who paid his expenses" (782–83). Supported by both Dorothea and his constituents, Will finds what he wants to do.

Will—like the hero of *Can You Forgive Her?*—learns from the woman he loves how he can pursue the public life whose issues have long fascinated her. The would-be artist, effete in his devotion to the beautiful, now becomes the practical politician committed to the useful. But an even more positive exchange has taken place here: in his marriage to Dorothea, Will has gained not only her money but also her ardor. As an "ardent public man," Will becomes appropriately described by the word that is used repeatedly in *Middlemarch* to characterize Dorothea, the term that becomes a kind of formulaic reference to her. Such ardor, by contrast, is designated as precisely what Lydgate lacks when he fails to be "more massive" than his wife (714). Will's encounters with Dorothea, however, save him from Lydgate's fate: they teach Will to adopt her burning desire for public good and to use her property to achieve it. Moreover, the famous line in the "Finale" to *Middlemarch* that responds in mock amazement to the idea that Dorothea's qualities have been wasted on Will exactly conveys the values attributed to women of the 1860s when they are deemed to give off the sweet scent of flowers: "Many who knew [Dorothea], thought it a pity that so substantive and rare a creature should have been absorbed into the life of another, and be only known in a certain circle as a wife and mother" (783). Like all those genteel female characters who precede her in the fiction of the decade, Dorothea is both rare and substantive, both spirit and matter. Even more specifically like the two Keith wives at the end of *The Clever Woman of the Family*, Dorothea has become, as wife and mother, a "substantial" woman and the source of substance in others.

The difference between the ending that *Middlemarch* envisions for one of its principal melancholics, a role among the members of a reformed Parliament in London, and the disappearances to unknown locations through which earlier characters like Felix Holt and Harold Transome simply vanish might be traced to the novel's status as a post-reform, post-1867 fiction. The Second Reform Act, despite its source in the Conservative ministry and the less-than-liberating effect it is now understood to have had on English society,[7] enfranchised both the artisans whom Gladstone had wanted to see come within the pale of the Constitution and many urban working-class men whose supposed lack of skill defined them solely in terms of their physical strength. Like many novels of the decade, *Middlemarch* wants to contemplate the value of such men only in their idealized embodiments—in this case, in the gentrified form of Caleb Garth, who supervises the work that other men do with their hands but who is himself not above getting his own hands dirty. The "wretched hand-loom weavers in Tipton and Freshitt," the kind of "residuum" still deemed beyond the pale after 1867, are represented as being nowhere visible in this novel, much less smelled (307); but Garth and his idealized "close contact" with materiality stand for the manly qualities that both Will and the pre-1867 Constitution lack.

In a contribution to *Essays on Reform* (1867), R. H. Hutton explained that the "coldness" of those in power toward the "artisans of the towns" who would be enfranchised by an extension of the suffrage was a response to "what is strongest and most manly in [the] character" of such workers (27). Hutton's emphasis on strength and manliness is, I think, apposite, though the term *coldness* hardly conveys the significance that high-Victorian novels, *Middlemarch* prime among them, find in the strength and substance associated with artisanal life. Felix Holt, the pseudo-artisan whose manhood is relentlessly diminished by the romance plot in which he becomes entwined, is less the epitome of such vitality than he is its opposite. Yet the difference between the role that Dorothea's money makes possible for Will Ladislaw and that granted Felix Holt by his wife's inheritance might be more adequately explained by the passage of the reform bill that intervened between the writing of their two stories. The same argument would apply to the difference between Will's profession as a politician and the positions of unsullied leisure that characters like John Harmon and Ainslie Forbes come to occupy. After the electorate had been broadened to include the physicality and strength of working-class numbers, it would have been easier than it had been to imagine institutional politics as the proper arena for any character whose respectable manliness a novel takes pains to establish. In the years after 1867, politics could be portrayed as a vital form of manly business to which a genteel character might want to turn his hand.

In his 1870s commentary on the effects of the democracy that the reforms of the previous decade had portended, James Fitzjames Stephen proclaimed, "Strength, in all its forms, is life and manhood. To be less strong is to be less of a man, whatever else you may be" (199). Walter Bagehot invoked similar terms in his 1872 account of the Second Reform Act, which had transformed the Constitution through an exchange that made "the possessors of the 'material' distinctions of life" the superiors of those conventionally identified as their betters, "those who possess the *im*material distinctions." According to Bagehot, a fight between such opponents would be one that those defined by their immateriality would lose (5: 178, 174). Such formulations, which articulate truths taken to be self-evident in Victorian culture, explain the odd last act of John Harmon in *Our Mutual Friend*, the working gentlemen of *Hard Cash* and *Put Yourself in His Place*, the trained athlete of *Lizzie Lorton*, and, by contrast, relatively effete melancholics like Pip and Evan and Arthur Vincent, as well as the supposedly working-class hero of *Felix Holt*. Stephen's and Bagehot's commentaries, like Eliot's practice in *Middlemarch*, also place in the context of institutional politics the values that emerge from the osmology of high-Victorian fiction. Those who have substance smell; those who smell them do not. Substance, as a form of strength, as proof of physical potency, may be demeaned by those who lack it, but the olfactory encounters of daily life tend to prove not only its inescapability but also its worth. If Dickens, as his office boy attested, was a man "who lived a lot by his nose," he did so because he lived in a culture attuned to the messages borne by odors. The often implicit recognitions conveyed by the fictional osmology of the 1860s attest to the value of matter and of the men and women conceived of as matter. One political outcome of such common sense became evident when the Act of 1867 hesitantly began to enfranchise the workers whose labors and whose foods were imagined to be rich with the scents of substance.

APPENDIX

The novels surveyed for this study are listed below by title, along with their authors and the dates of their first publication in serial or book form (Sutherland, *Stanford Companion*). All these novels were at least partially written and/or published in the 1860s. This expansive definition of the decade justifies the inclusion here of Swinburne's *Love's Cross-Currents*, which did not appear for more than a decade after it was written in 1862 (E. Wilson 22); his *Lesbia Brandon*, which waited to be published for almost a century after 1864 when he began work on it; and Eliot's *Middlemarch*, the initial stages of several plots of which were written starting in the middle of 1869. See the Works Cited for the specific editions quoted in the text.

The Adventures of Philip, William Makepeace Thackeray, 1861–62
Armadale, Wilkie Collins, 1864–66
At Odds, Jemima, Baroness Tautphoeus, 1863
Aurora Floyd, Mary Elizabeth Braddon, 1862–63
Barrington, Charles Lever, 1862–63
The Belton Estate, Anthony Trollope, 1865–66
Beyond the Church, Frederick William Robinson, 1866
Can You Forgive Her? Anthony Trollope, 1864–65
Castle Richmond, Anthony Trollope, 1860
The Claverings, Anthony Trollope, 1866–67
The Clever Woman of the Family, Charlotte Mary Yonge, 1864–65
The Cloister and the Hearth, Charles Reade, 1861
Cometh up as a Flower, Rhoda Broughton, 1867
Cousin Phillis, Elizabeth Gaskell, 1863–64
De Profundis: A Tale of the Social Deposits, William Gilbert, 1864
The Doctor's Wife, Mary Elizabeth Braddon, 1864
East Lynne, Ellen Price [Mrs. Henry] Wood, 1860–61
Eleanor's Victory, Mary Elizabeth Braddon, 1863
Emilia in England [*Sandra Belloni*], George Meredith, 1864
Evan Harrington, George Meredith, 1860
Felix Holt, the Radical, George Eliot, 1866

Foul Play, Charles Reade and Dion Boucicault, 1868
Framley Parsonage, Anthony Trollope, 1860–61
Grasp Your Nettle, Eliza Lynn Linton, 1865
Great Expectations, Charles Dickens, 1860–61
Griffith Gaunt, or Jealousy, Charles Reade, 1865–66
Hard Cash, Charles Reade, 1863
He Knew He Was Right, Anthony Trollope, 1868–69
Hidden Depths, Felicia Skene, 1866
High Church, Frederick William Robinson, 1860
The House by the Churchyard, Sheridan Le Fanu, 1861–63
John Marchmont's Legacy, Mary Elizabeth Braddon, 1862–64
*Johnny Robinson: The Story of the Childhood and Schooldays of an "Intelligent
     Artisan"* [Thomas Wright], 1868
Lady Audley's Secret, Mary Elizabeth Braddon, 1862
The Lady's Mile, Mary Elizabeth Braddon, 1866
The Last Chronicle of Barset, Anthony Trollope, 1866–67
Lesbia Brandon, Algernon Swinburne, 1952
Linda Tressel, Anthony Trollope, 1867–68
Lizzie Lorton of Greyrigg, Eliza Lynn Linton, 1866
Lorna Doone, R. D. Blackmore, 1869
Lost and Saved, Caroline Norton, 1863
Lost Sir Massingberd, James Payn, 1864
Lothair, Benjamin Disraeli, 1870
Love's Cross-Currents [*A Year's Letters*], Algernon Swinburne, 1877
Man and Wife, Wilkie Collins, 1870
Middlemarch, George Eliot, 1871–72
The Mill on the Floss, George Eliot, 1860
Miss Mackenzie, Anthony Trollope, 1865
Miss Marjoribanks, Margaret Oliphant, 1865–66
The Moonstone, Wilkie Collins, 1868
Mrs. Gerald's Niece, Lady Georgiana Fullerton, 1869
Nina Balatka, Anthony Trollope, 1866–67
No Name, Wilkie Collins, 1862–63
Not Wisely but Too Well, Rhoda Broughton, 1867
Orley Farm, Anthony Trollope, 1861–62
Our Mutual Friend, Charles Dickens, 1864–65
The Perpetual Curate, Margaret Oliphant, 1864
Phineas Finn, Anthony Trollope, 1867–69
Put Yourself in His Place, Charles Reade, 1869–70
Rachel Ray, Anthony Trollope, 1863
The Rector and the Doctor's Family, Margaret Oliphant, 1861
Rhoda Fleming, George Meredith, 1865
Romola, George Eliot, 1862–63

Salem Chapel, Margaret Oliphant, 1862–63
The Semi-Attached Couple, Emily Eden, 1860
Silas Marner, George Eliot, 1861
The Small House at Allington, Anthony Trollope, 1862–64
A Strange Story, Edward Bulwer-Lytton, 1861–62
The Struggles of Brown, Jones, and Robinson, Anthony Trollope, 1861–62
Sylvia's Lovers, Elizabeth Gaskell, 1863
Tom Brown at Oxford, Thomas Hughes, 1859–61
The Trial, Charlotte Mary Yonge, 1863
Two Marriages, Dinah Mulock Craik, 1867
Uncle Silas, Sheridan Le Fanu, 1864
Under Two Flags, Ouida [Marie Louise de la Ramée], 1867
The Vicar of Bullhampton, Anthony Trollope, 1869–70
The White Rose, G. J. Whyte-Melville, 1868
Wives and Daughters, Elizabeth Gaskell, 1864–66
The Woman in White, Wilkie Collins, 1859–60
Woodburn Grange, William Howitt, 1867

NOTES

Introduction

1. Critics who make smells their primary subject are relatively rare, Corbin and Rindisbacher providing the main exceptions to this rule, as do more recently A. Booth ("Scent") and Morrison ("Smelling Polyester"). Trotter is also alert to representations of smells ("New Historicism," *Cooking*), as are Wohl and Waters; Connor, Trotter's colleague in what they both call cultural phenomenology, explains, "I want critical writing to get back its sense of smell" (*CP*). An early important treatment of olfaction appears in Stallybrass and White, ch. 3; recent accounts of noxious smells in relation to Dickens's fiction are offered by Douglas-Fairhurst (132–37) and Lougy.

2. Most accounts of the sense of smell begin by elaborating on its ill repute. See Vroon (ch. 1) and W. Miller (66–79) for particularly lively accounts. On the "sensory biases of Western culture," see Howes, "Sensorial" 172; Le Guérer 153–75; Rindisbacher 149.

3. LeGuérer 27–34; on the Serer Ndut, see Classen, Howes, and Synnott 103. See also Classen, Howes, and Synnott, ch. 5; Classen, ch. 4.

4. Carpenter 473. Common sense as a philosophical position was articulated in the late eighteenth century by Thomas Reid and championed in the nineteenth by Sir William Hamilton, as Carpenter explains in his 1874 account (ch. 11).

5. These areas of interest in literary and cultural studies have been identified only relatively recently. Most historians seem to agree with the narrator of Patrick Süskind's *Perfume*, who refers to "the fleeting realm of scent" as "a domain that leaves no traces in history" (3). As Highmore points out, the "historicity of everyday sensation" is a subject "massively underdeveloped" in cultural studies (26). Yet such analysis can be traced back at least to Bourdieu's *Distinction* with its interest in the consumption of "cultural goods," a term that includes clothes and food as well as literature and art (see especially ch. 3). In a section called "OBJECT LESSONS," Bourdieu comments, "the social relations objectified in familiar objects . . . impress themselves through bodily experiences which may be as profoundly unconscious as the quiet caress of beige carpets or the thin clamminess of tattered, garish linoleum, the harsh smell of bleach or perfumes as imperceptible as a negative scent" (77). For an account of

various object-based studies, see Bill Brown, 190–91n16. For studies of the relation between objects and sensory perceptions in Victorian culture, see Connor, *CP*, *Dumbstruck*, and "Making"; Trotter, *Cooking*, "New Historicism"; Picker; I. Armstrong. On the sensual life of the bourgeoisie, see Gay. For a treatment of blushing as represented in nineteenth-century fiction, see O'Farrell.

   6. *Punch* 12/7/1867: 227; 4/26/1862: 166.

   7. As Rylance notes, "Victorian psychology was clearly overwhelmingly rationalist and intellectualist" (148), often avoiding the subject of the senses and their functions, despite the prominence of associationist emphases on "sensory and perceptual stimulation" (57). Boring, however, contends that the "English tradition . . . made perception the primary problem in psychology" (169). For accounts of the emerging science of psychology in the 1860s, see Dames 172–77; Rylance 70–71.

   8. Dimock 68. Even believers in the value of circumstantial evidence rely on their senses: if the footprint that Crusoe sees does not exactly constitute an experience of having seen a man (Welsh, *Strong* ix), it cannot become a form of evidence, circumstantial or otherwise, until it is seen. See Flint, *Victorians* 14–19, on the reliability of the vision that apprehends appearances. A similar faith animated one of the most extensive fads of the period, spiritualism (Owen 21–23; cf. Oppenheim, *Other* 39–44, 297–98, 312). When Lewes attacked the movement in an 1860 essay, he began by asserting, "Seeing *is* believing; and he that distrusts the evidence of his own sight, will have a difficulty in bringing forward evidence more convincing" ("Seeing" 381).

   9. The commentary in *The Senses* notes that the mere "names" of spring and summer conjure up "fragrances of fields" (131). The analysis offered by Victorian scientists reverses the direction of the process described in James Mill's associationist account of how sensations yield ideas (Rylance 59–60). Maudsley offers an extremely complicated explanation of the physiology that makes it possible for ideas to elicit physical sensations, afterward applying his theory to the arts (90–115). At least one twentieth-century critic seems to agree with Victorian conceptions of the physical effects of verbal stimuli: Terry notes that in reading Oliphant's *Salem Chapel*, "you can smell the ham and cheeses in Tozer's shop" (83).

   10. This passage has received quite a bit of critical attention, including commentaries by Gallagher (*Industrial* 237–43) and Trotter ("New Historicism" 36–40). My reading of this scene differs from such accounts by depicting Felix as explicitly constituted by his responses to odors, the perception of which he presumes himself to be above.

   11. W. Cohen, introductory remarks, "Matter out of Place," Modern Language Association, December 2002.

   12. Classen, Howes, and Synnott 95. This term is used by cultural anthropologists interested in founding a new field, an "anthropology of the senses" (Howes, "Sensorial" 167). Focusing on the senses as both the "bearers of culture" and the "shapers of culture" (Howes, *Varieties* 17), they examine "how

the senses are ordered by culture and express cultural values" (Classen 5). These anthropologists trace the roots of their intellectual endeavors to a 1967 article by Ong, who defined the sensorium, "a fascinating subject for cultural studies," as "in part determined by culture while at the same time it makes culture" (28). Functioning within an osmology, smells, though associated with dirt, are not treated like dirt. According to Douglas's well-known formulation in *Purity and Danger*, that substance defies categorization because it "is the by-product of a systematic ordering and classification of matter, in so far as ordering involves rejecting inappropriate elements" (36). Smells in high-Victorian fiction are routinely subjected to, not rejected by, such processes of "systematic ordering," on which Victorian culture placed a high value. In one of the first of the lectures that eventually came to make up *The Idea of a University*, John Henry Newman explains that human beings simply cannot use their senses without organizing all the impressions that they register, and he identifies that process as characteristic of the difference between "man" and "brute." According to Newman, the human mind is powerless to resist such impulses, and "*viewing* . . . the objects which sense conveys to the mind [and] throwing them into a system" is an elementary form of philosophy and science (60).

13. Williams, *Long* 47–48. On the difficulties of Williams's use of the term, see Williams, *Marxism* 132; Simpson 36, 43. In recent treatments of *Our Mutual Friend*, both Farrell and Morris invoke Williams's phrase and his approach, Morris using it as a way to place Dickens's novel in the context of "the main currents of feeling and social forces of the 1860s" (182). Influential studies as different as Bourdieu's *Distinction* and Crary's *Techniques of the Observer* make their cases by examining how their data constitute structures of feeling and sensation.

14. In Victorian usage, particularly in journalism, the term *encounter* could refer to a murderous conflict between two persons such as a duel or, on a larger scale, a battle (e.g., Altick, *Deadly Encounters* 11). The classic studies of encounters in modern Western society are Goffman's *The Presentation of Self in Everyday Life* and Sennett's *The Fall of Public Man*. The structure of encounter and the term itself have been used productively in historical and cultural criticism: e.g., Beer; Davidoff and Hall (450, pt. 3 passim); Gallagher and Greenblatt (6); P. Phelan (3–4); Wolfreys (5, 143); and Friedman (3–4, 9), who also offers an account of recent ethnographic theories of encounter (141–44). Cultural criticisms using approaches similar to those I adopt here include: W. Miller's analysis of current American society (ch. 9); and Jaffe's *Scenes of Sympathy*, which frequently uses the term *encounter*, although its focus on the specularity defined by the relation between a superior and the object of his or her sympathy or charity does not encompass the larger category of daily meetings that I call comparative encounters.

15. On the everyday, see Langbauer (19–33), who quotes Lefebvre's *Everyday Life in the Modern World* (98): "everyday insignificance can only become meaningful when transformed into something other than everyday life"

(cf. Lefebvre, *Critique* 246; Stewart 13–21). On the everyday as unrepresentable and its relations to class, see Highmore (19–24 and 103–4, respectively).

16. The exchanges that I treat here, though akin to monetary exchange, constitute a larger category of human interactions, both of which participate in a "universe of exchanges," to use the term offered by James Thompson, who in *Models of Value* (22) cites the idea from Simmel's *The Philosophy of Money* (see J. Thompson 206n21; Simmel 82–83). As Goux explains, exchange in any arena involves a "substitution" that creates "value or meaning" (224). See also Reddy's work on what he calls "monetary exchange asymmetry" (106, 94). For uses of the concept of exchange in relation to fiction, see N. Armstrong, *Desire* 117–18; Brantlinger, *Fictions*, ch. 4; cf. A. Anderson on reciprocity, 141, 197, 206–8, 226.

17. By contrast, both traditionally deferential eighteenth-century English culture and late-industrial, American democratic society have been described as involving encounters that, however different in their affective imports, ratify unchanging oppositions between their parties. See, respectively, Hadley, ch. 1; W. Miller, ch. 9. In both these accounts, what Hadley calls "face-to-face exchange" (15) and what Miller labels "the micropolitics of face-to-face interaction" (207) are the test of social organization.

18. On the meanings of these various terms, see Briggs, "Language" 49; Best ix–x; Gay, ch. 1; Cannadine, 101–2.

19. Although a range of factors—birth, education, occupation, income, habits, and manners—all contributed to a complicated system of inequalities, work and its material attributes were often seen as determinative. The occupational rankings that appeared in the census from 1841 on tended to confirm this role (Crossick 166; Hunt 1). See Baxter for a Victorian example of the difficulties of describing an "income-class" (7; cf. McClelland). Twentieth-century accounts tend to reject what is taken to be the simple economism of nineteenth-century formulations of class (see Cannadine 17). Central to such thinking has been Weber's conception of "status groups" as social formations that are "stratified according to the principles of their *consumption* of goods as represented by special styles of life" (rpt. Joyce, *Class* 39; cf. Hobsbawm, *Workers* 194).

20. *Felix Holt* 57–58. The relation between smell and class was widely recognized in the nineteenth century (Corbin, ch. 7 and 9; Le Guérer 26, 30), as have been more recently the political implications of olfactory responses (Le Guérer 27–34; Rindisbacher 22, 57; W. Miller, ch. 10; Classen, Howes, and Synnott, ch. 5; Stallybrass and White 140; Davidoff and Hall 383).

21. Poovey, in analyzing "the binary logic" of Victorian culture, identifies the dichotomy of gender as "*the* opposition upon which all the other opposi-tions claimed to be based" (*Uneven* 12), but a study of comparative encounters proposes that class deserves that distinction. The emphasis here counters attempts in recent historical and cultural studies to invalidate class as a descriptive or analytic category. Cannadine provides a good account of this

trend (8–17). For examples, see Joyce, *Democratic* 2; Calvert, ch. 8, 214; Reddy 31, 105. Stedman Jones's understandable rejection of class as simply or solely referential—"the *different* languages of class [do not] all share a single reference point in an anterior social reality" (*Languages* 7–8)—has been extended to involve a rejection of the category itself. Yet as Janowitz pointedly explains, "bourgeois ideology, in so far as it successfully universalizes itself, has an interest in denying the category of class altogether" (240). Moreover, even Joyce, who has mounted the most vigorous attack on class and who favors analyzing supposedly classless collectivities like "the human heart" and "the people" (*Democratic* 1, 63) proves the relevance of class analysis by using its terminology throughout his study of Victorian lives. Class is, as Dimock and Gilmour note of the concept, "continually problematic and problematically indispensable" (11). See Hoppen (4, 65) and Finn (187, 243) on the multiple determinants of Victorian identities.

22. As Langland puts the point, class is "inscribed on the body through characteristic postures, modes of speech, thought, and feeling" (60). Many valuable analyses of Victorian culture assume that the class distinctions of an industrialized society are predominantly a function of the relations between groups. Social historians characteristically speak of "the personal, face-to-face relationships of patronage" characteristic of eighteenth-century social organization as opposed to "the impersonal solidarities of class" (Perkin 51) and "the innumerable gradations of individual placings" of the former as opposed to the "more limited number of collective categories" characteristic of the latter (Cannadine 29). Cf. Hadley's work on nineteenth-century market society, which focuses on "factions" such as theatre audiences (56–57) or the poor as conceived by bureaucratic administrators (ch. 3). For discussions of how Victorians experienced and understood the structure of their society, see Mill 3: 758, 767, 896; 19: 447; Marx and Engels 80, 91; Neale 145–47; M. Booth 64; Gloag 147, 201–2. For analyses of this question, see Crossick 159–60; Hoppen 49–50; Joyce, *Class* 6–11; Neale 133–35. Cannadine offers the fullest treatment of class strucutures when he proposes that British society has been understood according to three models—as a hierarchy, as a tripartite division, and as a dichotomy between "them" and "us" (20), although his conclusion that notions of hierarchy predominated in the mid-Victorian period (101–3) is not confirmed by the evidence of comparative encounters.

23. W. Miller 68; Lougy 476–85; cf. Trotter on the "pure negativity of the nausea" that the sense of smell "provokes" ("New Historicism" 43).

24. Qtd. Stallybrass and White 139. In Chadwick's *Sanitary Report*, human beings become "human miasms" more capable than even "the effluvia from dead organic matter" of spreading disease through their stench (413). On the report see Poovey (*Making*, ch. 6) and Childers (ch. 5).

25. Corbin notes that in France from the middle of the nineteenth century, anxieties focused, not on smells as they had previously, but on dust and smoke (134). *Our Mutual Friend* seems to offer an instance of this relatively new

concern, as does *Tom Brown at Oxford*, which locates the "reek of the great city" in the "loathsome dust" of Rotten Row in Hyde Park (1: 308).

26. Some commentators take the success of such efforts for granted (e.g., Howes, "Olfaction" 144–46; Rindisbacher 20–22). Corbin, in his study of French olfactory culture, makes prominent their material successes even as he offers a perspective, which I extend here, that casts doubt on their psychological effectiveness.

27. Rindisbacher 116, 162. Cf. A. Booth, "Scent"; Sutherland, *Is* 196–98. Such late-nineteenth-century texts have proven to be of particular interest to cultural anthropologists and even scientists; see Classen 33; Classen, Howes, and Synnott 86; Stoddart 129.

28. Corbin makes this point in relation to the smells associated with nineteenth-century French bourgeois women (176).

29. See Morrison's "Smelling Polyester" for John Waters's experiments in odorama; Banes, on the use of odorants in "aroma design" in theatrical productions; and Drobnick, on high art that smells.

30. Both contemporaries and subsequent historians have characterized the 1860s and the longer mid-Victorian period, usually construed as beginning in the 1850s and ending in the 1870s, as times of peace and prosperity: London *Times* of 1865 (rpt. G. M. Young, facing 2: 502); Burn 17; Arnstein, ch. 5; Briggs, *Making*, ch. 8; Joyce, *Work* 52, 90; Cannadine 99; and in a more qualified form, Hoppen 234. Writing about sensation fiction, however, P. Gilbert refers to "the troubled" and "the anxious 1860s" (85, 89). See Hewitt for commentaries on this question.

31. For other characterizations of the 1860s as transitional, see the 1872 introduction to the second edition of Bagehot's *The English Constitution* 5: 166–67; *The Education of Henry Adams*, qtd. Burn 300; Stedman Jones, *Outcast*, ch. 13; Hobsbawm, *Age* 80, 160; Gallagher, *Industrial*, ch. 9; Nead; Trotter, *Cooking* 16, 29; Chase and Levenson, conclusion.

32. This perspective counters a dominant trend in Victorian studies, the identification of the modernity of urban experience as the hallmark of Victorian culture. See Nead 1–8; Parsons, ch. 1; Wolfreys 12–13; cf. Humpherys. As Plotz explains, London's growth in the first half of the nineteenth century "meant that chance encounters on [its] streets produced a new sort of social life, both a pleasant and a threatening urban anonymity" (1). Along with Plotz's work on crowds, see the studies of the sights and sounds on city streets (Nead; Picker) and of the social effects of the nature of urban dwellings and living arrangements (Chase and Levenson; Marcus; Hoppen 71). London in the 1860s constituted a particularly obvious locus for what I call comparative encounters simply because its great construction projects—railroad stations, the underground, and the Thames embankment—increased the daily contact between those living and working in the city. For London in the 1860s, see Stedman Jones, *Outcast* 161–3, 166–71, 180, 243; Nead, pt. 1, ch. 2. Stallybrass and White also comment on the London street as a "'mingle-mangle', 'a hodge-

podge'" (128). Even middle-class women were outdoors often enough regularly to meet and to be met (Nead 64–73; Nord 143–147). As Nead and Jaffe have separately argued, judging the status of a stranger on a city street could be a difficult, even perilous undertaking (Nead 72, 132–34; and Jaffe, *Scenes*, ch. 2; cf. Parsons 22–23). On the relative reliability of such visual signs, however, see N. Armstrong, *Fiction* 123, 127; cf. Flint, *Victorians* 14–19.

33. The meaning of the term *gentleman* has been widely canvassed (Castronovo, Gilmour, Girouard, A. Young). See also: Crossick 164–65; Burn 257; Newsom, *Charles Dickens* 149, ch. 7. Although a number of prominent considerations of Victorian middle-class culture have focused on its pretensions to the behavior and status of the aristocracy—N. Armstrong, *Desire* 160; Kucich, *Power* 51, 81; Staten—an analysis of comparative encounters reveals that the relation between the middle classes and their nearest superiors, the gentry, was more crucial—a judgment confirmed by the analysis provided by Davidoff and Hall.

34. The classic statement of how negative projection incorporates the "Other" is offered by Stallybrass and White: "The bourgeois subject continuously defined and re-defined itself through the exclusion of what it marked out as 'low'—as dirty, repulsive, noisy, contaminating. . . . The low was internalized under the sign of negation and disgust . . . return[ing] as the object of nostalgia, longing and fascination" (191). The explanatory force of this formulation is undeniable. Yet encounters and exchanges often demonstrate that the low is internalized, not through "negation and disgust" or even "longing and fascination," but through approbation and respect. Kucich also objects that "middle-class self-consciousness is not always a sublimated displacement of disturbing energies and desires" (*Power* 73). For revealing studies of the intricacies of such processes, see Jaffe's *Scenes of Sympathy*, which significantly complicates the model offered by Stallybrass and White (e.g., 19), and A. Anderson's reformulation of it in her adaptation of Habermas's model of "communicative action" (203–4; cf. 226). For a more conventional invocation of the concept of negative projection, see Herbert 169–84.

35. Bodenheimer, *Politics* 3. See Kay for a particularly useful definition of the political as encompassing both everyday behavior and the workings of the state (2–4).

36. Bain lamented that "much remains to be known" about "the *actions of odours*" on the nose (163; cf. *Senses* 133, 157), and twentieth-century psychophysiology has also been unable to explain how olfaction takes place (Geldard 483–84; Vroon 34, 51). See, however, Burr's account of the theories of Luca Turin. Many of the often speculative conclusions of Victorian commentators have been confirmed by the more recent work of zoologists, neurobiologists, and experimental psychologists. In the discussions that follow, I use the terms *smell* or *smelling* and *olfaction*, or *sensation*, and *perception* interchangeably, not distinguishing in the case of the first three terms, as some twentieth-century scientists do, between olfaction as specific to the olfactory organ and smell as

also encompassing responses of the trigeminal nerve and the vomeronasal organ
(Finger and Silver 4) or in the case of the last two terms, as Victorian scientists
rarely did, between a stimulus and a response to it.

Chapter 1

1. Twentieth-century science has located where olfaction happens, thereby
confirming many of the conclusions that Victorian commentators based on
speculation and the observation of everyday experience. The emotional nature
of olfactory response, not as often the subject of experimental research as it
might be (Lawless 128), has come to be understood in terms of its anatomical
origins. After olfactory stimuli are received by the cilia of the sensory nerves in
the olfactory organ high in the nasal cavity, they are processed in the rhinencephalon, close to the limbic system and the basal ganglia, seats, respectively, of
hormonal activity and autonomic or involuntary responses (Vroon 13; Howes,
"Olfaction" 132; Stoddart, ch. 2). These cerebral structures together govern
unconscious responses—emotions, automatic movements, appetites, and urges.
The olfactory system and those directly connected with it are prior in phyloge-
netic development to the other sensory systems of the human body, and
twentieth-century scientists often use almost Victorian terminology to speak of
olfaction as a function of the "deepest parts of our brain" (Stoddart 47) and
"the most primitive" nervous system in the body (Geldard 445; cf. Bain 21).
Moreover, what is true of phylogeny holds in ontogeny. Smell is the first sense
that develops in a fetus; complete by roughly the fifth month of gestation, it
presumably provides a human being's first sense experience by allowing the
unborn child to perceive the odor of amniotic fluid (Vroon 75, 21; Mennella
and Beauchamp 202; cf. Bain 23).

2. Again modern science has offered anatomical explanations of this
conclusion by insisting on the distinction between the older parts of the brain,
with which smelling is associated, and the faculties that make possible cogni-
tion and particularly language: smell has "relatively few direct connections with
the youngest part of the brain—namely, the left neocortex, a system which
houses, for example, 'language centers'" (Vroon 13; cf. Howes, "Olfaction"
132). Both science and language, then, would seem to be less able to deal with
olfactory experience than with visual information, and that has demonstrably
been the case in the long history of sensationistic philosophy and experimental
psychology (Boring 113–14). Odors as sensory stimulants famously resist
categorization, the process of ordering phenomena that is basic to scientific
method (Vroon 47–53, Geldard 454–58; cf. Lawless 156–60).

3. The "olfactory-verbal gap" is evident whenever experimental subjects
reveal that they can recognize smells without being able to name them (Lawless
151–53). See also Classen 56; W. Miller 67; Rindisbacher 64–65; Vroon 111.

4. Wilson's formulation exactly corresponds to Freud's later understanding
of smell in relation to Eros and Thanatos, for which see Rindisbacher 13–14,

103. For examples of the hedonic distinctions between smells, including those I offer here, see Classen 101; Classen, Howes, and Synnott, pt. 2; Vroon 76–77.

5. P. Phelan, ch. 1. As Phelan wittily puts it, "If representational visibility equal[ed] power, then almost-naked young white women should be running Western culture" (10). As Classen notes, "the 'other' is assigned an odour, but not usually allowed a voice" (149n29). See also Classen, Howes, and Synnott, ch. 5; Morrison, *Explanation*, ch. 1; Ed Cohen 32. Harvey offers a visual version of this argument when he treats the black that men wear as "the colour . . . without colour," the absence that is also "the signature of what they have: standing, goods, mastery" (10).

6. Geldard 458–62, Vroon 58–63. Whether this effect is the result of habituation or sensory fatigue is a question that modern science cannot yet answer (Lawless 141).

7. Chadwick 203. See also Poovey, *Making* 122; cf. P. Logan, ch. 6.

8. *Economic and Philosophic Manuscripts of 1844*, rpt. Baxandall and Morawski 52. See also *Selected Writings* 94, 152–54, 174.

9. For a different commentary on Marx's *Capital* as novelistic, see Cvetkovich, ch. 7.

10. On *Past and Present*, see Carlisle, "Introduction," *Factory Lives*. Similarly, Plotz analyzes Carlyle's *Chartism* by emphasizing the extent to which Carlyle sees in Chartist crowds an embodiment of "the 'deep dumb inarticulate want' of the English people" (137).

11. Rindisbacher makes this point in his discussion of a German novel of 1855, Gustav Freytag's *Soll und Haben*, emphasizing how smells in this particular text are used to maintain borders between "social and class lines, male and female realms" (57). None of the other novels that he treats in *The Smell of Books* resembles so closely the osmology of high-Victorian English fiction. Twentieth-century conceptions of smell tend to emphasize the ability of olfactory experience to erase borders; as Horkheimer and Adorno insist: "Of all the senses smelling . . . testifies most clearly to the urge to abandon and assimilate oneself to the other. . . . In the act of seeing one remains oneself, in smelling one dissolves" (qtd. Rindisbacher 151n17). As a physiological principle, this generalization requires qualification because, as a recent theorist on smell notes, the effects of olfaction are highly dependent on context and situation (Engen 86). For a revealing account of bodily borders and their permeability in Victorian culture, see H. Michie.

12. Again twentieth-century physiology specifies the anatomy on which such Victorian perspectives on olfaction were based: an odorant must penetrate the mucous layer at the top of the nasal passages before it can reach the cilia of the sensory nerves in the olfactory organ (Vroon 27–28); the mechanism for smelling is therefore both deep within the head and uniquely unprotected from assault (Cowart et al., 177). One twentieth-century psychologist contends that "of all the senses, smell probably best meets the basic function of a sense: making a distinction between *me* and *not me*"

(Vroon 185), but if that is so, the process of smelling depends on directly violating the distinction that it creates.

13. Qtd. Howes, "Olfaction" 136. For the role of smells in marking transitions, see Gell; Howes, "Olfaction," which discusses the perspectives on this function offered by Douglas and Turner (141–42).

14. Classen, Howes, and Synnott 83–84, 96. Waters surveys this association as it appears in Victorian literature (134–48; cf. ch. 9) and identifies it as a way of indicating female sexuality without violating the taboo against its mention (137). See also Classen 30–32; Corbin, ch. 11; Seaton 16–20; Davidoff and Hall 190–91, 374; Rindisbacher 82.

15. For discussions of the relations between gender and perfume, see Classen, Howes, and Synnott 36, 83; Corbin 68–70, 181–86. There is, of course, no necessary relation between the smells exuded by women and the heteronormativity typical of Victorian narratives. See, for instance, A. Booth's analysis of twentieth-century texts that pit language against the sensation of smell "to dislocate sexual identities" ("Scent," 17). In only one case that I know is a male character associated with an odor of vegetation. Squire Wentworth, who cannot keep track of the many children he has had by his successive wives, first appears in Oliphant's *The Perpetual Curate* as he walks beside a row of lime trees "in glorious blossom, filling the air with that mingling sense of fragrance and music which is the soul of [that] murmurous tree" (157). According to Linnaeus, lime trees give off the odor of sperm, which was thought in the nineteenth century to constitute "the essence of life" (Vroon 48; Corbin 36), so the squire here may be marked with the aroma of the fertility he seems unable to control.

16. The best-known speculation on this subject is that offered by Freud in the note to *Civilization and Its Discontents*, in which he links the lessening of the sexual power of smell in "civilized" human beings to their upright posture. For commentaries on Freud's analysis, see Mavor 64–66; W. Miller 70–78; Rindisbacher 103, 150–52; Stoddart 124–26. See also Stoddart's study in evolutionary biology for the speculation that the light floral scents of the perfumes now worn by women originated in the gendered division of labor among hunter-gatherers that relegated to women close contact with presumably odoriferous plants (161–67, 233).

17. Davidoff and Hall 281, 116. See also Poovey's analysis of the Victorian tendency to reduce women to their maternal instincts and reproductive organs (*Uneven* 7, ch. 2; *Making* 171).

18. The spiritual use to which odors can be put has been a focus of anthropological study (Howes, "Olfaction"; Gell; cf. Wilson 63, 85). Particularly interesting in relation to female sexuality are Gell's comments on smell as the sense that registers "moments . . . of *materialisation* and *dematerialisation*" and on its role in exciting desires for and expectations of "richer sensory content" (28). Cf. Stoddart, ch. 7.

19. From this perspective, the powerfully constitutive role in middle-class culture that studies in the last two decades have granted Victorian women as

the sources and arbiters of representation is put in question by the function that such women fulfill as bearers of matter. For classic statements of the relation between women and representation, see N. Armstrong, *Desire*; Poovey, *Uneven*; and Langland, who emphasizes the relative power of middle-class Victorian women by focusing on their centrality to "the privileging of representational value over use value, and the deployment of representations in managing class unrest" (6). Interestingly, the historical account offered by Davidoff and Hall, the third part of whose *Family Fortunes* treats the "encounters" of "daily life" (450), does not share this emphasis on the power of women in relation to representation.

20. Flint, *Woman* 12. Flint similarly notes that whether the discussion of the effect that reading had on women was "conducted by men or by women," it was "very frequently used to uphold or reinforce dominant patriarchal structures" (10).

Chapter 2

1. E. Cohen 27–28; cf. A. Miller 161–62. Possessing property, having complete control and discretion over it, was a central way of defining an individual man's freedom and power. See Nunokawa for an analysis of Georg Simmel's thinking on this question (77); Pocock for an explanation of the relation between different conceptions of property, personality, and masculinity; and Poovey for a discussion of the alienation suffered by all men under capitalism (*Uneven* 76–77). Analyses over the last twenty years of the cultural construction of individuals gendered male have revealed a wide variety of Victorian masculinities and a range of registers within which such constructions evolve: sexuality (E. Cohen, W. A. Cohen, Craft, Lane), social and moral values (Gilmour, Girouard), art and literature (Sussman), intellectual labor (Adams, Dowling), physicality (Cvetkovich, ch. 7; D. Hall; London), myth and history (Munich, Kestner, Girouard), mental disorder (Oppenheim, *"Shattered"*; J. Wood, ch. 2), religion (Vance), age (Robson), domesticity (Tosh, Sullivan). H. Michie helpfully coordinates many of these various analyses (412–19). Central to all these conceptions of middle-class masculinity are self-discipline and self-restraint. Most recent treatments of masculinity in the Victorian culture stress the various assertions of manhood typical of the period. Such assertions assume the "fragility of [a] masculinity" (Roper and Tosh 15) that is either "under stress" (Adams 25) or facing "dissolution" (Sussman 62), reflecting, as one commentator notes, "the high Victorian fascination with spectacles of male failure" (Sullivan 100). As Paul Morrison puts the point when commenting on a quotation from Trollope, "The excess in which the pursuit of masculinity issues always betrays the lack in which it originates" (*Explanation* 125). Danahay's perspective on the "masculine autobiography" of the Victorian period as a form based on "the ideal of autonomy and a corresponding nostalgia for the lost intimacy represented by community" (7) is aligned with my readings of Victorian fiction. Treatments of the economic

determinants of Victorian masculinities include Stearns's *Be a Man!* (ch. 4 and 5), the third chapter of Leverenz's study of the American Renaissance, and Sussman's treatment of art and literature in the context of industrialism (ch. 1) and the emerging commodity market (153–58). On this subject Davidoff and Hall take economic considerations seriously, treating them in relation to religious and moral issues; and the melancholia on which I focus here could be seen as the outcome of the developments that they analyze in *Family Fortunes*. As they demonstrate, the mid-Victorian ideal of gentility often drew in partial or contradictory ways on the traditional values presumably embodied by the land-holding gentry (73, 110, 227).

2. This point appears in almost every study of Victorian masculinities from Gay's (ch. 2) to D. Hall's *Fixing Patriarchy*, in which male anxieties of the 1860s are specifically analyzed as a response to collective action undertaken by middle-class women during that decade (177–78). Robson offers revealing analyses of the function of "the little girl" as a constituent of the identities of middle-class Victorian men. A. Young treats the relation between all women and lower-middle-class men as an "informal alliance . . . in their resistance to cultural and literary marginalization" (3).

3. Radden 39–40; Foucault notes that women were unlikely to suffer from melancholia, though if they did, their symptoms were more severe than those typical of men (*Madness* 120). According to mid-Victorian mad-doctor John Conolly, women were particularly prone to religious melancholy (rpt. Bourne Taylor and Shuttleworth 19–20). Only when it was labeled depression in the late nineteenth century was melancholy predominantly gendered as female (Radden 40–44). The male melancholic whose sufferings I analyze in this chapter had his female counterpart in the "love-mad woman," a convention examined by Small (see especially her treatment of Miss Havisham [ch. 6]). Cf. J. Wood, chs. 1 and 2.

4. Oppenheim, *"Shattered"* 27. For commentaries on nineteenth-century conceptions of melancholia, see Oppenheim, *"Shattered,"* passim; Radden, "Introduction." For uses of the terms *melancholia* and *melancholy* to analyze nineteenth-century texts, see Wiesenthal (ch. 4), who places Trollope's *He Knew He Was Right* in the context of the tradition of melancholia from Burton to Kristeva; and Lucas, who uses Kant's definition of the "man of melancholy disposition" to characterize Dickens. Kant's conception, which defines melancholy as a form of freedom, dignity, and self-respect untouched by time or the opinions of others (xii), contrasts markedly to the condition that I analyze here, therefore suggesting the range of meanings that attach to the term. For medical authorities like Prichard and Esquirol, for instance, melancholia remained synonymous with monomania (see Bourne Taylor and Shuttleworth 251–62). J. Wood (60–65) uses the term *hypochondriasis* to label some of the symptoms of the mental disorder that I identify as male melancholia.

5. The character type that I analyze here is related to the "feminine heroes" identified by Showalter (ch. 5), though it is a creation of both male and female

novelists and it is not endowed with the energy that she finds typical of such figures (136). The melancholic is also like the anxious and passive "hero" of the Waverley novels analyzed by Welsh, though the 1860s character reflects far different economic conditions than those that mold Scott's protagonists (*Hero* 38, 82–83).

6. On the relation between fictional narratives and medical discourse on mental disorders, see P. Logan; Shuttleworth 13–16; Small, ch. 2; Vrettos. The specific model that I follow here is Maudsley's, who usefully outlines the definitional difficulties involved in using the term *melancholy* (320–23).

7. Morrison's formulation comes from an earlier version of the second chapter of *The Explanation for Everything* (see 21–29). Welsh fully demonstrates the centrality of Hamlet to nineteenth-century characterization: "the ghost of Hamlet—the son and not the father—frequented the nineteenth century so often and so freely that it is difficult to imagine the course of literary history without him" (*Hamlet* 100). Arac offers a perspective on the identification of Hamlet as central to questions about character, though Arac does not see such melancholy as a specifically gendered quality ("Hamlet"). *Hamlet* provides the touchstone for Gallagher and Greenblatt's chapter on *Great Expectations* (ch. 6). For a more extensive analysis of the relation between the play and *Great Expectations* as a revenge novel, see Welsh, *Hamlet*, ch. 4. Also pertinent here is Welsh's identification of modernist Hamlets as writers (153–54, 158–59). Cf. J. Wood, ch. 2.

8. Nervous exhaustion was conceived by the psychophysiologists who commented on it as a condition particularly prevalent among middle-class men in commercial or professional occupations, and its causes were consistently identified as overwork and worry (Oppenheim, *"Shattered"* 152–58). The businessman Pole in Meredith's *Emilia in England* exemplifies the type: his "nervous disease" renders him, in the words of one of the more vulgar characters, "peaky and puky" (2: 199, 206); as the narrator notes, "melancholy had become a habit with" Pole (3: 37). In an uncharacteristically emotive passage of *The Senses and the Intellect*, Bain calls such a condition "nervous fatigue," whose "peculiar quality or tone cannot be seized by any descriptive phrase," though he does try to describe it by quoting Tennyson's "Mariana," "I am aweary, aweary, O God that I were dead" (123–24). Allen analyzes a similar depressive complaint that he calls "Massive Discomfort" (19). Oppenheim's discussion of "Manly Nerves" (*"Shattered,"* ch. 5) treats the gendered implications of nervous exhaustion, particularly in relation to conflicts between fathers and sons.

9. As Bourdieu has noted, the difference between the substantiality of working-class food and the more purely formal qualities of middle-class food clearly embodies class distinctions (199, 190).

10. *Great Expectations* 295, 294. For more symbolic readings of food in this novel, see two essays by Hardy and Watt, the former of whom finds in its depiction "the moral significances of everyday life" (352).

11. Gloag uses a phrase from the last chapter of *The Pickwick Papers* to epitomize this central Victorian value: in an early instance of the phenomenon that I am charting, the narrator there speaks of "every attention to substantial comfort" (qtd. xvi).

12. Newsom identifies Philip Pip as the character's legal name (*Charles Dickens Revisited* 52), a formulation supported by the conversational practices of the characters of the novel: Biddy, Jaggers, and Herbert call him "Mr. Pip," and Herbert specifies that Mr. Pip's first name is Philip. How the author of his own story names himself when he is telling it is open to debate.

13. Foucault, *Madness and Civilization* 212–14. See Cheyne, i, 121.

14. (1862 ed.), qtd. Radden 236–37. Interestingly, Smiles eliminated this passage from his 1866 edition of *Self-Help* (304), its irrelevance at that later date being perhaps made evident by the manliness demonstrated by those who participated in the volunteer movement, whose political implications I trace in "Picturing Reform." According to the *OED*, "Male Green-Sicknesse" is a condition recognized by Shakespeare in *Henry IV* and described in an early nineteenth-century medical text (*green sickness, greensick*).

15. "Mourning and Melancholia" 14: 245, 251. Hamlet, significantly, is the only specific example of melancholia offered by Freud in "Mourning and Melancholia" (246). The 1895 draft on melancholia treats the condition in relation to sexual "anaesthesia"; its most pertinent observations for the definition of melancholia presented here deal with its sources in passivity and powerlessness: "impotent [individuals] incline to melancholia" (1: 204). See Welsh, *Hamlet* 51–53. See also Butler's use of Freud's conception of melancholia to analyze gender identification (*Gender* 57–65) and as a basis for what she identifies as "*heterosexual melancholy*" (*Bodies* 234–35); cf. Litvak, ch. 1. Also related to my definition of melancholia is Kucich's contention that repression in Dickens's "gentrified (male) characters" is the source of their "social authority" (*Repression* 268–69).

16. See Radden 30–32; Batten, passim. Although Batten equates melancholy, despair, and ennui in ways that I resist, her study of Romantic melancholy parallels mine in its interest in the conjunctions of work, loss, and nostalgia in the context of commodity culture. Lepenies's sociology of melancholy treats only highly self-conscious and self-aware manifestations of melancholy, though relevant here is his identification of it as a disease of nineteenth-century bourgeois culture in Germany resulting from the impotence felt by those who never had opportunities to exercise political power (ch. 4).

17. See R. Thomas for an analysis of the interpenetration of economic and psychological models in Freud. My analysis of Pip coordinates with Thomas's treatment of the character (ch. 3).

18. The distinction between commodities and objects drawn by Jones and Stallybrass is pertinent here: capitalist culture fetishizes commodities, not objects; what governs social relations in such a culture is not the materiality of things but the abstractions consequent on their exchange value (7–8). In that

sense, I am describing the condition of the melancholic as a longing for an earlier state of social relations in which the objects made by an artisan had not yet become commodities.

19. As numerous historical studies reveal, gentility in the Victorian period was predicated on distancing oneself from the physical proximity of commodities (Wiener; Cain and Hopkins, ch. 1; Davidoff and Hall 229). As Welsh puts it, "Nineteenth-century gentility still posits a certain ease: on the assumption that just having something is better than making it" (*Hamlet* 130). Gilmour pertinently concludes his analysis of *Great Expectations* with a discussion of the "haunting knowledge of the social exclusions and psychological repressions that make gentility possible" (144). Scarry comments on such exclusions when she retells "imagistically" the story of the creation of commodities: the body of the worker touching the commodity he makes becomes enormous, "larger and more vivid" than it has been; the body of the capitalist as he touches the commodity begins "to evaporate, grow airy: he [is] spiritualized, and disappear[s]" (275). Though this retelling captures middle-class anxieties about substantiality and fears about the physicality of the working classes, it overlooks the extent to which capitalists are defined by not touching what workers make. Here again Freud's analysis of melancholia is suggestive: he notes that the ambivalence at its root either may be a function of the melancholic's mental "constitution" or it may "proceed . . . precisely from those experiences that involved the threat of losing the object." Freud also assigns the "struggles" created by such "object-loss" to the unconscious, "the region of the memory-traces of *things*" rather than words (14: 256–57).

20. The reading version of the novel that Dickens had printed but did not perform simply eliminates Estella from the story, thereby suggesting, pace Schor (ch. 6), Estella's irrelevance to its central plot, if not to the elaborations that turned that plot into the novel *Great Expectations*.

21. These encounters depend for their effect on the kind of iteration that Butler identifies as central to performativity, the way in which culturally constructed differences are enacted by individuals who repeatedly but most often unconsciously "'cite' the norm" of a system of inequalities to establish their identities within it (*Bodies* 232; cf. 234, *Gender* 140–41).

22. Interestingly, Dickens, in making Joe a blacksmith, has Pip reject a trade that was becoming more, not less, materially evident during the Victorian period. Because more roads were needed to link the places reached by railways, the number of horses increased (F. M. L. Thompson, "Nineteenth" 64) and, along with them, the work for blacksmiths. Between 1851 and 1901, the number of horses used in commerce quadrupled, and "Victoria's reign saw the apogee of the horse world" (Chartres and Turnbull 1: 314). Between 1831 and 1851, the number of blacksmiths in England and Wales therefore nearly doubled (Burnett 257, Mathias 239); and it was not until the 1870s that the rate of increase among blacksmiths began to be outstripped by the rate of the increase in the general population (Burnett 262). More important, blacksmiths

were typically well employed even when men in other crafts found opportunities for work becoming more scarce, their wages decreasing, and their control over the conditions of their labor diminishing rapidly. As urbanization continued and villages became smaller, the village blacksmith became more important as a local craftsman, and smaller and smaller local populations were able to support him as the significance and variety of his work increased. The phrase *blacksmith made* was a term of particular praise for the quality and often the specialization of a particular tool (Chartres and Turnbull 1: 321, 323). As more and more varied machines were developed for agricultural use, blacksmiths developed the skills that evolved into the new trade of engineering; by 1851, three hundred engineering firms, which had their origins in the work of country blacksmiths and foundries, were exhibiting their wares at the Great Exhibition (E. J. T. Collins 1: 203). As a smart lad with a certain amount of ambition, Pip might have grown up to enjoy, had he served out his apprenticeship with Joe, a life of material comforts as the reward for increasingly diverse, inventive, and presumably satisfying work.

23. For an influential and controversial account of the deleterious effects of the characteristic Victorian distaste for trade, see Wiener. His analysis of "the gentrification of the Victorian middle classes" (14) is supported by the osmology inherent in high-Victorian fiction. Hampden-Turner treats the twentieth-century survival of such attitudes in *Gentlemen and Tradesmen*, tracing British economic woes to the disdain for the material and the practical exhibited by "gentrified, merchantilist, *haute bourgeoisie* who manage and finance capitalism" (100). Davidoff and Hall nicely capture the ambivalence of Victorian culture toward commerce and manufacture, whose "physical objects" might be dirty but whose very "dirt and drama" might hold "a special fascination" (270). For discussion and qualification of Wiener's thesis, see Malchow 363–80.

24. On the relation between unproductive labor and writing, see Jaffe, *Scenes*, ch. 2, especially 67–69.

25. Mayhew seems to misread Mill's definition of productive labor. Mill does not equate it with work creative of "material objects," but with work creative of "material wealth" (2: 49–50). But Mayhew is correct in saying that Mill classes merchants and dealers as productive, as rightly placed among those who, in Mill's words, endow "external material things with properties which render them serviceable to human beings" because they deliver goods where they are needed (2: 47, 46).

26. Here again Pip's story is representative since middlemen were increasingly important in the Victorian economy. Yet Dickens is also careful to give Pip the opportunity to make his career as a middleman in a sector of the economy that became particularly successful by the early 1860s. The tonnage in and out of Britain doubled between the 1840s and 1860s; by 1850, 60% of the world's tonnage was registered in Britain. With the coming of iron ships at midcentury, whose capacity increased fourfold between 1850 and 1860, the

business opportunities for shipping seemed almost unlimited (Briggs, *Making* 399, 398, 395). Pip's final comments on the success of Clarriker and Co. are therefore, I think, understatements typical of his consistent pose of self-effacement. Cf. C. Brown 71–72. Dickens's sons at the time of his writing this novel faced quite different economic conditions (Carlisle, Introduction, *Great Expectations* 15–16).

27. Although Pip is as diffident about using the word *apprentice* in relation to Herbert as Herbert is in using the word *clerk* in relation to Pip, Pip's signing of articles "of which Herbert was the subject" (297) puts them on the same level: as Magwitch makes a gentleman, Pip, the former blacksmith's apprentice, makes his gentleman friend into an apprentice clerk. (For more positive readings of this relationship, see Sheehan 103; Robbins, "How to Be" 188–91.) Throughout the nineteenth century, the majority of clerks, particularly commercial clerks, were trained first as apprentices or junior clerks. In one bank in Liverpool, for instance, 84% of the clerks employed between 1850 and 1875 served apprenticeships before becoming full-fledged employees (G. Anderson 14). In 1871, 350 firms in Liverpool employed 420 salaried clerks and 950 apprentices; among brokers the proportion of apprentices to clerks was even higher: 400 brokers employed 300 clerks and 1000 apprentices (Lockwood 26). These youths, who began their work at between fourteen and seventeen years old, were miserably paid on the customary ground that they were being trained—a system that worked principally because they also believed that their training would lead to opportunities for steady work and even management or ownership of a company. The labor that such apprentices did was often menial or mind-numbingly repetitive (G. Anderson 20–21, 15). By the Victorian midcentury, particularly in brokerage firms, apprenticeship might mean years of service at the end of which there would be no regular position. What made conditions more difficult for many apprentice clerks was the presence in their offices of relatively wealthy sons of gentlemen—of merchants, bankers, professionals, even aristocrats—serving apprenticeships before their parents or relatives invested the capital that would make them partners in their own firms. They were "the crowning curses" of less fortunate apprentices (qtd. Lockwood 25): because they did not need a wage, such men depressed the income of those who did (G. Anderson 13–14); and their status was often marked by the fact that they, like Herbert at the counting house, worked for no salary at all. It was not unusual for such apprentices to bring with them large premiums, often hundreds of pounds (Klingender 5). Their gentlemanly educations and genteel prospects distinguished them from the vast majority of clerks who would spend their lives earning no more than £100 or £150 a year. As a contemporary put it, "These lucky gentlemen . . . may easily be distinguished by the observant as, early in the afternoon, they saunter homewards, weary and languishing, thoroughly convincing the onlooker that they consider work 'a horrid bore, you know'" (qtd. Lockwood 25).

28. On the relation between economic and psychological control, see Shuttleworth 35-37. On the economy figured as an unpredictable female force, see Brantlinger, *Fictions*; Walsh, who treats *Great Expectations* in the context of the midcentury's changing economic conditions.

29. Hobsbawm, *Age* 260, 250. Pettitt aligns Pip's characterization with Marx's thinking about the effects of a capitalist economy (245, 248-49).

30. Weiss, ch. 7; Hoppen, ch. 9; Lockwood 19; House 645. In 1851, only 44,000 men, approximately .8% of the workforce, were employed as clerks (Mathias 239, Lockwood 36). Stearns explains that the development of corporate capitalism replaced older forms of "economic manhood" and its "claims to property" with standards of individuality based on income (98).

31. Williams similarly generalizes Marx's point in *The Country and the City* when he explains that the "total character of what we know as modern society" has been "determined, in Britain, by capitalism," amounting for everyone concerned in "real social processes of alienation, separation, externality, abstraction" (295, 298).

32. Lowe 40. Cultural critics with significantly different goals focus on the connection between nostalgia and melancholy. Dever calls Collins's *The Woman in White* "a tour de force of melancholia, . . . a gesture to a phantasy of the historical past that secures the permanence of an unambivalently ideal love-object in the historical present" (110). T. Logan treats the typical Victorian nostalgia for life in a cottage (21-22, 218-19). S. Stewart examines the "social disease of nostalgia" by tracing the "relations of narrative to origin and object" (ix). Calling nostalgia "The Sadness Without an Object" (14-24), Stewart explains that "by the narrative process of nostalgic reconstruction the present is denied and the past takes on an authenticity of being"; yet that "past . . . has never existed except as narrative, and hence, always absent, that past continually threatens to reproduce itself as a felt lack" (23). Similarly, Hamlet in his mourning becomes a figure representative of modernity because, according to Welsh, "modernity assumes the loss of some priority . . . the loss of fathers, whether still living or not, [or] of prior customs, allegiances, governments, or literary conventions" (*Hamlet* xi). See Dames for an insightful account of nostalgia as an "absence," a form of memory that denies loss (4). Olfaction is the preeminent sensory modality for registering nostalgia since smells so powerfully evoke memories; see A. Booth, "The Scent" 3, 5; Engen 83, 86.

33. "Fictions" 102. For analysis of the "nostalgic subjectivity" of the style of *Great Expectations*, see G. Stewart 149-51.

34. On the stink of Walworth, where manure was stored for use in the countryside, and on pig-keeping as characteristic of poor urban workers, especially the Irish, see Wohl 82-83. See Hollington for a more positive reading of Wemmick's pig as a figure of providential and narrative recycling. Robbins analyzes the presentation of the pig in Wemmick's yard as a "subversion of the pig-keeping model of domesticity," which is exemplified by Joe

("How to Be" 184). Hollington also characterizes Walworth as a more salubrious place than I do (57–58).

35. F. M. L. Thompson, *Rise* 168; cf. Curran 9–10. Paroissien points out that the architecture of Wemmick's castle is an example of "cottage ornée," a style favored by "small property holders" in the late eighteenth century (228).

36. For an example of the argument that Wemmick exemplifies such an unhealthy division, see J. Phelan (126–27). Kelly notes that this "'split'" may serve as a "positive norm and a potential analogue to Pip" (146–47). Hollington analyzes Wemmick as an embodiment of an earlier and now lost economy like that represented in Joe's forge (58). To the extent that Wemmick combines a number of different modes of living, I agree with Clayton, who finds in him a figure of postmodernity (621–23).

37. Pip's status as an orphan is the starting point of both Brooks's classic essay on *Great Expectations* and Gallagher and Greenblatt's more recent analysis. See also Ginsburg, "Dickens."

Chapter 3

1. Staves points out that in a patriarchal society women "function as procreators and as transmitters of inheritance from male to male" (4). Nunokawa has analyzed the role of wives in Victorian fiction in relation to the fears aroused by the perpetual circulation of commodities. His analysis and mine share a number of terms and concerns—loss, security, property, possession—but he focuses on "a rhetorical effect," "the figure of a woman whose dimensions are defined less by the material shapes of house or body than by a lover's fond thoughts" (15, 13). Like Nunokawa, Schor emphasizes the symbolic nature of the substance that women represent: the good daughters of Dickens's fiction are associated with "property" defined as "value, meaning, the father's word" (4). For a different perspective on women, see E. Michie's discussion of Trollope's "association of women with [the materiality of] economics and men with asceticism" (86). In looking at such women as substance, bearers of children and property, I am offering an interpretation of their role more in line with that in Laqueur's *Making Sex* when he concludes that nineteenth-century medicine "tended to reduce woman's nature to woman's reproductive biology" (223). The role of women as property-owners in Victorian novels is related to a process that Poovey outlines: the representational value of women as metaphors, "represent[ing] and displac[ing] something they are not," allow them to "stand in for other forces beyond men's control," thus creating the "illusion . . . that what seems to be beyond man's control actually answers his deepest needs" (*Making* 167).

2. Ellis, qtd. Langland 72; Linton, "Womanly Dependence," qtd. Shanley 61; cf. Davidoff and Hall 315. See Hadley on the distinction between women as real property and commercial property (ch. 4). See Poovey on the relation between women as property and male alienation (*Uneven* 76–79).

3. Fears about slavery and prostitution were never far from conceptions of the marriage market, as both Nunokawa (5–7, 94–95) and Schor (186) have explained. See Holcombe, ch. 2.

4. A bride-price is given by the groom or his kin to the bride's kin. Rubin's well-known essay connects this practice in traditional societies with the modern, Western oppression of women. The term *bride-wealth* has been preferred by anthropologists who wish to avoid the implication that a price is being paid for human flesh (Levinson and Ember 1: 152), but both terms seem appropriate to a high-Victorian context if, as I have explained, the direction of the payment is understood as having been reversed. I use these terms instead of the more conventional phrases *dowry* and *marriage-portion* to emphasize the gendered quality of this exchange. Simmel explains that dowries replaced bride-prices when the division of labor between genders led to wives' being supported by their husbands (375–76).

5. Holcombe, ch. 1–3. See also Doggett 36–39; Poovey, *Uneven* 71–76. High-Victorian plots make none of the often dizzyingly complicated distinctions that actually determined the extent of an individual's power over possessions, differences among kinds of property (real and personal possessions, chattels real and choses in action) or kinds of land (freehold and copyhold), or legal systems (common law and equity). William Cohen treats such distinctions in a later novel, Trollope's *The Eustace Diamonds* (167–69), but I know of no comparable case in the fiction of the 1860s.

6. Holcombe, ch. 8; Shanley, ch. 2. Dolin treats fictional versions of the *feme sole* in his study of the ways in which women as property-owners vie against the norm of middle-class wives as propertyless. The central point here, I think, is the fantastic typicality of the former as well as the presence of the latter in high-Victorian fiction.

7. This perspective was confirmed in the mid-Victorian period by a parliamentary committee that explained that "agency is a mixed question of law and fact" (qtd. Cobbe, "'Criminals'" 124). Staves also makes the point that there is no necessary relation between "legal rules" and "social practice" (198).

8. Davidoff and Hall 209. The crucial distinction, as Parkin's extension of Marxist theory points out, is not between having some property and having none, but between what he calls property as capital and property as possessions: in the former case, one has legal power to use it to exclude others from the control of production; in the latter, it has no such use (53). Davidoff and Hall apply this distinction to mid-Victorian female gentility, explaining that women's "marital status always pre-empted their economic personality" (315). The distance between fiction and fact, as slippery and indispensable as those terms are, can be gauged by comparing the narrative patterns that I analyze here to what Tosh calls "the documentary record," which in his version of it demonstrates that in mid-Victorian culture women were seen as moral guides confined to the home and men as worldly creatures who often compromised their domestic roles in favor of work or public life. Tosh concludes specifically

that Victorian men were ultimately superior even to "women's moral superiority" (145). Malchow also uses historical records to point out that men in industry and commerce typically inherited property from their parents, not their wives (344).

9. Staves 214–15, 225–26; cf. Poovey, *Proper* 10–14.

10. Felix Holt's class position has been widely debated, the most influential contribution being Gallagher's analysis of his role as the embodiment of "pure value," an Arnoldian "alien" (*Industrial* 244). See also Williams, *Culture* 103–7; Fisher 149–50; Levine, "Introduction" ix–x. Bodenheimer analyzes the treatment of gentility in *Felix Holt* and summarizes its effects: "true elevation resides in the choice not to rise" (*Politics* 97). Wilt has argued that at the moment of the riots, Felix is "transform[ed] from working man with a stick to gentleman with a sword" (61). For an identification of Felix as working class, see Hobson. Class in *Felix Holt* depends on the economic, material conditions of work, but the work in question is not that with which Felix is identified at the beginning of the novel; rather, his class position is determined by his rejection of the conditions characteristic of the work of tradesmen. In effect, then, Felix, like the so-called unproductive worker of Victorian political economy, is produced by his distance from such men as the Treby brewers, Wace and Company.

11. Esther's status at the end of the novel has been a focus of feminist criticism of *Felix Holt* (for a summary, see Bode 770). Like Bode, I imagine that Esther will rule in the house that she and Holt come to inhabit; as Bode puts it, "it would not be a complete surprise to find the candles made of wax there" (786). Likewise, Wilt describes the couple as "relentlessly thriving, inevitably rising" (67). Kettle is one of the few critics to mention Esther's income, which he sees as a factor that undermines Felix's moral position (108). A. Booth does note that Esther "reserves a little of her wealth," emphasizing as more significant, however, her retention of her influence over Felix ("Not All" 156).

12. Two different readings of *Salem Chapel* agree in interpreting as symbolic Susan's maternal role: S. Jones calls it a "celebration of [the] maternal heroism" epitomized by both Susan and her mother (247), and Heller treats Susan as "an appropriate vessel not for a baby but for a newly authoritative [female] voice" (103).

Chapter 4

1. J. Hillis Miller, *Charles Dickens* 287. Arac counters that argument, noting "how little" the meetings in *Our Mutual Friend* "build plot" (*Commissioned* 169–74). Moretti offers a chart of the "encounters across class lines" in the novel (134).

2. Kincaid calls it "the increasingly silly and trite Wilfer-Harmon plot" (228); and like Kincaid, Glavin contrasts it to the Wrayburn-Hexam plot, cogently identifying Harmon's story as a "*parvenu* fiction of radical possibility"

as opposed to "a *plebian* fiction of equally radical *dearth*" (52–63). Cf. Cheadle, "The Late Novels" 84–85. Poovey sees the Harmon plot as relatively ineffective, existing in a "narrative vacuum," "almost completely cordoned off from the other plots" so that its resolution cannot "correct" the problems of "exploitation and fraud associated with speculation and debt" (*Making* 167). Other sources of dissatisfaction with this plot include Bella's transformation (see Syd Thomas) and the trick that Boffin's "pious fraud" perpetrates on the novel's readers, for an insightful analysis of which see Jaffe, *Vanishing*, ch. 5. See Ginsburg on the plot of *Our Mutual Friend* as one that deals with transformations, not resolutions (*Economies*, ch. 7).

3. *Fantasy* is the word that Poovey uses to describe the cultural work of *Our Mutual Friend*, though its "twin fantasies" become a "nightmare" (*Making* 180). Similarly, David uses the term *myth* to define the novel's "fable of regenerated bourgeois culture" (55). My reading of this novel focuses on many of the same issues examined by Poovey and by Gallagher in their quite different analyses of its treatment of the relation between masculinity and the economic system of the 1860s and between gender and commodification. Poovey and Gallagher, however, emphasize the role of women as, respectively, representations and commodities (*Making*, ch. 8; "Bioeconomics"), whereas I stress the bodily materiality upon which the representations of middle-class women in the novel insist. J. Hillis Miller similarly stresses "the unusual attention in this novel to elemental matter" ("Money" 75–77). On women as commodities in this novel, see A. Miller 135–38. Levine concludes that female characters like Bella "belong to a material world," but he sees that condition as the source of their inescapable "secondariness" (*Dying* 169).

4. Cheadle summarizes the previous criticism dealing with the kinds of work characteristic of the novel, adding to it by emphasizing the vitality and range of work done by the lowliest members of society ("Work"). Brantlinger points out the lack of "productive" work in *Our Mutual Friend* (*Fictions* 162). See A. Miller on the relation between work and play (ch. 4) and Shuman on the status of intellectual labor in the novel.

5. James 787. Poole makes this point at some length (xi–xx), but Bodenheimer argues persuasively that Dickens is confronting in this novel new concerns rather than old ones ("Dickens" 161–66).

6. My argument does not depend on deciding whether Victorian dust heaps typically contained human excrement. The inarguable presence in the mounds of kitchen leavings is sufficient to support my point about their inexplicable lack of odors. Sedgwick offers a good summary of the debate over whether dust heaps in the early 1860s contained human excrement (163–64); see also *Our Mutual Friend*, ed. Gill, 896–97n3; Brattin 27–28. According to Mayhew, dust did not include excrement, although the dustmen who worked by day carting household refuse might become after hours "nightmen" who cleaned out cesspools. The 1848 passage of the Nuisances Removal and Diseases Prevention Act made it illegal to dispose of night-soil, human excrement, in suburban

dust heaps (Cotsell, *Companion* 33–34); rather, it was to go straight into the
Thames. Those looking for human ordure will therefore be more likely to find
it in the Thames, where Harmon floats like a "turd," as Christopher Craft put
the point in the faculty discussions at the Dickens Project in August of 2000.

7. Both Penguin paperbacks, one edited by Stephen Gill (1971) and the
other by Adrian Poole (1997), offer useful information on the use in manufacture of the materials collected in dust heaps (respectively, 896–97n3; 805n20).
Yet the point of Dickens's depiction of the heaps is that they are not on their
way to such productive use. C. Bernstein puns that the mounds constitute a
"refuse-all," a resistance on the artist's part to accept the "loss" of the "material city" (207).

8. Cotsell reprints the drawing from the *Penny Illustrated Paper* depicting,
according to the accompanying text, thirty to forty women and girls working
the mounds (*Companion* 30; 31 [figure 2]). The *Illustrated London News* printed
a full-page, close-up image of a dust heap with one man shoveling, six women
sorting, and prominently in the foreground a large pig rooting in the trash. The
accompanying text begins by referring to the dust mounds in *Our Mutual
Friend* and Dickens's exaggeration of their value, though the writer concedes
that dust-contracting is no doubt a "lucrative trade," despite its being a dirty
one for its employees: "Sift[ing] the ashes from the cinders and small coal,
separating them at the same time from cabbage-stalks and potato-parings,
broken glass and potsherds, which are taken out by the hand and tossed
aside"—such labor is, the writer explains, "not very nice work" ("A London
Dustyard" 193, 191).

9. Frontispiece, vol. 2. Dickens had suggested to Stone an image of "the
Dustyard with the three mounds" (*Letters* 11: 87); but Stone, who was generally left to his own devices when choosing what to illustrate (e.g., *Letters* 10:
410), did not comply.

10. Mayhew contradicts himself in this account, implying first that the
heaps, particularly those composed of the rough dust used in agriculture, are
virtually valueless (2: 170), then in a table depicting the income of dust
contractors proving that the sale of dust brings in more than three times the
amount of the contracts for its removal. The average income of a dust contractor at the beginning of the 1850s Mayhew estimates to be approximately £800 a
year (2: 179).

11. Sedgwick 163–64. My commentary on *Our Mutual Friend* confirms
Sedgwick's emphasis on the extent to which "for Dickens the erotic fate of
every female or male is also cast in the terms and propelled by the forces of
class and economic accumulation" (165).

12. Dickens's treatment of this mansion confirms N. Armstrong's analysis
of the importance in nineteenth-century fiction of "a country house that is not a
country house" (*Desire* 69–75).

13. As Welsh notes of another cross-class contradiction in the novel, this
one involving Harmon and Betty Higden, Harmon's "reverence for Betty's

independence is not thought to conflict in any way with the prospect that he and Bella Wilfer will live happily every after on unearned income" (*City* 99).

14. Poovey puts a similar construction on the ironies of old Harmon's will, stressing John Harmon's active role in using the "opportunities [it offers] to make decisions for himself . . . to discover what he wants and calculate how to get it" (*Making* 166–67). Similarly, Gallagher grants John Harmon the power to "change illth into wealth" in her reading of the novel as an exploration of male identity in relation to the "commodity as dead body" or "life in abeyance" ("Bioeconomics" 56, 54, 58). See also Morris on the novel as "an ideological fiction of transcendence" (192) and Levine on its quest for "truth" (*Dying* 148–70).

15. Langland answers this question by explaining that Bella must prove herself "a disciplined helpmeet" or John Harmon risks "soon squander[ing] his wealth" (109). Dickens's portrayal of the Harmon wealth as "Inexhaust- ible," like the Harmon baby, casts doubt on such an explanation. More important is Langland's point that the depiction of Bella's time in the cottage is "a reinterpretation of woman's work as play, a corollary to the mystification of woman's work as 'duty'" (109). It is pointless play as well. Bella does not need to learn the household management that would allow her to run a comfortable home on a small income because Harmon has known that he will be rich long before Bella marries him, nor presumably does Bella need to learn to manage a large staff of servants since Mrs. Boffin may have that function in their Eminently Aristocratic Mansion. Cf. Shuman 159. Schor notes that "only by becoming property can [Bella] inherit," and she must be tested to prove that she has "the 'true golden gold' of female, wifely devo- tion" (178, 180).

16. The word *Baby* is the only item given such emphasis in the notes on the six chapters in the final double number (rpt. Cotsell, *Companion* 273).

17. Significantly, at the beginning of the dialogue in which Bella announces her pregnancy, she is described as a commodity: John "cared, beyond all expression, for his wife, as a most precious and sweet commodity that was always looking up, and that was never worth less than all the gold in the world" (667). His recognition that his wife, like Rose in *Evan Harrington*, is a piece of goods suggests that it is more difficult to reject the exchange of commodities than Harmon's youthful fleeing from his father would seem to effect. The narrator of *Our Mutual Friend* stresses the ironies by which the least apparently covetous characters in the novel, Boffin along with Harmon, can speak of value only in terms of commodities and gold.

18. Glavin notes that earlier in the novel Harmon has been unmanned when he becomes the object of other men's gazes (73). Gallagher concludes that *Our Mutual Friend* demonstrates how "lapses" and "breaks" in male identity "finally create the effect of an endlessly resilient and . . . emphatically male transcendent subject" ("Bioeconomics" 63), though the novel also seems to question the stability of such a subject even as an effect.

19. T. Logan 83, 96, 229; Gloag 33–34. A. Miller examines the implications in Dickens's having what John Forster called "the kind of interest in a house which is commonly confined to women" (ch. 4).

20. Ballard 1: 330; Lubbock 1: 387–88; cf. Padfield 20–21; Lewis 172, 188. See also Peck: "life at sea [was] built on the notion of manliness, in which strength was the only quality that really matters" (5). Almost as if he were echoing a Dickensian description, an early-twentieth-century commentator on the men of the Victorian merchant fleet speaks of their being "loose-limbed athlete[s]": "His half-shut hands had the grip of a grizzly bear" (Lubbock 1: 388, 391). Cotsell aptly notes that Harmon's time at sea is a "notional period of labor" in a "fairy-tale wish-fulfillment" ("Secretary" 132).

21. Bodenheimer, "Dickens" 170. Bodenheimer's analysis of the relation between Wrayburn and Headstone is a particularly good instance of a comparative encounter that becomes an exchange, and she uses those terms when she describes Wrayburn as coming "face-to-face [in an] encounter" with his lower-middle-class other, a violent "identity exchange" that grants the barrister his inferior's "primal energy to survive" (169–70).

22. Bodenheimer's recent treatment of Harmon is the exception to this rule ("Dickens" 170–73). Wrayburn and Headstone are the doubles usually given the most extensive attention. For an account of the criticism dealing with the novel's correspondences and doublings, see Farrell 797n50. Farrell describes Harmon as a character who undertakes "an authentic search for himself," succeeds because of his "purity and integrity," and achieves "liberation from the moral monstrosities that plague both self and society" in this novel (775, 778). Bodenheimer counters with a subtle exploration of the implications of such patterns, concluding that identity in *Our Mutual Friend* depends on a character's "recognition of . . . self-estrangement" ("Dickens" 174).

23. The phrase is from Wood's *East Lynne* (257); cf. Girouard 65. Braddon's *The Doctor's Wife* also speaks of a gentleman coming "from the supreme hand of Nature" (57).

24. Shuttleworth notes that the setting of *Lorna Doone* in the seventeenth century does not deter its author from attributing Victorian values to the hero so that the establishment of his manhood and "the drama of social ascendancy [are] projected through the workings of romance" ("Introduction," Blackmore xiv–xv).

25. Glavin emends Sedgwick's construction of the Headstone-Riderhood embrace as anal rape (169) by pointing out that the men face each other in the missionary position (59); Bodenheimer agrees ("Dickens" 169–70). In any case, Headstone's death grip is disconcertingly intimate.

26. David outlines how thoroughly social aggression is punished in *Our Mutual Friend* (58, 66). Kincaid notes that Wegg represents Podsnappery and the "dangerous values," selfishness and snobbery and cupidity, that put at risk trust and friendship (248, 250).

27. Shuman explains that in accordance with the educational reforms of the 1860s, Headstone conducts a "market-classroom" based on free-trade principles (166).

Afterword

1. Gallagher treats the "relationship between political and literary representation" in the 1860s in *The Industrial Reformation of English Fiction* (188; see ch. 9). See also Brantlinger, *Spirit*, ch. 10. Loesberg offers a different, though complementary attempt to align literary and political issues in "The Ideology of Narrative Form," which explains both sensation fiction and the debates over reform in the 1860s as ambivalent responses to conceptions of class (116–17).

2. Eliot, *Letters* 4: 236. The context in which *Felix Holt* was written may account for what A. Booth accurately calls its "hushed politics" ("Not All" 145). It may also explain the quality in the novel that Gallagher stresses, its attempt to envision a realm of "pure, disinterested politics" (*Industrial* 245), a politics that is abstract perhaps because it is unattainable.

3. Qtd. Clark 239. See Hall, McClelland, and Rendall 4–5, 98–99.

4. For political histories of the passage of the 1867 bill, see Smith and Cowling. Briggs (*Victorian People*, ch. 10) and Himmelfarb (ch. 13) offer comprehensive, though brief surveys of the events, and an early dissertation by Park examines a range of factors involved in the debates. Gillespie tells the story from the perspective of its working-class participants (ch. 9), as does R. Harrison (ch. 3). More recent explanations are offered by Hoppen 246–53; Evans, ch. 6; Joyce, *Democratic* 192–204; Biagini, ch. 5; Clark 237–43; Hall, McClelland, and Rendall. Harcourt and C. Hall both place the bill in a wide context of contemporaneous events and concerns, particularly those related to Britain's imperial ambitions, Harcourt stressing the Abyssinian campaign (99–104) and Hall, the examples of Jamaica and Ireland (Hall, McClelland, and Rendall, ch. 4).

5. This was Gladstone's chief argument for reform in 1866 (*Hansard* 182: 873; 183: 148). For versions of this argument, see Harcourt 104–8; Smith, ch. 1; R. Harrison 113–15, 119–23. Biagini rejects this theory, stating that the changes in attitude that took place during this period were those of "the ruling classes," not those of the "subaltern classes" (9). Concepts of the embourgeoisement of the working classes depend to some extent on the recently and widely challenged conception that there was a specific stratum of the so-called skilled working classes called the "labor aristocracy." Joyce ("Work" 173–75) reviews the studies of and questions about this formulation (cf. Biagini 8–10). Finn demonstrates effectively that the political ideals of middle-class radicals were as much changed by their exposure to popular views as the reverse (189, 244–53).

6. Clark cites Harcourt's work on Disraeli's imperialism to emphasize the "masculine defence of the empire" that workers might undertake, concluding,

"as a result of the 1866–7 Reform Acts debates, . . . politicians hoped to incorporate working-class masculinity into the Nation and defuse class conflict" (243). As I argue in "Picturing Reform," the reverse of such a formulation of cause and effect is also relevant: because workers were seen as central to the defense of the nation before the debates on reform, their enfranchisement seemed an acceptable outcome. Vernon speaks specifically of the "strength and sexual potency" of the "body" of the "masculine political subject," by which he indicates that subject's ability to father children ("Notes" 17).

7. The view that the act was a milestone in Britain's triumphant march toward democracy is open to doubt, as is its impact on the fortunes of the Liberal and Conservative parties. See Park 255–75; Smith 236–42; Evans, ch. 7. The crucial question here is not how many working men were enfranchised, but how much power over the composition of the House of Commons their votes in the boroughs actually gave them. Joyce finds the emergence beginning in 1867 of male "mass democracy . . . real enough" (*Democratic* 192), and Himmelfarb calls the 1867 act "the Great Reform Bill," the title usually accorded the 1832 measure, because it "transformed England into a democracy" (333). Yet Vernon argues convincingly that in the mid-Victorian period "English politics became progressively less democratic" (*Politics* 9, cf. 336–37), and Hoppen demonstrates that the act strengthened the Conservative party by making the county voters, traditionally conservative, "count . . . for more" (253). For a summary of this debate, see McWilliam 46–50.

WORKS CITED

Adams, James Eli. *Dandies and Desert Saints: Styles of Victorian Masculinity*. Ithaca: Cornell UP, 1995.

Allen, Grant. *Physiological Aesthetics*. London: Henry S. King, 1877.

Altick, Richard D. *Deadly Encounters: Two Victorian Sensations*. Philadelphia: U of Pennsylvania P, 1986.

Anderson, Amanda. *Tainted Souls and Painted Faces: The Rhetoric of Fallenness in Victorian Culture*. Ithaca: Cornell UP, 1993.

Anderson, Gregory. *Victorian Clerks*. Manchester: Manchester UP, 1976.

Arac, Jonathan. *Commissioned Spirits: The Shaping of Social Motion in Dickens, Carlyle, Melville, and Hawthorne*. New Brunswick: Rutgers UP, 1979.

———. "Hamlet, *Little Dorrit*, and the History of Character." *South Atlantic Quarterly* 87 (1988): 311–28.

Armstrong, Isobel. "Victorian Studies and Cultural Studies: A False Dichotomy." *Victorian Literature and Culture* 27 (1999): 513–16.

Armstrong, Nancy. *Desire and Domestic Fiction: A Political History of the Novel*. New York: Oxford UP, 1987.

———. *Fiction in the Age of Photography: The Legacy of British Realism*. Cambridge: Harvard UP, 1999.

Arnstein, Walter L. *Britain Yesterday and Today: 1830 to the Present*. 7th ed. Lexington, MA: D. C. Heath, 1996.

Bagehot, Walter. *The Collected Works of Walter Bagehot*. Ed. Norman St. John-Stevas. London: Economist, 1965–1986.

Bain, Alexander. *The Senses and the Intellect*. 1855. Rpt. Significant Contributions to the History of Psychology, 1750–1920, vol. A.4. Ed. Daniel N. Robinson. Washington, D.C.: University Publications of America, 1977.

Ballard, G. A. "The Navy." *Early Victorian England*. G. M. Young, ed. 1: 299–344.

Banes, Sally. "Olfactory Performances." *Drama Review* 45 (2001): 68–76.

Batten, Guinn. *The Orphaned Imagination: Melancholy and Commodity Culture in English Romanticism*. Durham: Duke UP, 1998.

Baxandall, Lee, and Stefan Morawski, eds. *Marx and Engels on Literature and Art: A Selection of Writings*. St. Louis: Telos, 1973.

Baxter, R. Dudley. *National Income: The United Kingdom*. London: Macmillan, 1868.

Beauchamp, Gary K., and Linda Bartoshuk, eds. *Tasting and Smelling*. San Diego: Academic Press, 1997.

Beer, Gillian. *Open Fields: Science in Cultural Encounter*. New York: Oxford UP, 1996.

Bernstein, Carol L. *The Celebration of Scandal: Toward the Sublime in Victorian Urban Fiction*. University Park, PA: Pennsylvania State UP, 1991.

Bernstein, Julius. *The Five Senses of Man*. 1876. New York: D. Appleton, 1881.

Best, Geoffrey. *Mid-Victorian Britain, 1851–1875*. New York: Schocken, 1972.

Biagini, Eugenio F. *Liberty, Retrenchment and Reform: Popular Liberalism in the Age of Gladstone, 1860–1880*. Cambridge: Cambridge UP, 1992.

Blackmore, R. D. *Lorna Doone: A Romance of Exmoor*. Ed. Sally Shuttleworth. Oxford: Oxford UP, 1994.

Bode, Rita. "Power and Submission in *Felix Holt, the Radical*." *Studies in English Literature* 35 (1995): 769–88.

Bodenheimer, Rosemarie. "Dickens and the Identical Man: *Our Mutual Friend* Doubled." *Dickens Studies Annual* 31 (2002): 159–74.

———. *The Politics of Story in Victorian Social Fiction*. Ithaca: Cornell UP, 1988.

Booth, Alison. "Not All Men Are Selfish and Cruel: *Felix Holt* as a Feminist Novel." *Gender and Discourse in Victorian Literature and Art*. Ed. Antony H. Harrison and Beverly Taylor. DeKalb: Northern Illinois UP, 1992. 143–60.

———. "The Scent of a Narrative: Rank Discourse in *Flush* and *Written on the Body*." *Narrative* 8 (2000): 3–22.

Booth, Michael R. *Theatre in the Victorian Age*. Cambridge: Cambridge UP, 1991.

Boring, Edwin G. *A History of Experimental Psychology*. 2nd ed. New York: Appleton-Century-Crofts, 1957.

Bourdieu, Pierre. *Distinction: A Social Critique of the Judgement of Taste*. Trans. Richard Nice. Cambridge: Harvard UP, 1984.

Bourne Taylor, Jenny, and Sally Shuttleworth, eds. *Embodied Selves: An Anthology of Psychological Texts, 1830–1890*. Oxford: Clarendon, 1998.

Braddon, Mary Elizabeth. *Aurora Floyd*. Intro. Jennifer Uglow. London: Virago, 1984.

———. *The Doctor's Wife*. Ed. Lyn Pykett. Oxford: Oxford UP, 1998.

———. *John Marchmont's Legacy*. Ed. Toru Sasaki and Norman Page. Oxford: Oxford UP, 1999.

———. *Lady Audley's Secret*. Ed. David Skilton. Oxford: Oxford UP, 1987.

———. *The Lady's Mile*. 2 vols. Leipzig: Bernhard Tauchnitz, 1866.

Brantlinger, Patrick. *Fictions of State: Culture and Credit in Britain, 1694–1994*. Ithaca: Cornell UP, 1996.

———. *The Spirit of Reform: British Literature and Politics, 1832–1867*. Cambridge: Harvard UP, 1977.

Brattin, Joel J. "Constancy, Change, and the Dust Mounds of *Our Mutual Friend*." *Dickens Quarterly* 19 (2002): 23–30.

Briggs, Asa. "The Language of 'Class' in Early Nineteenth–Century England." *Essays in Labour History*. Ed. Asa Briggs and John Saville. London: Macmillan, 1960. 43–73.

———. *The Making of Modern England, 1783–1867: The Age of Improvement*. New York: Harper and Row, 1959.

———. *Victorian People: A Reassessment of Persons and Themes 1851–67*. 1955. New York: Harper and Row, 1963.

Brontë, Charlotte. *Jane Eyre*. Ed. Beth Newman. Boston: Bedford, 1996.

Brooks, Peter. "Repetition, Repression, and Return: The Plotting of *Great Expectations*." *Reading for the Plot: Design and Intention in Narrative*. New York: Vintage, 1985. 113–42.

Broughton, Rhoda. *Cometh up as a Flower*. Stroud: Alan Sutton, 1993.

———. *Not Wisely but Too Well*. Stroud: Alan Sutton, 1993.

Brown, Bill. *A Sense of Things: The Object Matter of American Literature*. Chicago: U of Chicago P, 2003.

Brown, Carolyn. "'Great Expectations': Masculinity and Modernity." *English and Cultural Studies*. Ed. Michael Green. London: Murray, 1987. 60–74.

Burn, W. L. *The Age of Equipoise: A Study of the Mid-Victorian Generation*. New York: Norton, 1965.

Burnett, John, ed. *Annals of Labour: Autobiographies of British Working-Class People 1820–1920*. Bloomington: Indiana UP, 1974.

Burr, Chandler. *The Emperor of Scent: A Story of Perfume, Obsession, and the Last Mystery of the Senses*. New York: Random House, 2002.

Butler, Judith. *Bodies That Matter: On the Discursive Limits of "Sex."* New York: Routledge, 1993.

———. *Gender Trouble: Feminism and the Subversion of Identity*. New York: Routledge, 1990.

Cain, P. J., and A. G. Hopkins. *British Imperialism: Innovation and Expansion, 1688–1914*. London: Longman, 1993.

Calvert, Peter. *The Concept of Class: An Historical Introduction*. London: Hutchinson, 1982.

Cannadine, David. *The Rise and Fall of Class in Britain*. New York: Columbia UP, 1999.

Carey, Peter. *Jack Maggs*. London: Faber and Faber, 1997.

Carlisle, Janice, ed. Charles Dickens. *Great Expectations*. Boston: Bedford, 1996.

———. "Introduction." *Factory Lives*. Ed. James R. Simmons. Forthcoming, Broadview.

———. "Picturing Reform: High-Victorian Visual Politics." In progress.

Carlyle, Thomas. *Past and Present*. 1843. Ed. Richard D. Altick. Boston: Houghton Mifflin, 1965.

———. *Shooting Niagara: and After?* London: Chapman and Hall, 1867.

Carpenter, William B. *Principles of Mental Physiology*. 1874. New York: Appleton, 1891.

Castronovo, David. *The English Gentleman: Images and Ideals in Literature and Society*. New York: Ungar, 1987.

Chadwick, Edwin. *Report on the Sanitary Condition of the Labouring Population of Gt. Britain*. Ed. M. W. Flinn. Edinburgh: University P, 1965.

Chartres, J. A., and G. L. Turnbull. "Country Craftsmen." *The Victorian Countryside*. Ed. Mingay. 1: 314–28.

Chase, Karen, and Michael Levenson. *The Spectacle of Intimacy: A Public Life for the Victorian Family*. Princeton: Princeton UP, 2000.

Cheadle, Brian. "The Late Novels: *Great Expectations* and *Our Mutual Friend*." *The Cambridge Companion to Charles Dickens*. Ed. Jordan. 78–91.

———. "Work in *Our Mutual Friend*." *Essays in Criticism* 51 (2001): 308–29.

Cheyne, George. *The English Malady*. 1733. Rpt. New York: Scholars' Facsimiles and Reprints, 1976.

Chiel, Deborah. *Great Expectations*. New York: St. Martin's, 1998.

Childers, Joseph W. *Novel Possibilities: Fiction and the Formation of Early Victorian Culture*. Philadelphia: U of Pennsylvania P, 1995.

Christ, Carol T., and John O. Jordan, eds. *Victorian Literature and the Victorian Visual Imagination*. Berkeley: U of California P, 1995.

Clark, Anna. "Gender, Class, and the Nation: Franchise Reform in England, 1832–1928." *Re-reading the Constitution*. Ed. Vernon. 230–53.

Classen, Constance. *Worlds of Sense: Exploring the Senses in History and across Cultures*. London: Routledge, 1993.

Classen, Constance, David Howes, and Anthony Synnott. *Aroma: The Cultural History of Smell*. London: Routledge, 1994.

Clayton, Jay. "Is Pip Postmodern? Or, Dickens at the End of the Twentieth Century." *Great Expectations*. Ed. Carlisle. 606–24.

Cobbe, Frances Power. "'Criminals, Idiots, Women, and Minors.'" *'Criminals, Idiots, Women, and Minors.'* Ed. Hamilton. 108–31.

———. "'What Shall We Do with Our Old Maids?'" *'Criminals, Idiots, Women, and Minors.'* Ed. Hamilton. 85–107.

Cohen, Ed. *Talk on the Wilde Side: Toward a Genealogy of a Discourse on Male Sexualities*. New York: Routledge, 1993.

Cohen, William A. *Sex Scandal: The Private Parts of Victorian Fiction*. Durham: Duke UP, 1996.

Collins, E. J. T. "The Age of Machinery." *The Victorian Countryside*. Ed. Mingay. 1: 200–213.

Collins, Wilkie. *Armadale*. Ed. John Sutherland. London: Penguin, 1995.

———. *The Moonstone*. Ed. J. I. M. Stewart. Harmondsworth: Penguin, 1966.

———. *No Name*. Ed. Mark Ford. London: Penguin, 1994.

———. *The Woman in White*. Ed. Julian Symons. Harmondsworth: Penguin, 1974.

Connor, Steven. *CP or, a Few Don'ts (and Dos) by a Cultural Phenomenologist*. <http://www.bbk.ac.uk/eh/eng/skc/cp/cultcp.htm>. August 2003.

————. *Dumbstruck: A Cultural History of Ventriloquism*. Oxford: Oxford UP, 2000.

————. "Making an Issue of Cultural Phenomenology." *Critical Quarterly* 42 (2000): 2–6.

Corbin, Alain. *The Foul and the Fragrant: Odor and the French Social Imagination*. Cambridge: Harvard UP, 1986.

Cotsell, Michael. *The Companion to* Our Mutual Friend. London: Allen and Unwin, 1986.

————. "Secretary or Sad Clerk? The Problem with John Harmon." *Dickens Quarterly* 1 (1984): 130–36.

Cowart, Beverly J., I. M. Young, Roy S. Feldman, and Louis D. Lowry. "Clinical Disorders of Smell and Taste." *Tasting and Smelling*. Ed. Beauchamp and Bartoshuk. 175–98.

Cowling, Maurice. *1867: Disraeli, Gladstone and Revolution: The Passing of the Second Reform Bill*. Cambridge: Cambridge UP, 1967.

Craft, Christopher. *Another Kind of Love: Male Homosexual Desire in English Discourse, 1850–1920*. Berkeley: U of California P, 1994.

Crary, Jonathan. *Techniques of the Observer: On Vision and Modernity in the Nineteenth Century*. Cambridge: MIT P, 1990.

Crossick, Geoffrey. "From Gentlemen to the Residuum: Languages of Social Description in Victorian Britain." *Language, History and Class*. Ed. Penelope J. Corfield. Oxford: Basil Blackwood, 1991. 150–78.

Curran, Cynthia. *When I First Began My Life Anew: Middle-Class Widows in Nineteenth-Century Britain*. Bristol, IN: Wyndham Hall, 2000.

Cvetkovich, Ann. *Mixed Feelings: Feminism, Mass Culture, and Victorian Sensationalism*. New Brunswick: Rutgers UP, 1992.

Dames, Nicholas. *Amnesiac Selves: Nostalgia, Forgetting, and British Fiction, 1810–1870*. New York: Oxford UP, 2001.

Danahay, Martin A. *A Community of One: Masculine Autobiography and Autonomy in Nineteenth-Century Britain*. Albany: State U of New York P, 1993.

David, Deirdre. *Fictions of Resolution in Three Victorian Novels:* North and South, Our Mutual Friend, Daniel Deronda. New York: Columbia UP, 1981.

Davidoff, Leonore, and Catherine Hall. *Family Fortunes: Men and Women of the English Middle Class, 1780–1850*. Chicago: U of Chicago P, 1987.

Dever, Carolyn. *Death and the Mother from Dickens to Freud: Victorian Fiction and the Anxiety of Origins*. Cambridge: Cambridge UP, 1998.

Dickens, Charles. *Dombey and Son*. Ed. Peter Fairclough. London: Penguin, 1970.

————. *Great Expectations*. Ed. Margaret Cardwell. Oxford: Clarendon, 1993.

————. *The Letters of Charles Dickens*. Pilgrim Edition. Gen. eds. Madeline House and Graham Storey. Oxford: Clarendon, 1965–2002.

————. *Our Mutual Friend*. Ed. Adrian Poole. London: Penguin, 1997.

————. *The Uncommercial Traveller and Reprinted Pieces*. Intro. Leslie C. Staples. London: Oxford UP, 1958.

Dimock, Wai Chee. "Class, Gender, and a History of Metonymy." *Rethinking Class*. Ed. Dimock and Gilmore. 57–104.

Dimock, Wai Chee, and Michael T. Gilmore, eds. *Rethinking Class: Literary Studies and Social Formations*. New York: Columbia UP, 1994.

Disraeli, Benjamin. *Lothair*. Intro. Philip Guedalla. London: Peter Davies, 1927.

Doggett, Maeve E. *Marriage, Wife-Beating and the Law in Victorian England*. London: Weidenfeld and Nicolson, 1992.

Dolin, Tim. *Mistress of the House: Women of Property in the Victorian Novel*. Aldershot: Ashgate, 1997.

Douglas, Mary. *Purity and Danger: An Analysis of Concepts of Pollution and Taboo*. 1966. London: Routledge, 2002.

Douglas-Fairhurst, Robert. *Victorian Afterlives: The Shaping of Influence in Nineteenth-Century Literature*. Oxford: Oxford UP, 2002.

Dowling, Andrew. *Manliness and the Male Novelist in Victorian Literature*. Aldershot: Ashgate, 2001.

Drobnick, Jim. "Reveries, Assaults and Evaporating Presences: Olfactory Dimensions in Contemporary Art." *Parachute* 89 (Jan.–March 1998): 10–19.

Eliot, George. *Felix Holt, the Radical*. Ed. Fred C. Thomson. Oxford: Clarendon, 1980.

————. *The George Eliot Letters*. Ed. Gordon S. Haight. 9 vols. New Haven: Yale UP, 1954–1978.

————. *Middlemarch*. Ed. David Carroll. Intro. Felicia Bonaparte. Oxford: Oxford UP, 1998.

————. *The Mill on the Floss*. Ed. Gordon S. Haight. Oxford: Clarendon, 1980.

————. *Romola*. Ed. Andrew Sanders. Harmondsworth: Penguin, 1980.

————. *Silas Marner, The Lifted Veil, Brother Jacob*. Intro. Theodore Watts-Dunton. London: Oxford UP, 1969.

Engels, Friedrich. *The Condition of the Working Class in England*. Ed. Victor Kiernan. London: Penguin, 1987.

Engen, Trygg. *Odor Sensation and Memory*. New York: Praeger, 1991.

Evans, Eric J. *Parliamentary Reform in Britain, c. 1770–1918*. New York: Longman, 2000.

Farrell, John P. "The Partners' Tale: Dickens and *Our Mutual Friend*." *ELH* 66 (1999): 759–99.

Finger, Thomas E., and Wayne L. Silver, eds. *Neurobiology of Taste and Smell*. New York: John Wiley, 1987.

Finn, Margot C. *After Chartism: Class and Nation in English Radical Politics, 1848–1874*. Cambridge: Cambridge UP, 1993.

Fisher, Philip. *Making up Society: The Novels of George Eliot*. Pittsburgh: Pittsburgh UP, 1981.

Flint, Kate. *The Victorians and the Visual Imagination*. Cambridge: Cambridge UP, 2000.

———. *The Woman Reader, 1837–1914*. Oxford: Clarendon, 1993.

Foucault, Michel. *Madness and Civilization: A History of Insanity in the Age of Reason*. 1965. Trans. Richard Howard. New York: Vintage, 1973.

Freud, Sigmund. *The Standard Edition of the Complete Psychological Works*. Ed. James Strachey. London: Hogarth Press, 1953–74.

Friedman, Susan Stanford. *Mappings: Feminism and the Cultural Geographies of Encounter*. Princeton: Princeton UP, 1998.

Fullerton, Georgiana. *Mrs. Gerald's Niece*. 1869. Rpt. New York: Garland, 1976.

Gallagher, Catherine. "The Bioeconomics of *Our Mutual Friend*." *Subject to History: Ideology, Class, Gender*. Ed. David Simpson. Ithaca: Cornell UP, 1991. 47–64.

———. *The Industrial Reformation of English Fiction, 1832–1867: Social Discourse and Narrative Form*. Chicago: U of Chicago P, 1985.

Gallagher, Catherine, and Stephen Greenblatt. *Practicing New Historicism*. Chicago: U of Chicago P, 2000.

Gaskell, Elizabeth. *Sylvia's Lovers*. Ed. Andrew Sanders. Oxford: Oxford UP, 1982.

———. *Wives and Daughters*. Intro. Pam Morris. London: Penguin, 1996.

Gay, Peter. *The Bourgeois Experience: Victoria to Freud*, vol. 1: *Education of the Senses*. 1984. New York: W. W. Norton, 1999.

Geldard, Frank A. *The Human Senses*. 2nd ed. New York: John Wiley, 1972.

Gell, Alfred. "Magic, Perfume, Dream . . ." *Symbols and Sentiment: Cross-Cultural Studies in Symbolism*. Ed. Ioan Lewis. London: Academic Press, 1977. 25–38.

Gilbert, Pamela K. *Disease, Desire, and the Body in Victorian Women's Popular Novels*. Cambridge: Cambridge UP, 1997.

Gilbert, William. *De Profundis: A Tale of the Social Deposits*. 2nd ed. London: Alexander Strahan, 1866.

Gill, Stephen, ed. Charles Dickens. *Our Mutual Friend*. London: Penguin, 1971.

Gillespie, Frances Elma. *Labor and Politics in England, 1850–1867*. 1927. Rpt. New York: Octagon, 1966.

Gilmour, Robin. *The Idea of the Gentleman in the Victorian Novel*. London: George Allen and Unwin, 1981.

Ginsburg, Michal Peled. "Dickens and the Uncanny: Repression and Displacement in *Great Expectations*." *Great Expectations*. Ed. Rosenberg. 698–704.

———. *Economies of Change: Form and Transformation in the Nineteenth-Century Novel*. Stanford: Stanford UP, 1996.

Girouard, Mark. *The Return to Camelot: Chivalry and the English Gentleman*. New Haven: Yale UP, 1981.

Glavin, John. *After Dickens: Reading, Adaptation and Performance*. Cambridge: Cambridge UP, 1999.

Gloag, John. *Victorian Comfort: A Social History of Design from 1830–1900*. London: Adam and Charles Black, 1961.

Goffman, Erving. *The Presentation of Self in Everyday Life*. New York: Doubleday, 1959.

Goux, Jean-Joseph. *Symbolic Economies: After Marx and Freud*. Trans. Jennifer Curtiss Gage. Ithaca: Cornell UP, 1990.

Guiliano, Edward, and Philip Collins, eds. *The Annotated Dickens*. Vol. 2. New York: C. N. Potter, 1986.

Hadley, Elaine. *Melodramatic Tactics: Theatricalized Dissent in the English Marketplace, 1800–1885*. Stanford: Stanford UP, 1995.

Haight, Gordon S. *George Eliot: A Biography*. New York: Oxford UP, 1968.

Hall, Catherine, Keith McClelland, and Jane Rendall. *Defining the Victorian Nation: Class, Race, and Gender and the British Reform Act of 1867*. Cambridge: Cambridge UP, 2000.

Hall, Donald E. *Fixing Patriarchy: Feminism and Mid-Victorian Male Novelists*. London: Macmillan, 1996.

Hamilton, Susan, ed. *'Criminals, Idiots, Women, and Minors': Victorian Writing by Women on Women*. Peterborough: Broadview, 1995.

Hampden-Turner, Charles. *Gentlemen and Tradesmen: The Values of Economic Catastrophe*. London: Routledge and Kegan Paul, 1983.

Hansard's Parliamentary Debates. 3rd series, 175–86 (1864–1867).

Harcourt, Freda. "Disraeli's Imperialism, 1866–1868: A Question of Timing." *Historical Journal* 23 (1980): 87–109.

Hardy, Barbara. "Food and Ceremony in *Great Expectations*." *Essays in Criticism* 13 (1963): 351–63.

Harrison, Royden. *Before the Socialists: Studies in Labour and Politics, 1861–1881*. London, Toronto: Routlege and Kegan Paul, U of Toronto P, 1965.

Harvey, John. *Men in Black*. London: Reaktion Books, 1995.

Heller, Tamar. "'No Longer Innocent': Sensationalism, Sexuality, and the Allegory of the Woman Writer in Margaret Oliphant's *Salem Chapel*." *Nineteenth Century Studies* 11 (1997): 95–108.

Herbert, Christopher. *Culture and Anomie: Ethnographic Imagination in the Nineteenth Century*. Chicago: U of Chicago P, 1991.

Hewitt, Martin. *An Age of Equipoise? Reassessing Mid-Victorian Britain*. Aldershot: Ashgate, 2000.

Highmore, Ben. *Everyday Life and Cultural Theory: An Introduction*. London: Routledge, 2002.

Himmelfarb, Gertrude. *Victorian Minds*. New York: Knopf, 1968.

Hobsbawm, Eric. *The Age of Capital 1848–1875*. 1962. New York: Vintage, 1996.

———. *Workers: Worlds of Labor*. New York: Pantheon, 1984.

Hobson, Christopher Z. "The Radicalism of *Felix Holt*: George Eliot and the Pioneers of Labor." *Victorian Literature and Culture* 26 (1998): 19–39.

Holcombe, Lee. *Wives and Property: Reform of the Married Women's Property Law in Nineteenth-Century England.* Toronto: U of Toronto P, 1983.

Hollingshead, John. *Ragged London in 1861.* London: Smith, Elder, 1861.

Hollington, Michael. "Wemmick's Pig: Notes on the Recycling Economies of *Great Expectations.*" *QWERTY* 9 (1999): 51–60.

Hoppen, K. Theodore. *The Mid-Victorian Generation, 1846–1886.* New Oxford History of England. Oxford: Clarendon, 1998.

House, Humphry. "G. B. S. on *Great Expectations.*" *Great Expectations.* Ed. Rosenberg. 644–48.

Howes, David. "Olfaction and Transition." *The Varieties of Sensory Experience.* Ed. Howes. 128–47.

———. "Sensorial Anthropology." *The Varieties of Sensory Experience.* Ed. Howes. 176–91.

———, ed. *The Varieties of Sensory Experience: A Sourcebook in the Anthropology of the Senses.* Toronto: U of Toronto P, 1991.

Hughes, Thomas. *Tom Brown at Oxford: A Sequel to School Days at Rugby.* 2 vols. Boston: James R. Osgood, 1873.

Humpherys, Anne. "Knowing the Victorian City: Writing and Representation." *Victorian Literature and Culture* 30 (2002): 601–12.

Hunt, E. H. *British Labour History, 1815–1914.* Atlantic Highlands, NJ: Humanities Press, 1981.

Hutton, R. H. "The Political Character of the Working Class." *Essays on Reform.* London: Macmillan, 1867. 27–44.

Jaffe, Audrey. *Scenes of Sympathy: Identity and Representation in Victorian Fiction.* Ithaca: Cornell UP, 2000.

———. *Vanishing Points: Dickens, Narrative, and the Subject of Omniscience.* Berkeley: U of California P, 1991.

James, Henry. "Our Mutual Friend." *The Nation* 21 December 1865: 786–87.

Janowitz, Anne. "Class and Literature: The Case of Romantic Chartism." *Rethinking Class.* Ed. Dimock and Gilmore. 239–66.

Johnson, A. B. *The Physiology of the Senses; or, How and What We See, Hear, Taste, Feel and Smell.* New York: Derby and Jackson, 1856.

Jones, Ann Rosalind, and Peter Stallybrass. *Renaissance Clothing and the Materials of Memory.* Cambridge: Cambridge UP, 2000.

Jones, Shirley. "Motherhood and Melodrama: *Salem Chapel* and Sensation Fiction." *Women's Writing* 6 (1999): 239–50.

Jordan, John O., ed. *The Cambridge Companion to Charles Dickens.* Cambridge: Cambridge UP, 2001.

Joyce, Patrick, ed. *Class.* Oxford: Oxford UP, 1995.

———. *Democratic Subjects: The Self and the Social in Nineteenth-Century England.* Cambridge: Cambridge UP, 1994.

———. "Work." *The Cambridge Social History of Britain, 1750–1950.* 2 vols. Ed. F. M. L. Thompson. Cambridge: Cambridge UP, 1990. 2: 131–94.

————. *Work, Society and Politics: The Culture of the Factory in Later Victorian England*. Brighton: Harvester, 1980.

Kay, Carol. *Political Constructions: Defoe, Richardson, and Sterne in Relation to Hobbes, Hume, and Burke*. Ithaca: Cornell UP, 1988.

Kelly, Mary Ann. "The Functions of Wemmick of Little Britain and Wemmick of Walworth." *Dickens Studies Newsletter* 14 (1983): 145–49.

Kestner, Joseph A. *Masculinities in Victorian Painting*. Aldershot: Scolar P, 1995.

Kettle, Arnold. "'Felix Holt the Radical.'" *Critical Essays on George Eliot*. Ed. Barbara Hardy. New York: Barnes and Noble, 1970. 99–115.

Kincaid, James R. *Dickens and the Rhetoric of Laughter*. Oxford: Clarendon, 1971.

Kingsley, Charles. *Yeast*. Stroud: Alan Sutton, 1994.

Klingender, F. D. *The Condition of Clerical Labour in Britain*. 1935. New York: International, n.d.

Kucich, John. *The Power of Lies: Transgression in Victorian Fiction*. Ithaca: Cornell UP, 1994.

————. *Repression in Victorian Fiction: Charlotte Brontë, George Eliot, and Charles Dickens*. Berkeley: U of California P, 1987.

Lane, Christopher. *The Burdens of Intimacy: Psychoanalysis and Victorian Masculinity*. Chicago: U of Chicago P, 1999.

Langbauer, Laurie. *Novels of Everyday Life: The Series in English Fiction, 1850–1930*. Ithaca: Cornell UP, 1999.

Langland, Elizabeth. *Nobody's Angels: Middle-Class Women and Domestic Ideology in Victorian Culture*. Ithaca: Cornell UP, 1995.

Laqueur, Thomas. *Making Sex: Body and Gender from the Greeks to Freud*. Cambridge: Harvard UP, 1990.

Lawless, Harry T. "Olfactory Psychophysics." *Tasting and Smelling*. Ed. Beauchamp and Bartoshuk. 125–74.

Lefebvre, Henri. *Critique of Everyday Life*. Vol. 1. Trans. John Moore. London: Verso, 1991.

————. *Everyday Life in the Modern World*. Trans. Sacha Rabinovitch. New York: Harper and Row, 1971.

Le Fanu, Sheridan. *Uncle Silas*. Ed. W. J. McCormack. Oxford: Oxford UP, 1981.

Le Guérer, Annick. *Scent: The Mysterious and Essential Powers of Smell*. Trans. Richard Miller. New York: Random House, 1992.

Lepenies, Wolf. *Melancholy and Society*. Trans. Jeremy Gaines and Doris Jones. Cambridge: Harvard UP, 1992.

Lever, Charles. *Barrington*. London: Chapman and Hall, 1863.

Leverenz, David. *Manhood and the American Renaissance*. Ithaca: Cornell UP, 1989.

Levine, George. *Dying to Know: Scientific Epistemology and Narrative in Victorian England*. Chicago: U of Chicago P, 2002.

————. "Introduction." *Felix Holt*. New York: W. W. Norton, 1970. ix–xxi.

Levinson, David, and Melvin Ember, eds. *Encyclopedia of Cultural Anthropology*. 4 vols. New York: Henry Holt, 1996.

Lewes, George Henry. *The Physiology of Common Life*. 2 vols. Edinburgh: William Blackwood, 1859–60.

————. "Seeing is Believing." *Blackwood's Edinburgh Magazine* 88 (1860): 381–95.

Lewis, Michael. *The Navy in Transition, 1814–1864: A Social History*. London: Hodder and Stroughton, 1965.

Linton, Eliza Lynn. *Grasp Your Nettle*. 3 vols. London: Smith, Elder, 1865.

————. *Lizzie Lorton of Greyrigg: A Novel*. New York: Harper and Brothers, 1866.

————. "The Wild Women: As Politicians." *'Criminals, Idiots, Women, and Minors.'* Ed. Hamilton. 188–97.

Litvak, Joseph. *Strange Gourmets: Sophistication, Theory, and the Novel*. Durham: Duke UP, 1997.

Lockwood, David. *The Blackcoated Worker: A Study in Class Consciousness*. 2nd ed. Oxford: Clarendon, 1989.

Loesberg, Jonathan. "The Ideology of Narrative Form in Sensation Fiction." *Representations* 13 (1986): 115–38.

Logan, Peter Melville. *Nerves and Narratives: A Cultural History of Hysteria in Nineteenth-Century British Prose*. Berkeley: U of California P, 1997.

Logan, Thad. *The Victorian Parlour*. Cambridge: Cambridge UP, 2001.

London, Bette. "Mary Shelley, *Frankenstein*, and the Spectacle of Masculinity." *PMLA* 108 (1993): 253–67.

"A London Dustyard." *Illustrated London News* 62 (1873): 191, 193.

Lougy, Robert E. "Filth, Liminality, and Abjection in Charles Dickens's *Bleak House*." *ELH* 69 (2002): 473–500.

Lowe, Donald M. *History of Bourgeois Perception*. Chicago: U of Chicago P, 1982.

Lubbock, Basil. "The Mercantile Marine, 1830–65." *Early Victorian England*. Ed. G. M. Young. 1: 379–414.

Lucas, John. *The Melancholy Man: A Study of Dickens's Novels*. 1970. Sussex: Harvester, 1980.

Malchow, H. L. *Gentlemen Capitalists: The Social and Political World of the Victorian Businessman*. Stanford: Stanford UP, 1992.

Marcus, Sharon. *Apartment Stories: City and Home in Nineteenth-Century Paris and London*. Berkeley: U of California P, 1999.

Marx, Karl. *Capital: A Critique of Political Economy*. Vol. 1. 1867. Intro. Ernest Mandel. Trans. Ben Fowkes. London: Penguin, 1976.

————. *Selected Writings*. Ed. David McLellan. Oxford: Oxford UP, 1977.

Marx, Karl, and Friedrich Engels. *The Communist Manifesto*. 1848. Ed. A. J. P. Taylor. Trans. Samuel Moore. London: Penguin, 1967.

Mathias, Peter. *The First Industrial Nation: An Economic History of Britain, 1700–1914*. 2nd ed. London: Routledge, 1983.

Maudsley, Henry. *The Physiology and Pathology of the Mind.* 1867. Rpt. Significant Contributions to the History of Psychology, 1750–1920, vol. C.4. Ed. Daniel N. Robinson. Washington, D.C.: University Publications of America, 1977.

Mavor, Carol. "*Odor di Femina*: Though You May Not See Her, You Can Certainly Smell Her." *Cultural Studies* 12 (1998): 51–81.

Mayhew, Henry. *London Labour and the London Poor.* 1861–62. 4 vols. Rpt. New York: Dover, 1968.

Mayne, R. G. *Expository Lexicon of the Terms, Ancient and Modern, in Medical and General Science Including a Complete Medico-Legal Vocabulary.* London: John Churchill, 1860.

McClelland, Keith. "Time to Work, Time to Live: Some Aspects of Work and the Re-formation of Class in Britain, 1850–1880." *The Historical Meanings of Work.* Ed. Patrick Joyce. Cambridge: Cambridge UP, 1987. 180–209.

McWilliam, Rohan. *Popular Politics in Nineteenth-Century England.* London: Routledge, 1998.

Mennella, Julie A., and Gary K. Beauchamp. "The Ontogeny of Human Flavor Perception." *Tasting and Smelling.* Ed. Beauchamp and Bartoshuk. 199–221.

Meredith, George. *Emilia in England.* 3 vols. London: Chapman and Hall, 1864.

———. *Evan Harrington.* London: Bradbury, Evans, 1866.

———. *Rhoda Fleming. A Story.* 3 vols. London: Tinsley Brothers, 1865.

Michie, Elsie B. "Buying Brains: Trollope, Oliphant, and Vulgar Victorian Commerce." *Victorian Studies* 44 (2001): 77–97.

Michie, Helena. "Under Victorian Skins: The Bodies Beneath." *A Companion to Victorian Literature and Culture.* Ed. Tucker. 407–24.

Mill, John Stuart. *Collected Works of John Stuart Mill.* Gen. ed. John Robson. Toronto and London: U of Toronto P, Routledge and Kegan Paul, 1963–1991.

Miller, Andrew H. *Novels behind Glass: Commodity Culture and Victorian Narrative.* Cambridge: Cambridge UP, 1995.

Miller, J. Hillis. *Charles Dickens: The World of His Novels.* 1958. Bloomington: Indiana UP, 1969.

———. "Money in *Our Mutual Friend.*" *Victorian Subjects.* New York: Harvester Wheatsheaf, 1990. 69–77.

Miller, William Ian. *The Anatomy of Disgust.* Cambridge: Harvard UP, 1997.

Mingay, G. E., ed. *The Victorian Countryside.* 2 vols. London: Routledge and Kegan Paul, 1981.

"Modern Mysticism." *Quarterly Review* 190 (1899): 79–102.

Moretti, Franco. *Atlas of the European Novel, 1800–1900.* London: Verso, 1998.

Morris, Pam. "A Taste for Change in *Our Mutual Friend*: Cultivation or Education?" *Rethinking Victorian Culture.* Ed. Juliet John and Alice Jenkins. London: Macmillan, 2000. 179–94.

Morrison, Paul. *The Explanation for Everything: Essays on Sexual Subjectivity.* New York: New York UP, 2001.

————. "Smelling Polyester." Unpublished manuscript.

Munich, Adrienne Auslander. *Andromeda's Chains: Gender and Interpretation in Victorian Literature and Art*. New York: Columbia UP, 1989.

Nead, Lynda. *Victorian Babylon: People, Streets, and Images in Nineteenth-Century London*. New Haven: Yale UP, 2000.

Neale, R. S. *Class in English History, 1680–1850*. Oxford: Basil Blackwell, 1981.

Newman, John Henry. *The Idea of a University*. Ed. Frank M. Turner. New Haven: Yale UP, 1996.

Newsom, Robert. *Charles Dickens Revisited*. New York: Twayne, 2000.

————. "Fictions of Childhood." *The Cambridge Companion to Charles Dickens*. Ed. Jordan. 92–105.

Nord, Deborah Epstein. *Walking the Victorian Streets: Women, Representation, and the City*. Ithaca: Cornell UP, 1995.

Nunokawa, Jeff. *The Afterlife of Property: Domestic Security and the Victorian Novel*. Princeton: Princeton UP, 1994.

O'Farrell, Mary Ann. *Telling Complexions: The Nineteenth-Century English Novel and the Blush*. Durham: Duke UP, 1997.

Oliphant, Margaret. *Miss Marjoribanks*. Ed. Elisabeth Jay. London: Penguin, 1998.

————. *The Perpetual Curate*. Intro. Penelope Fitzgerald. London: Virago, 1987.

————. *The Rector and the Doctor's Family*. Intro. Penelope Fitzgerald. New York: Penguin, 1986.

————. *Salem Chapel*. Intro. Penelope Fitzgerald. New York: Penguin, Virago, 1986.

Ong, Walter J. "The Shifting Sensorium." 1967. *The Varieties of Sensory Experience*. Ed. Howes. 25–30.

Oppenheim, Janet. *The Other World: Spiritualism and Psychical Research in England, 1850–1914*. Cambridge: Cambridge UP, 1985.

————. *"Shattered Nerves": Doctors, Patients, and Depression in Victorian England*. New York: Oxford UP, 1991.

Orwell, George. *The Road to Wigan Pier*. Foreword Victor Gollancz. 1937. New York: Harcourt Brace, 1958.

Ouida [Marie Louise de la Ramée]. *Under Two Flags*. London: Chatto and Windus, 1912.

Owen, Alex. *The Darkened Room: Women, Power and Spiritualism in Late Victorian England*. Philadelphia: U of Pennsylvania P, 1990.

Padfield, Peter. *Rule Britannia: The Victorian and Edwardian Navy*. London: Routledge and Kegan Paul, 1981.

Park, Joseph H. *The English Reform Bill of 1867*. New York: Columbia UP, 1920.

Parkin, Frank. *Marxism and Class Theory: A Bourgeois Critique*. London: Tavistock, 1979.

Paroissien, David. *The Companion to* Great Expectations. Mountfield, East Sussex: Helm Information, 2000.

Parsons, Deborah L. *Streetwalking the Metropolis: Women, the City, and Modernity*. Oxford: Oxford UP, 2000.

Peck, John. *Maritime Fiction: Sailors and the Sea in British and American Novels, 1719–1917*. New York: Palgrave, 2001.

Perkin, Harold. *Origins of Modern English Society*. 1969. London: Ark, 1986.

Pettitt, Clare. "Monstrous Displacements: Anxieties of Exchange in *Great Expectations*." *Dickens Studies Annual* 30 (2001): 243–62.

Phelan, James. *Reading People, Reading Plots: Character, Progression, and the Interpretation of Narrative*. Chicago: U of Chicago P, 1989.

Phelan, Peggy. *Unmarked: The Politics of Performance*. London: Routledge, 1993.

Picker, John M. *Victorian Soundscapes*. New York: Oxford UP, 2003.

Plotz, John. *The Crowd: British Literature and Public Politics*. Berkeley: U of California P, 2000.

Pocock, J. G. A. "The Mobility of Property and the Rise of Eighteenth-Century Sociology." *Theories of Property: Aristotle to the Present*. Ed. Anthony Parel and Thomas Flanagan. Waterloo, Ontario: Wilfrid Laurier UP, 1979. 141–66.

Poole, Adrian, ed. Charles Dickens. *Our Mutual Friend*. London: Penguin, 1997.

Poovey, Mary. *Making a Social Body: British Cultural Formation, 1830–1864*. Chicago: U of Chicago P, 1995.

———. *The Proper Lady and the Woman Writer: Ideology as Style in the Works of Mary Wollstonecraft, Mary Shelley, and Jane Austen*. Chicago: U of Chicago P, 1984.

———. *Uneven Developments: The Ideological Work of Gender in Mid-Victorian England*. Chicago: U of Chicago P, 1988.

Radden, Jennifer, ed. *The Nature of Melancholy: From Aristotle to Kristeva*. Oxford: Oxford UP, 2000.

Reade, Charles. *The Cloister and the Hearth: A Tale of the Middle Ages*. New York: Modern Library, n.d.

———. *Hard Cash: A Matter-of-Fact Romance*. Library Edition. London: Chatto and Windus, 1895.

———. *Put Yourself in His Place*. Library Edition. London: Chatto and Windus, 1896.

Reddy, William M. *Money and Liberty in Modern Europe: A Critique of Historical Understanding*. Cambridge: Cambride UP, 1987.

Richards, Thomas. *The Commodity Culture of Victorian England: Advertising and Spectacle, 1851–1914*. Stanford: Stanford UP, 1990.

Rindisbacher, Hans J. *The Smell of Books: A Cultural-Historical Study of Olfactory Perception in Literature*. Ann Arbor: U of Michigan P, 1992.

Robbins, Bruce. "How to Be a Benefactor Without Any Money: The Chill of Welfare in *Great Expectations*." *Knowing the Past: Victorian Literature and Culture*. Ed. Suzy Anger. Ithaca: Cornell UP, 2001. 172–91.

———. *The Servant's Hand: English Fiction from Below*. New York: Columbia UP, 1986.

Robson, Catherine. *Men in Wonderland: The Lost Girlhood of the Victorian Gentleman*. Princeton: Princeton UP, 2001.

Roper, Michael, and John Tosh, eds. *Manful Assertions: Masculinities in Britain since 1800*. London: Routledge, 1991.

Rosenberg, Edgar, ed. Charles Dickens. *Great Expectations*. New York: W. W. Norton, 1999.

Rubin, Gayle. "The Traffic in Women: Notes on the 'Political Economy' of Sex." *Toward an Anthropology of Women*. Ed. Rayna R. Reiter. New York: Monthly Review Press, 1975. 157–210.

Rylance, Rick. *Victorian Psychology and British Culture, 1850–1880*. Oxford: Oxford UP, 2000.

Scarry, Elaine. *The Body in Pain: The Making and Unmaking of the World*. New York: Oxford UP, 1985.

Schor, Hilary M. *Dickens and the Daughter of the House*. Cambridge: Cambridge UP, 1999.

Seaton, Beverly. *The Language of Flowers: A History*. Charlottesville: UP of Virginia, 1995.

Sedgwick, Eve Kosofsky. *Between Men: English Literature and Male Homosocial Desire*. New York: Columbia UP, 1985.

Sennett, Richard. *The Fall of Public Man*. New York: Knopf, 1977.

"Sensation Novels." *Quarterly Review* 113 (1863): 481–514.

The Senses. London: Religious Tract Society, 1853.

Shanley, Mary Lyndon. *Feminism, Marriage, and the Law in Victorian England*. Princeton: Princeton UP, 1989.

Sheehan, Paul. "Marx, Money, and Monstrosity in *Great Expectations*." *QWERTY* 9 (1999): 97–104.

Showalter, Elaine. *A Literature of Their Own: British Women Novelists from Brontë to Lessing*. Princeton: Princeton UP, 1977.

Shuman, Cathy. "Invigilating *Our Mutual Friend*: Gender and the Legitimation of Professional Authority." *Novel* 28 (1995): 154–72.

Shuttleworth, Sally. *Charlotte Brontë and Victorian Psychology*. Cambridge: Cambridge UP, 1996.

Simmel, Georg. *The Philosophy of Money*. Ed. David Frisby. Trans. Tom Bottomore and David Frisby. 2nd ed. London: Routledge, 1990.

Simpson, David. "Raymond Williams: Feeling for Structures, Voicing 'History.'" *Cultural Materialism: On Raymond Williams*. Ed. Christopher Prendergast. Minneapolis: U of Minnesota P, 1995. 29–50.

Skene, Felicia. *Hidden Depths*. Rpt. *Use and Abuse, Hidden Depths*. New York: Garland, 1975.

Small, Helen. *Love's Madness: Medicine, the Novel, and Female Insanity, 1800–1865*. Oxford: Clarendon, 1996.

Smiles, Samuel. *Self-Help*. 1866. Ed. Asa Briggs. London: John Murray, 1958.

Smith, Adam. *The Wealth of Nations*. 1776. Ed. Edwin Cannan. Chicago: U of Chicago P, 1976.

Smith, F. B. *The Making of the Second Reform Bill*. Cambridge: Cambridge UP, 1966.

Sperber, Dan. *Rethinking Symbolism*. Trans. Alice L. Morton. Cambridge: Cambridge UP, 1974.

Stallybrass, Peter, and Allon White. *The Politics and Poetics of Transgression*. Ithaca: Cornell UP, 1986.

Staten, Henry. "Is *Middlemarch* Ahistorical?" *PMLA* 115 (2000): 991–1005.

Staves, Susan. *Married Women's Separate Property in England, 1660–1833*. Cambridge: Harvard UP, 1990.

Stearns, Peter N. *Be a Man! Males in Modern Society*. New York: Holmes and Meier, 1979.

Stedman Jones, Gareth. *Languages of Class: Studies in English Working Class History, 1832–1982*. Cambridge: Cambridge UP, 1983.

———. *Outcast London: A Study in the Relationship between Classes in Victorian Society*. 1971. London: Penguin, 1992.

Stephen, James Fitzjames. *Liberty, Equality, Fraternity*. Ed. R. J. White. Cambridge: Cambridge UP, 1967.

Stewart, Garrett. "Dickens and Language." *The Cambridge Companion to Charles Dickens*. Ed. Jordan. 136–51.

Stewart, Susan. *On Longing: Narratives of the Miniature, the Gigantic, the Souvenir, the Collection*. Baltimore: Johns Hopkins UP, 1984.

Stoddart, D. Michael. *The Scented Ape: The Biology and Culture of Human Odour*. Cambridge: Cambridge UP, 1990.

Sullivan, Sheila. "Spectacular Failures: Thomas Hopley, Wilkie Collins, and the Reconstruction of Victorian Masculinity." *An Age of Equipoise?* Ed. Hewitt. 84–108.

Süskind, Patrick. *Perfume: The Story of a Murderer*. Trans. John E. Woods. London: Penguin, 1987.

Sussman, Herbert. *Victorian Masculinities: Manhood and Masculine Poetics in Early Victorian Literature and Art*. Cambridge: Cambridge UP, 1995.

Sutherland, John. *Is Heathcliff a Murderer? Great Puzzles in Nineteenth-Century Literature*. Oxford: Oxford UP, 1996.

———. *The Stanford Companion to Victorian Fiction*. Stanford: Stanford UP, 1989.

Swinburne, A. C. *The Novels of A. C. Swinburne: Love's Cross-Currents, Lesbia Brandon*. Intro. Edmund Wilson. New York: Noonday, 1963.

Tautphoeus, Jemima, von. *At Odds*. Philadelphia: J. B. Lippincott, 1886.

Terry, R. C. *Victorian Popular Fiction, 1860–80*. London: Macmillan, 1983.

Thackeray, William Makepeace. *The Adventures of Philip*. Oxford Thackeray, vol. 16. Ed. George Saintsbury. London: Oxford UP, n.d.

———. *The Newcomes*. Oxford Thackeray, vol. 14. Ed. George Saintsbury. London: Oxford UP, n.d.

Thomas, Ronald R. *Dreams of Authority: Freud and the Fictions of the Unconscious*. Ithaca: Cornell UP, 1990.

Thomas, Syd. "'Pretty Woman, Elegantly Framed': The Fate of Bella Wilfer in Dickens's *Our Mutual Friend*." *Dickens Quarterly* 14 (1997): 3–23.

Thompson, E. P. *The Making of the English Working Class*. 1963. New York: Vintage, 1966.

Thompson, F. M. L. "Nineteenth-Century Horse Sense." *Economic History Review*, new ser., 29 (1976): 60–81.

———. *The Rise of Respectable Society: A Social History of Victorian Britain, 1830–1900*. Cambridge: Harvard UP, 1988.

Thompson, James. *Models of Value: Eighteenth-Century Political Economy and the Novel*. Durham: Duke UP, 1996.

Tosh, John. *A Man's Place: Masculinity and the Middle-Class Home in Victorian England*. New Haven: Yale UP, 1999.

Trollope, Anthony. *An Autobiography*. Ed. Michael Sadleir and Frederick Page. Oxford: Oxford UP, 1980.

———. *Can You Forgive Her?* Pref. Sir Edward Marsh. Oxford: Oxford UP, 1973.

———. *Castle Richmond*. Ed. Mary Hamer. Oxford: Oxford UP, 1989.

———. *The Claverings*. Intro. Norman Donaldson. New York: Dover, 1977.

———. *Framley Parsonage*. London: Penguin, 1993.

———. *He Knew He Was Right*. Ed. Frank Kermode. London: Penguin, 1994.

———. *The Last Chronicle of Barset*. Ed. David Skilton. London: J. M. Dent, 1993.

———. *Miss Mackenzie*. Ed. A. O. J. Cockshut. Oxford: Oxford U P, 1988.

———. *Nina Balatka [and] Linda Tressel*. Ed. Robert Tracy. Oxford: Oxford UP, 1991.

———. *Orley Farm*. London: Oxford UP, 1951.

———. *Phineas Finn: The Irish Member*. Ed. Jacques Berthoud. Oxford: Oxford UP, 1982.

———. *Rachel Ray*. Intro. Ben Ray Redman. New York: Knopf, 1952.

———. *The Struggles of Brown, Jones and Robinson*. London: Penguin, 1993.

Trotter, David. *Cooking with Mud: The Idea of Mess in Nineteenth-Century Art and Fiction*. Oxford: Oxford UP, 2000.

———. "The New Historicism and the Psychopathology of Everyday Modern Life." *Critical Quarterly* 42 (2000): 36–58.

Tucker, Herbert F., ed. *A Companion to Victorian Literature and Culture*. Oxford: Blackwell, 1999.

Vance, Norman. *The Sinews of the Spirit: The Ideal of Christian Manliness in Victorian Literature and Religious Thought*. Cambridge: Cambridge UP, 1985.

Van Dyke, Catherine. "A Talk with Charles Dickens's Office Boy: William Edrupt of London." *Bookman* 53 (1921): 49–52.

Vernon, James. "Notes towards an Introduction." *Re-reading the Constitution: New Narratives in the Political History of England's Long Nineteenth Century*. Cambridge: Cambridge UP, 1996. 1–21.

————. *Politics and the People: A Study in English Political Culture, c. 1815–1867*. Cambridge: Cambridge UP, 1993.

Vrettos, Athena. *Somatic Fictions: Imagining Illness in Victorian Culture*. Stanford: Stanford UP, 1995.

Vroon, Piet. *Smell: The Secret Sharer*. With Anton van Amerongen and Hans de Vries. Trans. Paul Vincent. New York: Farrar, Straus and Giroux, 1997.

Walsh, Susan. "Bodies of Capital: *Great Expectations* and the Climateric Economy." *Victorian Studies* 37 (1993): 73–98.

Waters, Michael. *The Garden in Victorian Literature*. Aldershot: Scolar P, 1988.

Watt, Ian. "Oral Dickens." *Dickens Studies Annual* 3 (1974): 165–81.

Weiss, Barbara. *The Hell of the English: Bankruptcy and the Victorian Novel*. Lewisburg: Bucknell UP, 1986.

Welsh, Alexander. *The City of Dickens*. Oxford: Clarendon, 1971.

————. *Hamlet in His Modern Guises*. Princeton: Princeton UP, 2001.

————. *The Hero of the Waverley Novels with New Essays on Scott*. 1963. Princeton: Princeton UP, 1992.

————. *Strong Representations: Narrative and Circumstantial Evidence in England*. Baltimore: Johns Hopkins UP, 1992.

Wiener, Martin J. *English Culture and the Decline of the Industrial Spirit, 1850–1980*. Cambridge: Cambridge UP, 1981.

Wiesenthal, Chris. *Figuring Madness in Nineteenth-Century Fiction*. London and New York: Macmillan and St. Martin's P, 1997.

Williams, Raymond. *The Country and the City*. New York: Oxford UP, 1973.

————. *Culture and Society, 1780–1950*. 1958. New York: Harper and Row, 1966.

————. *The Long Revolution*. 1961. Rpt. Westport, CT: Greenwood, 1975.

————. *Marxism and Literature*. Oxford: Oxford UP, 1977.

Wilson, Edmund. "Swinburne of Capheaton and Eton." *The Novels of A. C. Swinburne*. 3–37.

Wilson, George. *The Five Gateways of Knowledge*. Cambridge: Macmillan, 1856.

Wilt, Judith. "Felix Holt, the Killer: A Reconstruction." *Victorian Studies* 35 (1991): 51–69.

Wohl, Anthony S. *Endangered Lives: Public Health in Victorian Britain*. Cambridge: Harvard UP, 1983.

Wolfreys, Julian. *Writing London: The Trace of the Urban Text from Blake to Dickens*. London: Macmillan, 1998.

Wood, Mrs. Henry [Ellen Price]. *East Lynne*. Ed. Sally Mitchell. New Brunswick: Rutgers UP, 1984.

Wood, Jane. *Passion and Pathology in Victorian Fiction*. Oxford: Oxford UP, 2001.

"Work." *Cornhill* 2 (1860): 599–614.

[Wright, Thomas.] *Johnny Robinson: The Story of the Childhood and Schooldays of an "Intelligent Artisan." By "The Journeyman Engineer."* 2 vols. London: Tinsley Brothers, 1868.

Yonge, Charlotte M. *The Clever Woman of the Family*. New York: Penguin, 1986.

Young, Arlene. *Culture, Class and Gender in the Victorian Novel: Gentlemen, Gents and Working Women*. London and New York: Macmillan and St. Martin's P, 1999.

Young, G. M., ed. *Early Victorian England, 1830–1865*. 2 vols. London: Oxford UP, 1934.

INDEX